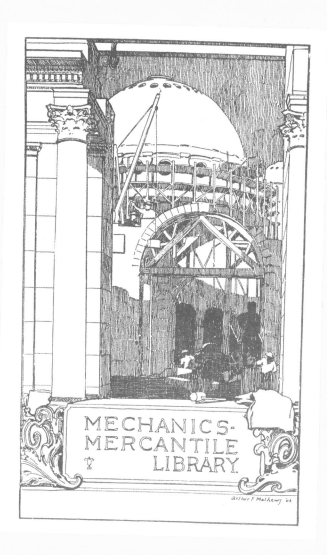

MECHANICS-
MERCANTILE
LIBRARY.

CONTESTED WATERS

JEFF WILTSE Contested Waters

A SOCIAL HISTORY OF SWIMMING POOLS IN

AMERICA THE UNIVERSITY OF NORTH CAROLINA PRESS CHAPEL HILL

Set in Scala and Eagle types by Tseng Information Systems, Inc.
Manufactured in the United States of America

This book was published with the assistance of the
THORNTON H. BROOKS FUND of the University of
North Carolina Press.

The paper in this book meets the guidelines for permanence
and durability of the Committee on Production Guidelines for
Book Longevity of the Council on Library Resources.

Library of Congress Cataloging-in-Publication Data
Wiltse, Jeff.
Contested waters : a social history of swimming pools
in America / Jeff Wiltse.
     p. cm.
Includes bibliographical references and index.
ISBN-13: 978-0-8078-3100-7 (cloth : alk. paper)
1. Swimming Pools—Social aspects—United States.
2. Swimming pools—United States—History. I. Title.
GV838.53.S85W55 2007
306.4′81—dc22   2006031021

11 10 09 08 07   5 4 3 2 1

To Ann,

My love

CONTENTS

ILLUSTRATIONS

ACKNOWLEDGMENTS

I never would have begun this book had it not been for Jacqueline Jones, my adviser at Brandeis University. I still remember sitting in her office, timidly describing an idea to research the history of swimming pools that I had literally dreamed up over a Thanksgiving weekend in Hershey, Pennsylvania. If she had responded the way almost everyone else did—with incredulous laughter—I would have abandoned the idea. Instead, she confidently replied, "That's it." Thereafter, Jackie was generous with her time, thoughtful in her criticism, and unfailingly supportive. Michael Willrich befriended and mentored me during graduate school. He offered enlightening criticism of an early version of the manuscript and taught me how to be a professional historian. Howard Chudacoff was a model of professional generosity and kindness. I am deeply indebted to Brandeis University for supporting my work on this project with the Rose Crown Fellowship, the Graduate School of Arts and Sciences' Dissertation Year Fellowship, and the Louis, Frances, and Jeffrey Sachar Research Grant.

The research for this book took me all over the northern United States, where I encountered many memorable and generous people. Librarians at the Free Library of Philadelphia, Martin Luther King, Jr. Library in Washington, D.C., Harvard University's Lamont Library, and the St. Louis Public Library were especially helpful. A special thanks to recreation department officials in Elizabeth, New Jersey, who let me climb up into the attic at city hall to search through dusty old boxes. Emily Varner, archivist at the Trumbull County Archives in Warren, Ohio, also deserves special thanks. She spent hours searching the courthouse basement for the pleadings of an important legal case. She finally found them minutes after I had left and came running down the street after me, shouting and waving her arms. Thank you, Joseph Plechavy and Duane Shipman, for chatting with me about your experiences at municipal pools during the 1930s. Christina Cruse, Jan Lovell, Deborah Cribbs, Sony Onishi, Christopher Farris, Carrie Meade, and Mary Milinkovich went out of their way to find photos that appear in the book.

Many friends and colleagues read all or parts of the manuscript at various stages and improved it through their comments and suggestions. Clark Hantzmon, Brian McCarthy, Mike Fein, Dana Comi, and Julie Frank helped me get started on the project in our Brandeis writing group. Ben Irvin, Molly McCarthy, Eben Miller, Hillary Moss, and Paul Ringel offered valuable feedback on chapter 5 at a critical point. Kay, Garry, and Paul Crane read everything I sent them with three pairs of passionately critical eyes. They have also supported my intellectual development in countless other ways. The anonymous reader for the University of North Carolina Press provided a thoughtful and incisive assessment of the manuscript. It was filled with spot-on recommendations that helped guide me through the final revision.

My colleagues in the history department at the University of Montana have been exceptionally supportive. Thanks in particular to Richard Drake, John Eglin, Dan Flores, Linda Frey, Harry Fritz, Anya Jabour, Paul Lauren, Ken Lockridge, Michael Mayer, Kevin Ostoyich, and Pamela Voekel. Jody Pavilack deserves special thanks. Her close reading of the manuscript and perceptive questions helped me solve several perplexing structural problems. Diane Rapp responded to my many demands on her time with good cheer and impeccable competence. Thanks also to Tom and Anne Boone for their support of faculty research. The College of Arts and Sciences at the University of Montana provided generous support that enabled the timely completion of the book and allowed me to acquire the rights to reproduce several additional photos.

Sincere thanks to everyone at the University of North Carolina Press, especially my editors Sian Hunter and Ron Maner. Sian was a dedicated advocate for the book, offered valuable suggestions during the final revision, and always put my mind at ease with her friendly emails and phone calls. Ron responded to my many queries with sound judgment and good humor. I could not have hoped for a better publishing experience.

I am fortunate to have a loving and supportive family. My parents, Johannah and John Wiltse, opened every possible door, encouraged me to pursue my own interests, and always trusted that I knew what I was doing. They also taught me to be honest, hardworking, and appreciative, which has served me well in life and in the writing of this book. Brenda and Walter Hiester lovingly accepted me into their family and have encouraged and supported me in many thoughtful ways. Ann Hiester Wiltse has shared her life with me through the entire journey of writing this book. Scholarship can be a lonely enterprise, but thanks to her I never felt alone. Every time I discovered a critical piece of evidence, had an analytical epiphany, or phrased something just right, I most wanted to tell her. I guess that's love. Ann also read every chapter multiple times and spent countless hours helping me clarify my writing and thinking. Her mark is on every page. Daniel and Rose bring me indescribable joy every day. "Daddy, daddy, daddy" is the second most wonderful thing that has ever been said to me.

CONTESTED WATERS

"JUST DON'T TOUCH THE WATER"

In 1898 Boston's mayor Josiah Quincy sent Daniel Kearns, secretary of the city's bath commission, to study Philadelphia's bathing pools. Philadelphia was the most prolific early builder of municipal pools, operating nine at the time. All but three were located in residential slums and, according to Kearns, attracted only "the lower classes or street gamins." City officials had built the austere pools during the 1880s and early 1890s—before the germ theory of disease transmission was popularly accepted—and intended them to provide baths for working-class men and women, who used them on alternating days. The facilities lacked showers, because the pools themselves were the instruments of cleaning. Armed with the relatively new knowledge of the microbe, Kearns was disturbed to see unclean boys plunging into the water: "I must say that some of the street gamins, both white and colored, that I saw, were quite as dirty as it is possible for one to conceive." While the unclean boys shocked Kearns, blacks and whites swimming together elicited no surprise. He commented extensively on the shared class status of the "street gamins" and their dirtiness but mentioned their racial diversity only in passing. Nor did racial difference seem to matter much to the swimmers, at least not in this social context. The pools were wildly popular. Each one recorded an average of 144,000 swims per summer, or about 1,500 swimmers per day.[1]

Fifty-three years later, the scene at a municipal pool in Youngstown, Ohio, was quite different. A Little League baseball team had won the 1951 city championship and decided to celebrate at the local pool. The large facility was situated within the sylvan beauty of the city's Southside Park, not in a residential slum. The pool itself was surrounded by a broad deck and grassy lawn, both of which provided swimmers ample space to play games or lie in the sun. The pool was clearly intended to promote leisure, not cleanliness. To celebrate their baseball victory, coaches, players, parents, and siblings showed up at the pool, but not all were admitted. One player, Al Bright, was denied entrance because he was black. The lifeguards forced him to sit on the lawn outside the fence as everyone else played in the pool. The unwritten rule was clear, one guard told the coach, "Negroes are not permitted in the pool area." After an hour had passed, several parents pleaded with the guards to let Al into the pool for at least a couple of minutes. Finally, the supervisor relented; Al could "enter" the pool as long as everyone else got out and he sat inside a rubber raft. As his teammates and other bystanders looked on, a lifeguard pushed him once around the pool. "Just don't touch the water," the guard constantly reminded him, "whatever you do, don't touch the water."[2]

How is it that so much had changed in those fifty years?

At its heart, this book answers that question. It explains how and why municipal swimming pools in the northern United States were transformed from austere public baths—where blacks, immigrants, and native-born white laborers swam together, but men and women, rich and poor, and young and old did not—to leisure resorts, where practically everyone in the community except black Americans swam together.[3] As the opening vignettes suggest, this social, cultural, and institutional transformation occurred during the first half of the twentieth century and involved the central developments of the period: urbanization, the erosion of Victorian culture, Progressive reform, the emergence of popular recreation, the gender integration and racial segregation of public space, and the sexualization of public culture. In short, the history of swimming pools dramatizes America's contested transition from an industrial to a modern society.

But the story does not end there. A second social transformation occurred at municipal swimming pools after midcentury. Black Americans challenged segregation by repeatedly seeking admission to whites-only pools and by filing lawsuits against their cities. Eventually, these social and legal protests desegregated municipal pools throughout the North, but desegregation rarely led to meaningful interracial swimming. When black Americans gained equal access to municipal pools, white swimmers generally abandoned them for private pools. Desegregation was a primary cause of the proliferation of private swimming pools that occurred after the mid-1950s. By the 1970s and 1980s, tens of millions of mostly white middle-class Americans swam in their backyards or at suburban club pools, while mostly African and Latino Americans swam at inner-city municipal pools. America's history of socially segregated swimming pools thus became its legacy.

Throughout their history, municipal pools served as stages for social conflict. Latent social tensions often erupted into violence at swimming pools because they were community meeting places, where Americans came into intimate and prolonged contact with one another. People who might otherwise come in no closer contact than passing on the street, now waited in line together, undressed next to one another, and shared the same water. The visual and physical intimacy that accompanied swimming made municipal pools intensely contested civic spaces. Americans fought over where pools should be built, who should be allowed to use them, and how they should be used.

This is a very different view of urban space than presented by historians John Kasson, Kathy Peiss, and David Nasaw. They characterize commercial amusements at the turn of the twentieth century—such as Coney Island, dance halls, and movie houses—as social melting pots that rather painlessly dissolved earlier class and gender divisions but reinforced racial distinctions. According to Nasaw, "'going out' meant laughing, dancing, cheering, and weeping with strangers with whom one might—or might not—have anything in common. . . . Only persons of color were excluded or segregated from the audience." Kasson makes essentially the same point when he concludes that commercial amusements "help[ed] to knit a heterogeneous audience into a cohesive whole."[4]

Just the opposite was true at swimming pools early in the twentieth century. Northerners' use of municipal pools throughout the Progressive Era reinforced class and gender divisions but not racial distinctions. Cities strictly segregated pools along gender lines, and people from different social classes almost never swam together. In many cases, middle-class northerners fought vigorously to ensure that working-class swimmers did not intrude upon their recreation spaces. By contrast, blacks and working-class whites commonly swam together, often without conflict.

All this changed during the 1920s, when northerners redrew the lines of social division at municipal pools. Different social classes of whites and both sexes plunged into the same pools and simultaneously excluded black Americans. This social reconstruction had many causes. The Great Black Migration contributed to the onset of racial segregation at pools by intensifying residential segregation in northern cities and heightening perceptions of black-white racial difference. Conversely, economic prosperity and the decline in European immigration mitigated perceptions of class and ethnic difference. Middle-class northerners generally became willing to swim in the same pools with working-class whites because they did not seem as poor, foreign, or unhealthy as before. Also, municipal pools became more appealing to the middle class during the 1920s because cities redesigned them as leisure resorts and typically located them in open and accessible parks rather than residential slums. At the same time, municipal officials began permitting males and females to swim together because they intended the new resort pools to promote family and community sociability. The concerns about intimacy and sexuality that had necessitated gender segregation previously did not disappear during the 1920s; rather, they were redirected at black Americans in particular. Whites in many cases quite literally beat blacks out of the water at gender-integrated pools because they would not permit black men to interact with white women at such intimate public spaces. Thus, municipal pools in the North continued to be intensely contested after 1920, but the lines of social division shifted from class and gender to race.

Historians have largely ignored this racial contest over public space in northern cities after 1920, focusing instead on housing, work discrimination, and schools. John McGreevy, for example, recently concluded that "racial violence in the North centered on housing and not, for the most part, on access to public space."[5] This book tells a different story. The imposition of racial segregation at municipal pools was a violent and contested process in the North. Blacks and whites battled one another with their fists as well as with bats, rocks, and knives. Racial segregation succeeded not because black Americans acquiesced, but because white swimmers steadfastly attacked black swimmers who entered pools earmarked for whites and because public institutions—namely the police and courts—enforced the prejudice of the majority rather than the rights of minority.

The social reconstruction of municipal pools between 1920 and 1940 marked a fundamental shift in northern social values and patterns of social interaction. During the Gilded Age and Progressive Era, the difference between people with "black" skin and those with "white" skin was a less significant social distinction than class. Furthermore, what we now think of as "race" was a less significant public social division than gender, class, and even generation. That changed during the 1920s, when race emerged as the most salient and divisive social distinction. Northern cities became fundamentally more integrated along class, gender, and generational lines, yet more segregated along racial lines. This racial division persisted throughout the rest of the twentieth century, despite court-ordered desegregation and the civil rights movement.[6]

Northerners also contested public culture at municipal pools. During the late nineteenth century, working-class boys battled with Victorian public officials to determine the use and function of these new institutions. Public officials intended municipal pools to be used "seriously" as baths and fitness facilities. They were supposed to instill the working classes with middle-class values and habits of life. In defiance of these expectations, working-class boys transplanted their boisterous and pleasure-centered swimming culture from natural waters and defined municipal pools as public amusements. In doing so, they undermined Victorian public culture and helped popularize the pleasure-centered ethos that came to define modern American culture.[7] During the 1920s and 1930s, swimmers refashioned attitudes about the body and cultural standards of public decency by what they wore and how they presented themselves at municipal pools. City officials attempted to dampen the sexual charge sparked by mixed-gender use and to limit exhibitionism and voyeurism by mandating conservative swimsuits. They could not, however, control popular demand. The acceptable size of swimsuits shrank during the interwar years and pools became eroticized public spaces. As a result, public objectification of the body became implicitly acceptable, and public decency came to mean exhibiting an attractive appearance rather than protecting one's modesty. The female nakedness and overt sexuality that pervade contemporary American culture originated, in part, at swimming pools. In these ways, ordinary Americans reshaped public culture by what they did and what they wore at municipal pools.

Municipal swimming pools were extraordinarily popular during the 1920s, 1930s, and 1940s. Cities throughout the country built thousands of pools—many of them larger than football fields—and adorned them with sand beaches, concrete decks, and grassy lawns. Tens of millions of Americans flocked to these public resorts to swim, sunbathe, and socialize. In 1933 an extensive survey of Americans' leisure-time activities conducted by the National Recreation Association found that as many people swam frequently as went to the movies frequently. In other words, swimming was as much a part of Americans' lives as was going to the movies.[8] Furthermore, Americans attached considerable cultural significance to swimming pools during this period. Pools became emblems of a new, distinctly modern version of the good life that valued leisure, pleasure, and beauty. They were, in short, an integral part of the kind of life Americans wanted to live.

This story of tens of millions of Americans flocking to municipal pools, reshaping cultural standards, and redefining the meaning of the good life presents a very different view of modern American culture than offered by most historians. William Leach, Gary Cross, and Richard Fox and T. J. Jackson Lears are unanimous in arguing that consumption and commercialism became the dominant cultural ethos in twentieth-century America, effectively wiping out all competing public cultures. In their introduction to *The*

Culture of Consumption, Fox and Lears claim that "consumption became a cultural ideal, a hegemonic 'way of seeing' in twentieth-century America." Additionally, many cultural historians characterize Americans as passive receivers of this consumer culture supposedly created and popularized by marketers, movie producers, merchants, and entrepreneurs. As William Leach argues in *Land of Desire*, "the culture of consumer capitalism may have been among the most non-consensual public cultures ever created . . . it was not produced by 'the people' but by commercial groups in association with other elites."[9] This was not the case at municipal swimming pools, where ordinary Americans helped create a vibrant public culture not primarily focused on spending money and consuming goods.

Finally, the history of swimming pools reveals changes in the quality of community life and the extent of civic engagement in modern America. From the 1920s to the 1950s, municipal pools served as centers of community life and arenas for public discourse. Hundreds and sometimes thousands of people gathered at these public spaces where the contact was sustained and interactive. Neighbors played, chatted, and flirted with one another, but they also fought with one another over who should and should not be allowed to swim and what sorts of activities and clothing were appropriate for this intimate public space. In short, community life was fostered, monitored, and disputed at municipal pools. The proliferation of private swimming pools after the mid-1950s, however, represented a retreat from public life. Millions of Americans abandoned public pools precisely because they preferred to pursue their recreational activities within smaller and more socially selective communities. Instead of swimming, socializing, and fighting with a diverse group of people at municipal pools, private-pool owners fenced themselves into their own backyards. The consequences have been, to a certain extent, atomized recreation and diminished public discourse.

〜〜〜〜 This study focuses on the history of municipal swimming pools in the northern United States. I chose to focus on municipal pools because they enabled me to study the public lives of Americans from many different— and often overlapping—social groups: working-class whites, women, African Americans, immigrants, children, and the middle class. At one time or another, Americans from all these social groups frequented municipal pools and contested their use. This book also examines and interprets the history of private swimming pools, but mostly when that history is necessary for understanding what occurred at municipal pools. I chose to focus on the northern United States in order to make the research more manageable, and because I wanted to tell a coherent story rather than interpret regional variation. I have, however, defined the northern United States broadly, including cities such as Baltimore, Washington, D.C., and St. Louis. These cities certainly have a southern heritage, but the history of their municipal pools followed a very similar pattern to that of cities further north. Likewise, the pattern occurred not only in large cities but in smaller municipalities as well. It turns out that what happened at municipal pools, whether in St. Louis and Chicago or in Newton, Kansas, and Elizabeth, New Jersey, was all quite similar.

CHAPTER I

A "PECULIAR KIND" OF BATH

THE ORIGIN OF MUNICIPAL POOLS

IN AMERICA

The growing popularity of the public [swimming] baths quite justifies the experiment. They should be established in all parts of the city. An expenditure of public money for the promotion of personal cleanliness among the poorer classes is a most profitable sanitary investment. — *Editorial,* Philadelphia Evening Bulletin *(1888)*

Philadelphia opened one of the earliest municipal pools in America on June 21, 1884, at the intersection of Twelfth and Wharton Streets. The "swimming bath," as it was commonly called, was so popular with the boys and young men of this immigrant, working-class neighborhood that they regularly waited an hour in line to enter. During the first few days, the crowd outside the pool often became unruly. The youths argued, fought, and tried to sneak ahead of one another in line. On the night of June 24, the usual ruckus escalated into a small riot. It started when the superintendent informed the expectant swimmers that they would not be admitted that evening because the pool was already filled to capacity. As the crowd grew incensed, the superintendent retreated inside the building and bolted the door. According to a local newspaper, the fifty or so young men who had been turned away "concluded to override his authority by the superiority of their numbers." They tore the door from its hinges and knocked down the fence that surrounded the pool. The city had stationed a police detail at the pool in anticipation of disorderly behavior, but the four officers were no match for the angry crowd. They were "tossed about like little bits of driftwood in rough water." Police reinforcements eventually restored order "with a liberal application of their clubs," but not before the pool and the reputation of the bathers had been severely damaged. The *Philadelphia Evening Bulle-*

tin editorialized that "the good [the pool] has accomplished amongst the unwashed down-town youths has been more than counterbalanced by the harm a certain gang of roughs has seen fit in their ignorant and brutal natures to inflict." Commissioner of City Property William Dixey, whose department administered the pool, promised that "if such conduct is kept up," he would "close the house and keep it closed."[1]

The small riot that accompanied the opening of the Twelfth and Wharton Bath captures in microcosm the contested early history of municipal pools in the United States. Municipal pools originated during the last third of the nineteenth century as public baths. They were quintessential Victorian reforms. Large northern cities located them within residential slums and intended them to promote cleanliness, refinement, and modesty among the urban poor. Public baths were necessary because the urban poor lacked bathing facilities in their homes, and middle-class northerners had come to see dirtiness as a sign of disease, immorality, and disorder. A physically unclean person, they believed, was an agent of pestilence and a likely criminal, loafer, and drunk. By promoting the "bathing habit" among the urban poor and instilling them with middle-class values, reformers and public officials assumed that municipal pools would help counteract the rising rates of disease, crime, and pauperism that accompanied urban growth during the mid- to late nineteenth century.[2]

The "unwashed down-town youths" who plunged into the Twelfth and Wharton Bath, however, viewed municipal pools differently. They flocked to the pool and waited in long lines to enter not because they were eager to bathe or adopt middle-class values, but because they were excited to roughhouse in the water. Swimming had been a popular activity among working-class boys and young men throughout the nineteenth century. They swam in the lakes, rivers, and bays that surrounded most American cities and created a plebeian and masculine swimming culture that violated Victorian norms. They swam in the nude, they swore, they fought, and they evaded authority. Municipal pools brought working-class swimmers face-to-face with the cultural expectations of middle-class Americans and the social policies of civic leaders. Cities attempted to control what the "bathers" did in the pools through elaborate rules and poolside police officers. But, as the riot reveals, the boys and young men who controlled the natural waters around American cities were determined to control the artificial waters as well. They attempted to transplant their rowdy swimming culture to these new public spaces and transform municipal pools into public amusements. In the end, they did just that.

When working-class boys and young men plunged into the nation's first municipal pools, they brought with them a distinct swimming culture developed by earlier generations. Beginning in the late eighteenth century, plebeian boys commandeered urban lakes and rivers as their play domain. They stripped naked, splashed and shouted, and roughhoused in the water. Their behavior was sufficiently offensive to provoke a public response in several cities. In 1786 Boston passed an ordinance that prohibited swimming on the Sabbath. The law noted that it was "boys" in particular who were "prophan[ing]" [sic] the Lord's Day.[3] New York City passed an ordinance in 1808 forbidding daytime swimming in the East River. As the wording of the law explained, swimmers were "extremely offensive to spectators."[4] In 1820 J. G. Coffin sent a letter to Boston public officials complaining that the practices of local swimmers were "opposed to the decorum and purity of the social state."[5] The raucous behavior of these youngsters, and especially their naked bodies, offended other citizens and led most Americans at the time to associate swimming with rebelliousness and indecency.[6]

Even as urban America was transformed during the nineteenth century by industrialization, large-scale immigration, and technological advances, this swimming culture passed—in remarkably similar form—from one generation of plebeian boys to the next. Natural-water swimmers later in the century were just as immodest, defiant, and boisterous as their predecessors. One boy in Milwaukee received much notoriety in 1878 because he "was in the habit of stripping upon the bank of the river and assuming the pose of Michael Angelo's Slave just as the little river steamer hove in sight with her load of women and children."[7] Most swimmers and bathers did not flaunt their naked bodies like this fellow, but few went out of their way to hide themselves from the public gaze. Newspaper reports from the period also emphasized the "insulting language" that was common among the swimmers, noting in particular the verbal attacks they directed at those who happened to pass by.[8]

The *New York Times* offered an elaborate description of working-class boys' nineteenth-century swimming culture in a 1900 feature article. On an early summer Saturday along the East River, "a dozen or more boys were diving and splashing around, having water fights and making no small commotion, when suddenly a tall police officer hove in sight." New York still prohibited daytime swimming within its city limits, but, as the *Times* commented, "the boys care about as much for the law as the seagull that ventures up from the bay to see what is going on." When the blue-clad officer ordered the naked boys out of the water, a fourteen-year-old redhead replied, "come an' git us, will yer, Mister Cop?" The swimmers then quickly disappeared underneath the pier. As the officer leaned over the edge to see where the boys had gone, "a mass of spray flew up and struck the guardian of the law squarely amidships, causing him to jump back so quickly that his helmet flew off into the water." Predictably, one of the boys plucked the helmet from the surface and disappeared back beneath the pier. Smarting from defeat, the officer turned and skulked off the pier. The *Times* recognized that the whole episode—the naked swimmers, the fighting and splashing, and then the confrontation with the officer—exemplified a transmitted culture among urban, working-class boys. It all occurred, the paper noted, "according to a prescribed custom that has been handed down from the time when there was not any ferry at all at Fulton Street."[9]

A prolonged public debate that occurred in Milwaukee during the late 1850s clearly reveals the social and cultural tensions public swimming generated during the nineteenth century. As New York and Boston had done previously, Milwaukee passed an ordinance in 1856 that restricted public swimming and bathing. The law forbade any person from entering Lake Michigan or the Milwaukee River during the daytime or at a spot "within sight of any dwelling house, public walk, pier, or other place of business."[10] Like many nineteenth-century statutes, the law was not strictly enforced.[11] Residents who lived near the waterfront wrote several letters to the *Milwaukee Sentinel* charging that "men and boys . . . bath[ed] in the race in broad day light" with impunity. In response, the newspaper spearheaded a campaign to get local authorities to vigorously enforce the statute. In a June 25, 1858, editorial, the paper reiterated its readers' complaints, proclaiming that "the ordinance which was designed to prevent bathing within the limits of the city in exposed places, is shamefully violated every day, and we have, as yet, heard of no case of punishment for the offence."[12]

The paper objected to public swimming because the naked boys transgressed the Victorian public culture that middle-class Americans were constructing at the time. The *Sentinel* observed that, "In the evenings, particularly when so many ladies and gentlemen are out walking upon the bluffs, the shore is usually lined with naked boys, some of them big enough to be called men." By presenting their bodies "quite exposed to the public gaze," especially within view of "ladies and gentlemen," the swimmers were, according to the paper, "without any . . . regard for decency."[13] While nudity, profanity, and roughhousing were comfortable parts of male working-class culture at the time, they were antithetical to the Victorian conception of "decency," which emphasized modesty and self-restraint.[14]

The *Sentinel*'s complaint brought about the desired effect—local authorities began vigorously enforcing the anti-swimming law. One day after the editorial appeared, the municipal court was clogged with "lads" and "youngsters" caught swimming in the lake and river. Two days later twenty-six more "men and boys" were hauled before the judge and fined two dollars each for swimming within the city limits.[15] The large number of offenders revealed just how prevalent natural-water swimming was and suggests that the city did not strictly enforce the law because doing so would have preoccupied the police and overwhelmed the courts.

Public swimmers in Milwaukee resisted this assault on their favorite "summer sport." Over the next several years, they wrote numerous letters to the *Sentinel* defending what they claimed was their right to swim when, where, and how they pleased. One letter signed simply "boys" complained about the crackdown and asked rhetorically where they should swim if not in the Milwaukee River or Lake Michigan.[16] Not letting this opportunity pass without lecturing the "boys," the *Sentinel* instructed them to swim at the dam, which, being a considerable distance outside the city, was acceptable for day swimming. The paper then reminded the youngsters why they were such a nuisance: "Boys are not always young Apollos or Cupids when their breeches are off, and taste for the fine arts has not yet been sufficiently cultivated—even if the boys were each an Adonis—to permit so much statuary running loose under the eyes of the public."[17] A few days later, "Some More Boys" responded that if not allowed to swim, they may as well "put on frocks and give up being boys."[18] For them, swimming was an essential part of male adolescence.

Bathing in the Milwaukee River was as important to some of the city's working-class men as swimming was to its boys. A quartet of Irish immigrants expressed their opposition to the swimming ordinance in a letter to the *Sentinel* written for them by their employer. These common laborers viewed the law and the controversy over it very much in class terms. The ordinance, they claimed, was an attempt by "the aristocracy . . . to oppress the poor men." Broad indictments aside, their complaint reveals how the law unfairly burdened the poor. They described how each evening they finished their labor "wearied and dirtied by the toil of the day, needing a refreshing plunge." If denied access to the river, they had no other place to bathe. Unlike the "ladies and gentlemen" who favored the law, they did not have baths in their homes nor could they afford the cost of admission to a private bathhouse. The four laborers reasoned that it was unjust for the city to deprive them of their only means of bathing in order to protect the sensibilities of citizens wealthy enough to bathe in private.[19]

The Irish immigrants identified a central paradox of Victorian culture. During the mid- to late nineteenth century, preachers, domestic advice manuals, and popular magazines disseminated this system of values that emphasized piety, self-restraint, modesty, and cleanliness.[20] These values reflected the material and social circumstances of the middle class. They could, quite literally, afford to live according to these prescriptions. Americans who lived under different material circumstances could not. Modesty was not possible for a family of six living in a two-room tenement. Similarly, as the Irish laborers pointed out, "respectable" (meaning private) bathing was not practical for families who lived in homes without running water and were too poor to frequent private bathhouses. The Irish laborers were as committed to personal cleanliness as any of their middle-class critics, perhaps more so. They made daily trips to the Milwaukee River despite the possibility of a significant fine and argued publicly in defense of their "natural right" to bathe. Because of their material circumstances, however, they violated middle-class directives of privacy and decency.

Anti-swimming ordinances, such as those in Boston, New York, and Milwaukee, were a common public response to natural-water swimming and bathing during the nineteenth century. If vigorously enforced, they had the potential to curb these activities. A minimum two-dollar fine was a costly penalty. The ordinances, however, did not have that effect. Cities only sporadically enforced the laws, and most swimmers and bathers did not let the threat of arrest deter them. The four Irish laborers declared at the end of their letter that they would continue bathing at the Spring Street Bridge regardless of the law and advised fellow citizens "who didn't like their persons" not to look at them.[21] Other swimmers and bathers expressed similar defiance every time they plunged naked into a river or lake. Throughout the nineteenth century, urban waters provided working-class males with public spaces to recreate and bathe, to articulate class-specific values and sensibilities, and to contest the prevailing cultural order.

During the nineteenth century, swimming divided along several social lines, the most conspicuous being gender. When "Some More Boys" commented that they might as well "put on frocks and give up being boys" if not allowed to swim, they correctly identified natural-water swimming as a male activity. Contemporaneous references to urban swimmers and bathers invariably mention "lads," "boys," and "men and boys," but not lasses, girls, or women. One exception is revealing. In 1858 a reporter for the *Milwaukee Sentinel* was "terribly shocked" when he "unexpectedly [came] in full view of two buxom lasses, who appeared to be greatly enjoying a cool bath at the foot of Wisconsin Street."[22] The newspaperman's shock correctly suggests that this was not a common sight. One factor that limited working-class women's access to natural water was their inability to afford suitable bathing garments. While working-class boys and young men enthusiastically ignored this impediment by stripping naked, their sisters, wives, and mothers did not. Male public nudity was a nuisance; female nudity was taboo. Furthermore, urban lakes and rivers were marked as male public spaces during the nineteenth century. If a female did not let the nakedness and profanity of male swimmers keep her from plunging into natural water, she would have stigmatized herself as disreputable and unwomanly. More generally, nineteenth-century women's use of urban public space was circumscribed by cultural constructions of gender at the time. Females were not absent from public space, as Mary Ryan has shown in *Women in Public*, but they were typically segregated in their use of urban space, especially when it involved recreation.[23] Until facilities existed where women could swim separately from men, women's access to water remained restricted.

Swimming also divided along class lines. Prior to the 1850s, middling and well-to-do Americans rarely plunged into natural waters for recreation or amusement.[24] In addressing the middle-class readers of the *New England Magazine*, a commentator noted in 1832 that "there are so few people who can swim at all."[25] In addition to the fear of drowning, powerful social and cultural prejudices kept Americans concerned about their respectability from plunging into natural water. For one, swimming was associated with rowdy and indecent plebeians. As a commentator noted in 1803, "prejudices [against swimming] have almost established it as a law of decorum" to refrain from the activity.[26] Recall J. G. Coffin's comment in 1820 that the behavior of local swimmers was "opposed to the decorum and purity of the social state."[27] Swimming was also taboo among middling Americans during the first half of the nineteenth century because they associated it with amusement and physical vigor. In some parts of the country, especially the Northeast, deeply rooted religious and political beliefs proscribed activities undertaken for pleasure or physical stimulation.[28] Recreation was acceptable only when it was directed toward spiritual or mental development. Recreation for pleasure's sake or for physical exercise was considered dangerous to the piety of Christians and the prosperity of the young nation. As Thomas Wentworth

Higginson noted, "there is in the community an impression that physical vigor and spiritual sanctity are incompatible."[29] These cultural dictates held considerable sway with northerners and prejudiced many of them against swimming. In one case, according to Higginson, a young minister in New England lost his parish because he was found swimming in the Merrimac River.[30]

Swimming became socially acceptable among the middle and upper classes around midcentury. One cause was the advent of vacationing. Beginning in the 1840s, employers gave "brain workers" paid time off from work. At the same time, the expanding network of railroads made travel more affordable and convenient than it had been before. Many in the expanding urban middle class chose to spend their vacation time at an increasing number of seaside resorts and rural retreats. Commonly referred to as "watering places," these vacation spots were typically located on or near natural bodies of water. Swimming and wading in the water quickly became popular activities at these resorts.[31] As a result, prejudice against swimming weakened. Even the bulwarks of middle-class morality began to condone the activity. In 1858 Godey's Lady's Book published an instructional article that endorsed swimming as a "healthy pastime," even for middle-class women. The magazine did not, however, indiscriminately condone swimming. The article delineated with whom its readers should swim and where. According to Godey's, the most appropriate place to swim was at the seashore among one's social peers, certainly not in urban lakes or rivers.[32] Once swimming became acceptable for the middle class, the social aspects of it needed to be addressed by the engineers of Victorian morality.

A simultaneous development further broadened the appeal of swimming. Urban Americans became increasingly conscious of the virtues of physical fitness during the mid-nineteenth century. Many commentators concluded that city life and sedentary occupations were eroding the health and weakening the strength of the nation's urban population, especially middle-class men. To cure their frailty, doctors and even preachers prescribed weight lifting, calisthenics, gymnastics, and swimming. "For this once," Thomas Wentworth Higginson encouraged Atlantic Monthly readers in 1861, "lock your brains into your safe, at nightfall, with your other valuables; don't go to the Chess-Club; come with me to the gymnasium."[33] Termed "muscular Christianity," the midcentury fitness movement also had a spiritual dimension, which helped overcome earlier associations of physical stimulation with sin. Devotees linked exercise with postmillennialism, believing that strengthening the body was a prerequisite of progress and human perfection. "The soul is made healthier, larger, freer, stronger," Higginson claimed, "by hours and days of manly exercise."[34] Exponents of muscular Christianity identified swimming as a particularly beneficial form of exercise. Higginson referenced swimming throughout a series of *Atlantic Monthly* articles, suggesting at one point that it was the best form of outdoor exercise. Unlike most activities, he explained, swimming strengthened the entire body.[35]

This burgeoning interest in physical fitness caused entrepreneurs in several cities to open the nation's first swimming pools. These privately owned, indoor pools were almost always part of a larger fitness and social club. One pool opened in 1859 at Hlasko's Institute for Physical Fitness in Philadelphia. Patrons purchased membership "certificates" for fifteen dollars that entitled them to "use of the swimming bath for the first two seasons, or to instructions in gymnastics for six months, or to four months' instruction in dancing, or to two tickets for the junior soirees next season."[36] Another early pool was at the Chicago Natatorium and Institute for Physical Culture. It was long and narrow with three springboards at one end. Men and women both used the pool but at different times. The institute also provided a walking track, rowing machines, and "health-lifts." Instructional classes were available in swimming, gymnastics, and etiquette.[37] As the cost of membership at Hlasko's Institute and the classes in etiquette at the Chicago Natatorium suggest, these early swimming pools catered to the middle and upper classes.

By the third quarter of the nineteenth century, Americans across the social spectrum plunged into water. Different classes of Americans, however, took to different waters. In rural and small-town America, where class distinctions were not as salient as in cities, people generally shared the same "swimmin' holes." Swimming among America's burgeoning urban population, however, was far more socially divided. The rich ventured into water at fashionable resorts such as Saratoga Springs and Newport. The urban middle class swam at less fashionable (and less expensive) vacationing spots along the New England coast and the New Jersey shore. They also exercised and learned to swim at private club pools. The working classes, on the other hand, took to the natural waters that surrounded them. Boys and young men from the lower social orders appropriated urban lakes and rivers as their public spaces. They created and passed along from one generation to the next a vibrant swimming culture that expressed their class and gender-specific values and sensibilities. However, the increasing social diversity of swimmers after mid-century did not mean that swimming had become a popular or widespread activity. In fact, it remained relatively uncommon throughout the nineteenth century, except among working-class boys.

〰〰 Public pools originated at the same time as private pools but served a different function for a different social class. Whereas the Chicago Natatorium functioned as a sport and fitness facility for the urban middle class, the earliest public pools functioned as baths for the urban poor. They were essentially large community bath tubs. Cities and private charities began providing public baths in the 1850s and 1860s because that is when middle-class reformers and public officials came to see personal cleanliness as a public necessity, not just a cultural preference. They assumed that dirtiness caused the spread of diseases, moral degeneracy, and urban disorder. By promoting cleanliness among the poorest and dirtiest residents, they expected public baths—including pools—to combat many of the urban problems that had became so conspicuous.

The mid-nineteenth century was a period of dramatic and problematic urban growth. Northern cities became increasingly crowded and unhealthy as foreign immigrants and rural migrants seeking work and opportunity flooded in. Between 1830 and 1860, the population of Philadelphia climbed from 161,271 to 565,529, Boston from 61,392 to 177,840, St. Louis from 5,852 to 160,773, and Milwaukee from virtually no population to 45,246.[38] These cities were unprepared to cope with the rush of immigrants and migrants and the social problems they created. The newcomers overwhelmed the physical infrastructure of their adopted cities, which did not have sufficient housing, sewage, water, or relief services to support them. As a result, the rates of disease and death grew ghastly high. During the same period, northern cities began to segregate along class lines. Many in the middle and upper classes gathered in exclusive residential areas or migrated out to the periphery of cities, creating "streetcar suburbs." The working classes, on the other hand—which included blacks, native-born white laborers, and most immigrants—clustered into downtown residential areas. These overcrowded neighborhoods became the poorest, dirtiest, and most unhealthy sections of cities. In short, they became slums.[39]

These immigrant and working-class slums appeared menacing to the middle class. Journalists and social workers detailed the gambling, prostitution, drunkenness, and vagrancy that, according to them, characterized life in the slums. At the same time, popular fiction writers sensationalized stories of urban crime. Historian Paul Boyer contends that this "wicked city" stereotype shaped middle-class Americans' impression of tenement life during the mid-nineteenth century. Magazines and newspapers expressed widely felt fears that the working classes and their "vices" posed a threat to the Victorian social and moral order. Many of the urbanites who moved out to the new streetcar suburbs did so in order to escape the danger, disorder, and immorality that they associated with cities.[40]

Commentators and social critics also expressed concern about the material conditions within the slums. In 1845 physician John H. Griscom vividly described the physical squalor that characterized working-class life in his influential study, *The Sanitary Condition of the Laboring Population of New York*. According to Griscom, entire families crowded into single-room dwellings, without windows or other means of ventilation. Filth accumulated throughout their homes. "Every corner of the room, of the cupboards, of the entries and stairways, piled up with dirt. The walls and ceilings, with the plaster broken off in many places, exposing the lath and beams, and leaving openings for the escape from within of the effluvia of vermin, dead and alive, are smeared with the blood of unmentionable insects, and dirt of all indescribable colours." Griscom also pointed out that the inhabitants were just as filthy as their homes because, without running water, they could not bathe. "The deficiency of water and the want of a convenient place for washing," Griscom wrote, "are very serious impediments in the way of improvement."[41]

After shocking his readers with descriptions of "how the other half lived," Griscom lent his authority to two beliefs gaining currency among the middle class at the time. First, he warned that the "pestiferous places" in which the poor lived posed a significant health risk not only to their unfortunate inhabitants, but to citizens of all classes who resided or worked in the city: "I will only add . . . that disorders arising and fostered in these low places, will sometimes become so virulent as to extend among and jeopardize the better classes of citizens." Griscom also affirmed that the "immoral" behavior of the urban poor was inextricably linked to the physical environment in which they lived. "Physical evils," Griscom told his readers, "are productive of moral evils of great magnitude and number."[42]

These two assumptions—that the slums were the source of citywide epidemics and that physical squalor cultivated moral degeneracy—led Victorian reformers to attempt to improve conditions within the slums. Municipal governments formed health departments, opened almshouses, and built city hospitals.[43] Private charity organizations lobbied for tenement reform, opened free medical dispensaries, and undertook countless studies of tenement life.[44] Reformers also encouraged city governments and private charity organizations to promote personal cleanliness among the working classes. A report issued in 1860 by a special committee formed to investigate bathing practices in Boston advised the city to "initiate some plan which may give the masses an opportunity for habitual and economical bathing,—being convinced that moral purity and mental refinement are its natural concomitants."[45] Magazines and newspapers also encouraged public officials to address the bathing needs of "the people." An 1849 article in the *New York Evening Post* posited that "no greater service can be done to persons in necessitous circumstances than to give them the opportunity of preserving perfect cleanliness in their persons and clothing."[46]

Middle-class Americans' desire to promote cleanliness among the urban poor was frustrated, however, by the lack of bathing facilities. The 1860 report on bathing in Boston enumerated the impediments that prevented the city's poor from washing themselves regularly. First of all, "the men, women, and children belonging to the laboring classes" lacked bathing facilities in their homes. The committee also found that commercial bathhouses were too expensive for working-class Bostonians. The "masses" were left with no alternative except to plunge, where available, in natural water. Some did so with delight, but there were several problems with this practice. Outdoor bathing was only practical during part of the year. Few, if any, were hearty enough to bathe in the Charles River from October to April. Furthermore, the Charles River and Boston Harbor were not easily accessible to many residents.[47] Another impediment that the Boston bathing committee did not mention was the increasingly polluted condition of rivers and lakes in many cities. Sewage and industrial waste drained and seeped into urban waters, which limited their suitability for bathing.

Private charity organizations and city governments opened the nation's first public pools in order to provide the working classes with accessible and suitable places to bathe. The New York Association for Improving the Condition of the Poor (AICP) opened the People's Bath in 1852 on the Lower East Side, in the heart of the most densely populated slum in the city. The AICP was founded in 1843 by a group of Protestant merchants, manufacturers, and professionals intent on improving the lives of the urban poor by providing them short-term alms and instilling them with middle-class values and habits, such as cleanliness.[48] The People's Bath included a pool, tub baths, and laundry facilities. The AICP charged bathers a fee to use the pool and tubs because it believed that a free bath would promote dependence and shiftlessness, whereas a "small" charge would promote self-respect and self-reliance. At five and ten cents, however, the AICP made the price of dignity and independence too high. The poor could not afford to bathe regularly, and the facility closed in 1861 due to a lack of patronage.[49]

Boston was the first U.S. city to provide public baths. In its 1860 report,

Boston's Joint Special Committee on Public Bathing Houses advised the city to provide "cheap plunge bath[s] for poor men and boys . . . in various parts of the city."[50] By plunge baths, the committee meant in-ground pools. The committee claimed that the pools would improve both the health and morality of the city's poor. "If public bathing-places were provided at points easy of access, and the prices of baths fixed so that the poorest could afford their use as an habitual necessity, might not we expect that many thousands would receive daily benefit, not only as a measure of health, but as an inducement to self-respect and refinement, and consequent elevation in the scale of society."[51] Bostonians had to wait several years for the baths, however, as the Civil War diverted public attention and money from this and other civic projects.

The building of public baths took on special urgency after the war because many in Boston feared an outbreak of cholera. In 1866 Charles W. Slack, chairman of the city's bathing committee, wrote to the board of alderman urging it to quickly pass an order allocating $10,000 for the building of several baths in order to defend the city from the disease: "With the apprehension generally entertained of the approach of the cholera the ensuing season, our resident population seem nearly unanimous in support of the measure."[52] Slack and other middle-class Bostonians favored public baths because they associated communicable diseases such as cholera, tuberculosis, and yellow fever with dirtiness. The prevailing belief at the time, known as the zymotic theory of disease, held that disease agents were foul-smelling vapors given off by unclean substances. This theory stigmatized the urban poor. Commentators identified them as the agents of pestilence precisely because they rarely bathed. Their dirty bodies and clothes supposedly transported diseases throughout the city.[53] Reformers and civic leaders in Boston assumed that the baths would protect the overall public health by providing large tubs in which the city's poor could wash away the dirt and disease.

The city opened six baths during the summer of 1866, but none was a pool. Five were "river baths," attached to bridges crossing the Charles River, and one was a "beach bath," located at the end of L Street in South Boston on Dorchester Bay. City officials chose to build natural-water baths rather than in-ground pools, because they considered the pools to be too expensive.[54] The river baths, however, did resemble pools. They were enclosed wooden structures, with wooden tanks submerged into the Charles River that measured fifteen feet wide, twenty-five feet long, and four feet deep. The boards that composed the tanks were spaced with one to two inch gaps to allow the river water to flow in and out naturally. The L Street Beach Bath consisted of

Harvard Bridge Bath, Boston, circa late 1800s. U.S. Department of Commerce and Labor, *Bulletin of the Bureau of Labor,* September 1904.

a small changing room, and a fenced in section of the beach where bathers entered the bay. All six baths were quite popular, in large part because they were free. That first summer, Bostonians took over 436,000 baths at the six facilities. So many people frequented the river baths in particular that bathers often waited in long lines, clogging up the streets and "seriously impeding the public travel while awaiting their turn."[55]

While the baths were primarily intended to serve the city's "poor men and boys," they attracted a broad cross section of citizens. About 15 percent of the bathers were female. They used the baths during the middle morning and afternoon, whereas males bathed early in the morning, at midday, and in the evening. This temporal division clearly accommodated men's work schedule.[56] Bathers also represented all social classes. Boston's different social classes, however, frequented different baths. The L Street Beach Bath, which was located on the city's periphery and not accessible by street car, attracted well-to-do Bostonians, including a "large number of ladies." The Warren Bridge Bath, on the other hand, drew from the North End's working-class population. The West Boston Bridge Bath, located close to Cambridge and the West End, attracted young, low-level white-collar and skilled blue-collar workers, including many "clerks and in-door mechanics." The Arch Wharf and Dover Street Bridge Baths—which were the two most heavily used facilities—attracted mostly Irish immigrants from East Boston.[57]

The city's bathing committee attributed these class divisions not just to the city's segregated social geography but also to the type of bathing experience each facility offered. "It was soon found," the committee noted in its 1866 *Report*, "that the peculiar locations *and conveniences* of the several baths attracted a distinctive class of bathers."[58] Well-to-do Bostonians "resorted thither" to the L Street Bath because they could lounge "upon a beautiful beach." The West Boston Bridge Bath, which attracted young middle-class bathers, was used for "general swimming purposes," according to the committee. The committee described the two baths frequented by Irish immigrants as exclusively for bathing, adding that "large throngs of the foreign population came regularly, and with evident advantage."[59] The men who composed Boston's Joint Special Committee on Free Bathing Facilities clearly viewed public swimming and bathing in class-specific terms. Resorting on a beach was for the rich, swimming was for middle-class men, and public bathing was for the urban poor.

In 1868 Boston opened the first municipal pool in the United States. A local newspaper described it as an "experiment, the first [bath] of this peculiar kind." The indoor facility, located on Cabot Street in the Boston Highlands section of Roxbury, was an austere wooden structure measuring forty by eighty feet. It contained two twenty by twenty-four foot pools, divided by a partition, and forty-eight dressing rooms. Each pool could accommodate thirty to forty bathers at a time. One was exclusively for males and the other for females. The bathing committee never explicitly explained or justified the gender segregation, probably because people at the time needed no such explanation. Public life in general divided along gender lines—for both the middle and working classes—and social conventions mandated that the sexes be separate in an activity such as bathing.[60]

The Cabot Street Bath had neither showers nor tubs because the pools were the instruments for cleaning. Bathers plunged their dirty bodies into the water and rubbed their skin clean. The recently finished Cochituate waterway, which supplied fresh water to Boston, made the pools feasible. Because of frequent emptying and refilling, the pools required over 2.7 million gallons of water during their first two months of operation. The facility was also quite expensive to build. It cost $7,315, several thousand dollars more than a river bath. City officials chose to build the comparatively expensive pools in order to provide year-round bathing and to transport the benefits of bathing to the working-class residents of Boston Highlands, who lived a considerable distance from the natural-water baths on the Charles River and Dorchester Bay.[61]

From the start, the city's bathing committee was concerned about how bathers would behave at the pool. It established regulations intended to ensure orderly and gentlemanly use. The committee forbade smoking, "profanity," and "noisy conversations." It also warned bathers that they would be arrested for "defacing the dressing rooms, fences, or tanks." The committee explained in its annual report that these rules were intended to establish the boundaries of "propriety and decorum" for a public bath. The city even stationed a police officer "in constant attendance" at the bath to "preserve order and enforce [the] regulations." City officials clearly did not want working-class bathers transplanting their raucous natural-water swimming culture to this new public space.[62]

Unlike the river baths, which attracted large numbers of children and adults, the pool bath attracted almost exclusively children. Boys bathed in their pool 56,007 times in 1869, girls 16,306, men 2,210, and women only 277 times.[63] Children thus accounted for nearly 97 percent of the baths. This was not an unusual year. In 1870 boys and girls accounted for 96 percent of the baths.[64] By comparison, boys and girls accounted for 73 percent of the visits to the city's river and beach baths in 1869.[65] This was a significant majority but not close to their virtual ubiquity at the Cabot Street Bath. Although not conclusive, these figures suggest that the working-class residents of Boston Highlands viewed the pools as children's playgrounds rather than baths for working men and women.

America's first municipal pool was short-lived. Boston's city council closed the Cabot Street facility only eight years after it opened, despite continued heavy use. During its last summer of operation, 1876, the pools attracted more than 80,000 bathers. Although the council did not explain its decision to close the facility, two explanations seem likely. Because of frequent emptying and refilling, a cost not incurred at the river baths, the pools were expensive to operate. Second, the pools were not serving their intended function as baths for dirty working men. The city council was apparently not willing to spend large sums of money to provide play facilities for working-class children. Protecting public health was an accepted municipal function in the 1870s but providing amusement for the working classes was not.[66] Still, the council perhaps foresaw that artificial pools had a future. Instead of tearing down the structure, it merely floored over the tanks and turned the building into a wardroom and evening school.[67] Twenty-two years later, the city did in fact tear up the flooring and refill the pools so a new generation of children could splash along Cabot Street.

Just as in Boston, Philadelphia first attempted to provide baths for its working-class residents by building river baths. The city opened its first river bath in 1881 and operated three by 1883—two on the Delaware River and one on the Schuylkill.[68] All three were located near waterfront slums. Philadelphia mayor Samuel King justified the river baths as having "great sanitary value" for the entire city. He believed that they would improve the overall health and morals of the city by enabling the city's dirtiest residents to wash themselves regularly.[69] Local newspapers applied the same hope to the river baths. The *Philadelphia Evening Bulletin* editorialized in 1883 that "public baths are great moral and sanitary agents" and encouraged the city to build more of them.[70]

Philadelphia did build more baths but not in the rivers. From 1884 to 1892 the city opened six outdoor pools in different sections of the city. This building spree represented the most significant commitment to municipal pools in nineteenth-century America. The tanks were made of asphalt and varied in depth from three to six feet. At roughly forty feet wide and seventy feet long, the tanks were much larger than those at Boston's Cabot Street facility and actually permitted bathers to swim around in the water.[71] Although the pools could accommodate swimming, city officials conceived them as public baths "to aid citizens in maintaining cleanliness free of cost."[72] Just like Boston's Cabot Street Bath, Philadelphia's pools were intended to transport the benefits of bathing to citizens who lived too far from natural-water baths to make regular trips. The first pool was located on the corner of Twelfth and Wharton Streets in the heart of South Philadelphia. It was almost exactly a mile and quarter from both the Delaware and Schuylkill Rivers. Residents of this neighborhood had no easy access to the river baths or unauthorized swimming spots along the waterfront. If city officials wanted the poorer residents of the central districts to clean themselves regularly, they needed to bring the baths to them. In-ground pools did precisely that.

All six of the pools opened between 1884 and 1892 were located within working-class neighborhoods. The families that lived around the Twelfth and Wharton pool, for example, were mostly Irish immigrants, and the men typically worked at semiskilled jobs. They were millworkers, factory laborers, blacksmiths, railroad hands, shoemakers, painters, tailors, and machinists. Thomas Cunningham, his wife Rose, their five school-age boys, and a niece lived a couple of row houses down from the pool. Thomas, who worked as a street contractor, and his wife both emigrated from Ireland. Right next to the pool lived William Buchanon, his wife, Ann, their son, and two daughters. William was a second-generation Irish immigrant, while Ann emigrated from Scotland. He was sixty-nine and worked as a dyer, but was frequently unemployed. His three children were all in their thirties but still lived at home.[73]

The city's second pool, opened in 1885, was located near South Street Bridge in West Philadelphia. The row houses and rear tenements in this area of the city were filled with multiple families and many borders. Most of the men who lived near the pool identified themselves as "laborers" or "teamsters." Few were skilled craftsmen and almost none were clerks or held other white-collar jobs. Boardinghouses and saloons, often located next door to one another, were common in the neighborhood. Louis Phillips, for example, operated a saloon at 3057 Chestnut Street, a couple of blocks from the pool. Next door, Samuel Young and his wife Lizzie ran a boardinghouse. The ten men who boarded with the Youngs were typical for the neighborhood. Three were stonecutters, two were blacksmiths, one was a common laborer, another was a cigar maker, one was a molder, another a plasterer, and the last was a bartender, probably at Phillips's place. Five were first- or second-generation Irish immigrants, and one had emigrated from England.[74]

By locating the pools within immigrant, working-class neighborhoods, city officials effectively segregated their use along class lines. While studying Philadelphia's pools in 1898, Daniel Kearns, secretary of the Boston bath commission, found that only "the lower classes or street gamins" used them. Furthermore, he was shocked by the filthy bathers and the murky water in the pools. He reported back to Boston mayor Josiah Quincy: "People enter the water immediately after disrobing, clean or unclean as they may be, and I must say that some of the street gamins, both white and colored, that I saw, were quite as dirty as it is possible for one to conceive."[75] Not surprisingly, middle-class Philadelphians did not venture into the slums to bathe or swim in these pools. They had baths in their homes and would have been just as repulsed by the filthy "street gamins" as Kearns.

Use of Philadelphia's early pools did not, however, divide along racial lines. None of the six pools were located within the city's principal black neighborhood as identified by W. E. B. Du Bois in his classic sociological study *The Philadelphia Negro*; however, as Kearns noted, blacks and whites bathed together. Kearns's report not only indicated that the pools were racially integrated; it also revealed his attitude about mixed-race bathing. He was not surprised or offended that blacks and whites used the pools together. Further-more, blacks, immigrants, and native-born white laborers themselves did not seem to mind sharing this intimate space with one another. Neither bath department reports nor newspaper articles mention racial conflict and, perhaps most telling, the pools were very popular. Each one recorded an average of 144,000 baths per summer.[76] In the social context of a municipal pool, race was not an insurmountable social divide at the time, at least not in Philadelphia.

Despite their popularity among the working classes, the pools did not function as city officials intended. Men and women who toiled in industrial factories and labored along Philadelphia's dirty streets constituted a relatively small percentage of the bathers. Attendance figures reveal that "boys" plunged into the pools far more than "men," and that females rarely entered the pools at all. In its first summer, boys took 81 percent of the baths at the Twelfth and Wharton facility and men took 17 percent; women and girls—who bathed on separate days from males—took 2 percent.[77] The same was true at the other pools. Boys took 85 percent of the baths at the Thirty-second and South Street pool during its first several summers. Men accounted for 13 percent, while girls and women accounted for only 1 percent of the baths.[78] By 1891 boys had become even more prevalent. City officials reported that they accounted for 1.119 million of the 1.284 million total baths that summer. Almost nine out of every ten "bathers" was a boy.[79] Just like urban lakes and rivers, Philadelphia's municipal pools were male, adolescent, working-class spaces.

Boys flocked to the pools because they were excited to swim and play in the water, not because they were eager to bathe. Newspaper articles invariably mentioned the excitement expressed by the boys even as they waited in long lines to enter. In 1884 the *Philadelphia Evening Bulletin* noted "the joy [the opening of one of the pools] has occasioned amongst the unwashed down-town youths."[80] A few years later, the same paper described the "great delight" the pools brought to boys who lived nearby.[81] Local reformer Franklin Kirkbride likewise recognized that boys frequented the pools to amuse themselves rather than to clean their bodies when he lamented in 1899 that "most of their patrons are younger men . . . who simply desire to get amusement from swimming."[82] Whereas city officials and reformers intended the pools to promote cleanliness and middle-class morality among the toiling masses, the reality was that they provided summer recreation for working-class youths.

Milwaukee was the second most prolific builder of municipal pools during the late nineteenth century, opening three between 1889 and 1903. The history of its "natatoriums" shows more clearly the pleasure-centered pattern of use that developed at early municipal pools.[83] Milwaukee's first pool, located on Prairie Street in the city's West Side, opened August 14, 1889, but no one entered the water that day. The "city fathers" were supposed to take the ceremonial first dip, but, according to a local newspaper, they "were unable to brave the curious looks of the crowd and were afraid of the water."[84] Without their business suits and hats, they did not feel nearly so comfortable with the public gaze upon them. They understood what Thorstein Veblen would later call "dress as an expression of the pecuniary culture."[85] Clothing advertised social standing, especially in the anonymity of late nineteenth-century metropolises. As the *Milwaukee Sentinel* recognized, the pool stripped swimmers of this class distinction: "In the wide scope for judging human nature in—practically speaking—*puris naturalibus* there is no better place than the same tank full of dripping heads, for there, the varying adornments and artificialities of every day life being laid aside, men and boys alike show up as God intended them to be and none can hypocritically vaunt his own perfections, unless they really exist, and none can mutely extol himself as people do in the outer world by habiting themselves in swagger garments upon the very correct hypothesis that fine feathers occasionally make fine birds."[86] Unadorned by the accoutrements of wealth and status, what remained were the bare essentials of, in this case, manhood.

The aldermen's unwillingness to plunge into the pool that first day symbolized their inability to determine the function and usage of this new public space. Just as in Philadelphia, boys flocked to the pool for amusement, not to wash themselves. A few months after the pool opened, a reporter for the *Sentinel* spent an entire Saturday at the West Side Natatorium and recorded his observations in a feature article. On that day, rambunctious swimmers filled the pool.[87] Most were boys, but a few men played in the water as well. All were naked, just like the boys who swam in the Milwaukee River and Lake Michigan. The most popular and conspicuous swimmer was a big-bellied man, who, according to the reporter, brought "unlimited enjoyment" to the younger swimmers. The man floated on his back in the middle of the pool, "letting himself out as a buoy." One lucky youngster got to sit on his stomach and play king of the hill, while other "weary and panting urchins" held onto his limbs.[88]

The pool also served as a stage for boys to act out male, adolescent rituals. One group of youngsters observed the pool scene from the second-floor walkway, making fun of swimmers already in the water. "Them's the greenhorns,"

Greenbush Natatorium, Milwaukee, Wisconsin, circa 1895.
Courtesy of Milwaukee Public Library, neg. 417662.

mocked one of the boys. Another pointed out a particularly feeble young man and commented, "I wouldn't be creepin' round dere an' shiverin like dat dude." The *Sentinel* reporter recalled that this timid young man "looked like a picture in a tailor's pattern book" when he entered the natatorium; but, stripped of his clothes, he became the butt of jokes and ridicule. "Dudes suffer frightfully in the naked ordeal of the bath," he concluded. When the gang of boys finally entered the water, they continued their verbal assault on timid swimmers. With some quick thinking and crafty acting, however, a boy named Bill exacted some revenge on the bullies. He pretended not to know how to swim and submitted to their ridicule. Bill warily entered the deep water in response to their jeers, and then flailed about as though he was drowning. Frightened with guilt, the boys came to rescue him, but Bill deftly evaded their grasping hands and swam away with ecstatic delight shrieking "Yah! Yer didn't tink I could swim didn't yer."[89]

Such were the games boys played in the Milwaukee River and such were the games they played at the natatorium. Pools may have domesticated swimming, but working-class boys maintained cultural authority over the activity. Even in the supervised and regulated setting of a municipal pool, swimming continued to serve as an expression of adolescent independence and rebelliousness. After spending the day at the pool, the *Sentinel* reporter concluded that boys just "love to cast off the encumbrances of clothing and revel in the nudity of the noble savage." The swimmers "shone all over with untrammeled happiness and freedom."[90] Just as boys and young men commandeered nature's "swimmin' holes" as their play domain, the boys of the West Side did the same at the city's new concrete natatorium. They transplanted their natural water swimming culture to it and, in the process, defined municipal pools as centers of working-class amusement.

~~~~~ A very different swimming culture developed at private pools during the last quarter of the nineteenth century. Most private pools at the time were housed within exclusive athletic clubs, where wealthy men swam for sport and fitness. Women were typically excluded. The New York Athletic Club (NYAC) christened an exemplary private pool in 1885. It was an institution dedicated to exercise and serious competition. Members used the pool for lap swimming and frequently hosted swimming meets and water polo contests, including the 1895 national championship between the NYAC and the Chicago Athletic Association. More than just a place to exercise and compete, though, the pool was an emblem of luxury and exclusivity. The design of the pool reflected the wealth and status of the men who swam in it. One historian of the club suggested that even "the luxury-loving Romans" would have been envious. The pool was built of marble and tile, lit by a row of chandeliers, and enclosed by ornate railing. This first pool lasted only ten years. The NYAC rebuilt its clubhouse after the 1895 water polo national championship with an even larger and more ornate pool. The new tank was located in a large, vaulted-ceiling room, walled in white marble, decorated with marble pillars, and surrounded by a large gallery that permitted spectators to observe the athletic contests.[91]

The Young Men's Christian Association (YMCA) slightly democratized private pools at the end of the nineteenth century by making them affordable to middle-class young men. The first Y pool opened at the Brooklyn branch in

1885. Two years later, pools were included in branch buildings in Milwaukee and Detroit. By 1895, seventeen YMCA branches housed swimming pools.[92] Like other private pools, the Y pools promoted exercise and physical fitness. The Brooklyn-branch pool measured fifteen by forty-five feet and, according to officials, provided young men the "opportunity to learn and practice the art of swimming."[93] The Y pools, however, were much less luxurious than the NYAC pool. They were typically located in building basements and were quite austere. The Cleveland YMCA's pool, for example, was cramped by a low ceiling and surrounded by a narrow walkway and brick walls.[94]

The young men who swam in the Y pools were thoroughly middle class. In 1890 members of the Brooklyn branch consisted of 57 percent clerks, 19 percent mechanics, 10 percent students, 7 percent merchants, 4 percent "professional men," and only 3 percent laborers. Thus, 78 percent of the members were either white-collar workers or students. Furthermore, only the most prosperous among the branch's membership actually swam in the pool. The association had a graduated fee structure, so that only the most expensive membership permitted use of the pool. In 1890 a two-dollar annual fee enabled members of the Brooklyn branch to use the library and reading rooms and attend social and religious meetings. A five-dollar membership added the educational classes. Only those who paid fifteen dollars could swim in the pool and exercise in the gymnasium.[95] The fee structure thus perpetuated the class divisions that characterized swimming throughout the nineteenth century. Social and religious meetings were deemed appropriate for mechanics and laborers, but swimming for exercise and fitness was limited to young men who were middle class.

At the end of the nineteenth century, two distinct pool cultures existed in America. Working-class boys had created a play and pleasure-centered culture at municipal pools. Elite and middle-class men had developed a more serious and orderly culture at private pools that reflected the competitive and directed character of Victorian culture. Both, however, were masculine cultures that valued physical vigor and camaraderie. These two pool cultures collided around the turn of the twentieth century, when public officials in several cities redefined municipal pools as fitness institutions and encouraged both middle- and working-class residents to use them. Chapter 2 details this redefinition of municipal pools and examines the ensuing social and cultural conflict.

CHAPTER 2

"A MEANS OF PHYSICAL CULTURE"
THE REDEFINITION OF MUNICIPAL
POOLS DURING THE 1890S

Both kinds of swimming baths [indoor and outdoor] are not intended for cleansing purposes, but are adapted only for pleasurable and healthful muscular exercise of the body and limbs. Their object is rather to maintain or improve health by hardening the body. — William Paul Gerhard, **Modern Baths and Bathhouse** *(1908)*

On July 9, 1895, a group of local residents presented a petition to the West Chicago Park Board "with upwards of ten thousand signatures attached" requesting an outdoor pool in Douglas Park. Given the previous history of municipal pools, this was a curious request. Douglas Park was situated in the midst of a growing streetcar suburb several miles west of downtown Chicago, not the type of neighborhood in which earlier pools in Boston, Philadelphia, and Milwaukee were located. Furthermore, the middle-class families that lived near the park and signed the petition had tubs in their homes. They clearly did not want or need a public place to bathe. Instead, as the accompanying request for an attached "open-air gymnasium" suggested, they wanted a public place to exercise and recreate.[1]

The park board accepted the petition as "notification from the public of its preference" and built a pool complex clearly designed to promote sport and fitness rather than cleanliness.[2] The facility contained showers in the dressing rooms, which made the two pools superfluous as baths. The park board also surrounded each pool with a "promenade" that permitted spectators to watch the swimmers. These observation galleries would have been both unnecessary and inappropriate had the facility been a bath. Furthermore, the pools themselves were particularly well suited for exercise and athletic competition. At 55 by 120 feet and 55 by 60 feet, they were much larger than earlier municipal pools and could accommodate lap swimming and races. The pools also had several springboards, which challenged swimmers to perform acrobatic feats in the air.[3] In terms of location, design, and intended function, Chicago's Douglas Park Pool represented a radical departure from earlier municipal pools.

The pool was also novel in that the park board intended it to serve a diverse cross section of West Side residents. The opening ceremony symbolized this intention. Several different ethnic groups and social classes marched together in a parade that was the centerpiece of the ceremony. Bohemian, Polish, Slovenian, Norwegian, and German *Turner* societies led the procession, followed by representatives of Chicago's trade unions, and finally members of the Chicago Bicycle Club pedaled past the cheering crowd.[4] The speeches that followed further emphasized that all citizens were welcome at the pool. Walter Bogle, president of the West Chicago Park Board, told the crowd that the pool would be open to "every man, woman, and child who so desired to take advantage of it without the cost of a cent."[5] The democratic intentions of the park board were more than mere rhetoric. As Bogle indicated in his speech, admission to the pool was free. Furthermore, Douglas Park was accessible to a diverse population. It was bordered by a middle-class neighborhood but was also accessible from several nearby working-class sections of the city.[6] This was to be a quintessentially democratic public space.

The pool did in fact attract a diverse crowd, when it first opened. Newspaper reports emphasized the variety of swimmers. Small boys were "very conspicuous in the crowd that besieged the place," but they were not alone. "Men, women and girls joined in the house-warming," but the sexes did not swim together. Males swam in the larger tank and females in the smaller one. All social classes were represented as well. Well-to-do swimmers "rode in carriages" to the pool; those who owned bicycles "scorched down boulevard and park drives on wheels"; while those who could afford neither carriages nor bicycles "ambled leisurely along on foot."[7] With carriages, bikes, and shoes set aside, Chicagoans mingled on a more equal basis in the pool. As a newspaper headline proclaimed, Douglas Park Pool was indeed a place "Where All May Dip."[8]

Within a couple of years, however, the swimmers became much less diverse. In 1900 the park board began charging an entrance fee to Douglas Park Pool "owing to the excessive patronage with which it [had] been favored." The pools had become "hard to manage," and the board concluded that the best way to restore order was to reduce the number of swimmers. The fee did indeed curtail use, but not indiscriminately. It disproportionately affected the

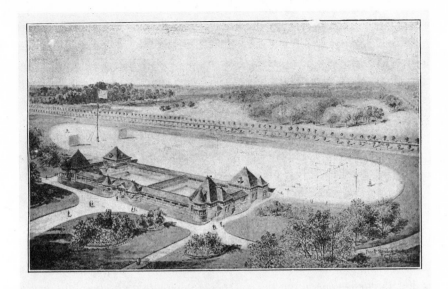

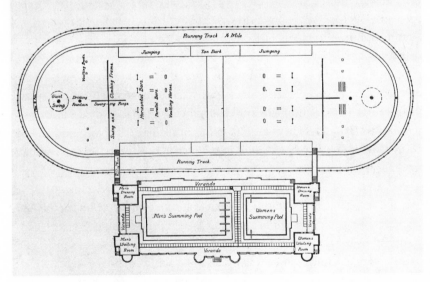

Drawing of Douglas Park Pool and Gymnasium, Chicago, circa 1895. Douglas Park Pool was one of the first municipal pools in the United States intended to function as an exercise and sport facility rather than a bath. U.S. Department of Commerce and Labor, *Bulletin of the Bureau of Labor*, September 1904.

working classes, especially the large number of boys who swam regularly.[9] They could least afford to pay the fee and thus swam less frequently or not at all. Middle-class swimmers, who could easily afford the charge, continued to swim as before. When park officials set out to restore order at the pools, they found it most expedient and probably most effective to exclude the poor. After all, it was the "scores of scantily attired youths, splashing and chattering" that caused most of the disorder.[10]

Douglas Park Pool exemplifies a redefinition of municipal pools that occurred during the mid- to late 1890s. In response to popular acceptance of the germ theory of disease transmission—which made pools obsolete as baths—and renewed enthusiasm for athletics and physical exercise among the urban middle class, residents and public officials in several northern cities reconceived municipal pools as sport and fitness facilities. Initially, city officials intended a broad cross section of citizens to use the new "swimming pools." They located them in parks and town squares, so middle-class residents would feel comfortable accessing them, and charged little or no entrance fee, so they were still affordable to the working classes. The pools did indeed attract a socially diverse crowd, but the cross-class use created problems. Working-class boys' rowdy and boisterous behavior offended pool administrators and middle-class swimmers. When public officials concluded that they could not reform the boys through cultural suasion or control them by stationing police officers poolside, they effectively excluded them by charging entrance fees. As a result, the social makeup of swimmers and the patterns of use at municipal pools drastically changed. Middle-class men replaced working-class boys as the typical municipal-pool swimmer, and the pools were used primarily for swimming instruction, exercise, and competitive sports.

～～～ The history of municipal pools abruptly changed during the mid- to late 1890s. The most direct cause was popular acceptance of the germ theory of disease. Previously, most doctors, scientists, and writers of popular health manuals linked infectious diseases such as typhoid, tuberculosis, and cholera with dirtiness. Reformers and public officials therefore believed that public baths—including pools—would reduce the risk of epidemics by promoting cleanliness among the poorest and, according to them, dirtiest urban Americans. By the mid-1890s, however, the germ theory of disease became accepted within the medical and scientific communities and then was widely reported to the general public. Medical studies showed that the source of diseases was actually invisible microbes that could be transmitted through casual contact such as shaking hands. Even more disconcerting, researchers found that these germs could pass from one person to another without the next victim ever making direct contact with the infected person. A carrier who drank from a common cup or touched a door handle might pass the disease on to the next person who drank from the cup or opened the door. According to historian Nancy Tomes, this "new bacteriology" expanded Americans' "mental map of potentially dangerous forms of intercourse" to include riding on a streetcar, mingling at an amusement park, and swimming in a pool. Pools were especially hazardous because studies showed that germs could live longer in water than on dry surfaces, and water served as a medium that could convey the disease to other victims.[11] As a result of this newly accepted understanding of how diseases were transmitted, pools suddenly became obsolete and downright dangerous as public baths.

Many cities consciously chose not to build municipal pools because officials now perceived them as threats to public health. In 1896 Boston mayor Josiah Quincy formed a "Committee on Public Baths" to investigate what types of baths would best serve the city's needs. After studying facilities throughout the United States and Europe, including Philadelphia's pools, the committee recommended showers "on account of the great economical and sanitary advantage which they offer" over pools.[12] The city eventually built a state-of-the-art facility in the South End that contained thirty-six shower baths, nine tubs, and no pool. Quincy hailed it as "the finest and most modern public bathing establishment on the continent."[13]

New York City likewise chose to build shower baths rather than pools during this period. The need for public baths in Manhattan was particularly acute. In 1894 the Tenement House Committee found that only 306 out of more than 250,000 tenement dwellers it surveyed had bathing facilities in their homes. As a remedy, the committee recommended that the city build several permanent bathhouses in "the crowded districts." A year later, Mayor William Strong organized a bath committee to undertake the project. As in Boston, the committee recommended facilities with lots of showers but no pool. Due to several delays, the first bathhouse did not open until 1901, but six more followed over the next five years. None contained a pool.[14] Whereas city officials, reformers, and newspaper commentators in the 1880s and early 1890s hailed pools as having "great sanitary value," many observers had, by the late 1890s, come to see them as threats to individual and public health.

The microbe, however, did not kill municipal pools entirely. A few cities continued to open new pools during the late 1890s, including Philadelphia, Chicago, and Brookline, Massachusetts.[15] Public officials in these cities, however, no longer intended them to function as baths. Instead, they redefined and redesigned them as sport and exercise facilities. They built showers into the changing rooms, so swimmers were clean before they entered the pool. They adorned the pools with "springboards," offered swimming instruction, and attached running tracks and gymnasiums. They even organized swimming clubs and hosted water polo matches and swimming competitions at the pools.

Municipal pools survived the discovery of the microbe and were redefined as swimming facilities in large part because the urban middle class was crazy about athletics and exercise at the time. Middle-class men in particular embraced competitive sports and physical fitness during the 1890s in order to combat their perceived frailty and loss of manliness. Many feared that sedentary occupations and comfortable life-styles were feminizing middle-class men and causing them to become weak and "overcivilized." In order to regain their strength and vigor, many clerks, merchants, managers, lawyers, academics, and even ministers started riding bicycles, playing sports, lifting weights, and swimming in pools. Bicycling, for example, became a phenomenon among the urban middle class at the end of the nineteenth century. Americans owned about 1 million bicycles in 1893 and 10 million seven years later. Middle-class cyclists used them mostly for exercise and recreation, not transportation. They founded bicycle clubs, entered races, and rode through the countryside. Bicycling became so popular that newspapers regularly devoted entire sections to the activity.[16] Gymnastics and weight lifting also surged in popularity at the end of the nineteenth century because they promoted strength and virility. Apostles of "physical culture," such as Eugen Sandow and Bernarr MacFadden, became iconic figures, representing the ideal, well-developed male that many sought to emulate through exercise.[17] According to historian Roy Rosenzweig, "the 1890s turned out to be the years in which America's middle and upper classes passionately embraced competitive sports and outdoor recreation."[18] The redefinition of municipal pools as swimming facilities was part of this passionate embrace. They offered fitness- and sports-crazed Americans a place to exercise and compete at swimming, diving, and water polo.

Municipal pools also survived the microbe because, by the mid-1890s, middle-class public officials and reformers had come to see sports and exercise as effective means for reforming the working classes. A laborer who regularly swam in a pool, they assumed, would expend surplus energy that might otherwise be directed toward antisocial behavior, such as crime and labor radicalism. A dedicated swimmer would also come to appreciate the virtues of self-discipline and hard work. Also, the physical stimulation of exercise would improve health and might even temper personal excesses, such as alcohol consumption and gambling. In short, Victorian public officials and reformers assumed that athletics and exercise would help transform laborers into "better" citizens, workers, and people by instilling them with middle-class values and character traits.[19]

Swimming pools were not effective reform institutions, however, because working-class boys—not public officials—controlled their use. As had occurred at the earlier bathing pools, young swimmers splashed, wrestled, and shouted in the water. But now, public officials found this rowdy behavior more obnoxious because it directly contradicted their intended function for the pools. When working-class boys misbehaved at the bathing pools, they were still getting clean. When they misbehaved at the swimming pools, they were clearly not learning the virtues of self-discipline and sobriety. Public officials responded by aggressively battling working-class boys for control of these public spaces, demanding that the pools be used in an orderly manner for serious purposes. When they determined that they could not control the rowdy boys, public officials excluded them by charging admission fees. In doing so, however, they abandoned the didacticism that was the cornerstone of Victorian public culture. Public officials excluded the working classes from the pools precisely because they could not reform or restrain them.

The early history of the Brookline, Massachusetts, "natatorium" exemplifies the redefinition of municipal pools as sport and exercise facilities and dramatizes the social and cultural conflicts that accompanied their use at the end of the nineteenth century. Brookline first considered building a municipal pool in the early 1880s. As in Boston and Philadelphia, the town intended the pool to function as a bath, where its poorer residents could wash themselves. The board of selectmen quickly abandoned the pool idea, however, concluding that it would cost too much to build and would drain too much of the town's supply of fresh water. They decided instead to build a natural-water bath in the "little stream" that ran along "the northerly side of the school-house lot on Boylston street." The town deepened and widened the stream in a spot close to the street and erected a small house over the pooled water. The bath opened in 1884.[20]

A few years later, the board of selectmen concluded that the stream bath no longer met the town's bathing needs. It was small, could only be used during the summer, and frequently became flooded. Furthermore, it was unsuitable for women and girls because voyeurs sometimes gathered on Boylston Street hoping to catch a glimpse of female bathers.[21] In 1890 the selectmen authorized a new Committee on Free Warm Baths to investigate possible alternatives. The committee studied baths in England, France, Philadelphia, and Boston and returned to the idea of building a permanent in-ground pool.[22] The town discussed the committee's report "at considerable length" during a town meeting. Two arguments swayed residents against the pool. Several citizens expressed concern that an indoor pool would be used mostly by boys for their own amusement rather than working men and women for bathing. Townspeople were also skeptical that the pool could be built for the $10,000 the committee estimated.[23] Unwilling to pay an unspecified amount of money for a public institution that they feared would serve only as a playground for boys and young men, the citizens of Brookline rejected the proposal.

The issue quieted until 1894, when the bath committee again recommended that the town construct a large public bath that would include an indoor pool. This time the committee identified the pool as a "swimming-bath" and emphasized that its "great value" was "as a means of physical culture and of acquiring an art [swimming] which saves many lives."[24] The pool was no longer for washing the poor; it would serve the entire community as an exercise and sport facility. In addition to the twenty-six by eighty foot pool, the Brookline Public Bath would also include showers, bathtubs, a spectator gallery overlooking the pool, and a running track. The combination bathhouse and swimming pool now appealed to the class of citizens who attended the town meetings. In 1895 they voted unanimously (248 to 0) to appropriate $15,000 for its construction.[25]

Brookline located the large structure on the "recreation ground of the town," adjacent to the high school and public playground. Bath committee chairman Walter Channing assumed that such a central location might surprise townspeople who still viewed the institution solely as a cleanliness bath. In order to explain the choice, he posed this question in the local newspaper: "We should not think of putting the town hall or the library in the worst section of the town, and why the bath-house?" The "bath-house" did not belong in the slums because it was much more than a bath. It served a variety of functions—bathing, sports, exercise, and swimming instruction—that encompassed the needs of all townspeople. In order to attract "bathers of all classes, from all quarters of the town," Channing explained, the facility had to be centrally located.[26]

When the Brookline Public Bath finally opened on New Year's Day, 1897, city officials undertook a comprehensive effort to instruct residents how to use the swimming pool in particular. The message was clear: the pool was for

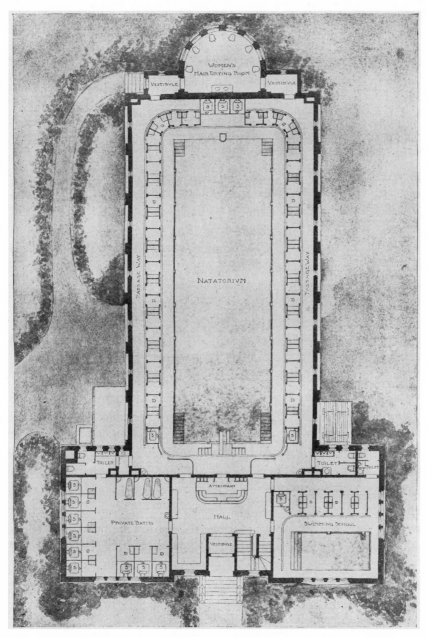

Plan of Brookline Public Bath, Brookline, Massachusetts, circa 1897. Even though the pool was housed within the town's "bath" house, it was intended to function as a swimming pool. U.S. Department of Commerce and Labor, *Bulletin of the Bureau of Labor*, September 1904.

sport and exercise, not play or bathing. The opening ceremony served as the first lesson. Hundreds of citizens crowded into the facility to watch a series of elaborate exhibitions.[27] Lionel Street, a well-known local sportsman, demonstrated proper swimming strokes and several ways to rescue someone who was drowning. Next, members of the newly formed Brookline Swimming Club exhibited fancy dives from the springboard, performed water gymnastics, and played a demonstration water polo match.[28] After opening day, the committee continued to educate the townspeople on the proper uses of the pool. It published a series of articles in the local newspaper touting swimming as a sport, as exercise, and as an important life-saving skill.[29] The bath committee also hired retired rear admiral George Belknap to deliver an address on swimming to students at Brookline High School. In his lecture, Belknap emphasized the utility of swimming, declaring that "readin, ritin, rithmetic, and swimmin'" should be the "obligatory requirements of primary education." He also told the students that the new pool was "the result of the indomitable purpose and untiring industry of the generations who have toiled and wrought on this soil from the earliest days of the Commonwealth to this time."[30] Belknap thus made clear to these young men and women that swimming had more in common with education and the work ethic of their forefathers than with frivolous amusement.

City officials intended the swimming pool to be a democratic institution, but not a social melting pot. They invited the whole town to swim in it but implemented a complicated usage and pay schedule that encouraged the different levels of Brookline society to swim at different times. Three days a week—Tuesdays, Wednesdays, and Saturdays—use of the pool was free, two and a half days a week admission cost fifteen cents, and on Thursday evenings swimmers had to pay twenty-five cents.[31] This fee structure enabled swimmers to segregate themselves along class lines. Those of moderate means could choose to swim on the days when entrance was fifteen cents, while the rich could afford to swim Thursday evenings. The town's poor had no real choice but to swim on the free days. While the fee structure clearly shows that the bath committee did not want to force the rich to swim with the poor, it shows just as clearly that the committee members intended the pool to serve the entire community. Town leaders thus sanctioned exercise for all social classes, even while enabling them to swim separately.

The bath committee also made class distinctions in an effort to maintain sanitary conditions at the pool. Because the pool opened after popular acceptance of the germ theory, the committee mandated that every swimmer must "take a warm shower-bath with soap and . . . wash his feet" before entering the water. Patrons who paid fifteen or twenty-five cents to use the pool, however, were permitted to wear their own swimsuits, whereas "only suits and towels furnished by the establishment [were permitted] on free days."[32] The committee apparently trusted that those who paid to use the pool—the middle and upper classes—would surely have clean swimsuits but feared that the suits worn by those who frequented the pool on free days—the working classes—were likely dirty and unsanitary.

As the committee expected, working-class boys filled the pool when admission was free. "On those days," noted committee chairman Walter Channing, "the town 'small boy' swarmed in large numbers."[33] Their use of the pool, however, offended the members of the bath committee. In its first annual report, the committee described the boys as "rude and boisterous" and characterized their activities in the water as "reckless and rough."[34] Channing explained the underlying cause of the problem to the local newspaper. According to him, the sons of the "laboring man" came to the pool "to have a good time" rather than for the constructive uses outlined by the committee. The reason, he surmised, was that they "had had no previous education as to what a [pool] was for."[35] These boys had apparently not read the newspaper articles or heard Admiral Belknap's lecture.

The bath committee did, however, post "Natatorium Rules and Regulations" that should have made it clear to them that the pool was not a place to have a good time. The committee virtually banned play in the pool. One rule mandated "[q]uiet and gentlemanly deportment will be expected in all patrons of the establishment. Yelling, running, pushing in the water, and other boisterous or dangerous practices will not be tolerated." The committee also discouraged leisurely use of the pool. Swimmers could spend no more than thirty minutes in the water per visit, and posted signs advised them to stay active while in the pool: "Do not stand still in the water to talk, but keep moving after entering the water, and if tired go and dress immediately."[36]

These rules and regulations reflected the class-specific values of the bath committee members. The committee consisted of representatives of Brookline's established elite. Six of the nine members were later included in a short list of Brookline's "Prominent Men Past and Present." Three were also listed in the Boston Social Registry, a definitive mark of high social status at the time. The chairman of the committee, Walter Channing, was a renowned doctor from a prominent Boston family that included William Ellery Channing and Margaret Fuller. He belonged to several exclusive social organizations, including the Boston Union Club, the University Club, and the Country Club at Brookline. James Codman was a wealthy world traveler who retired from active business pursuits at age twenty-six. Several members of the committee gained social and political prominence through their "old middle class" occupations. James Hand started a small painting enterprise in the 1850s that quickly grew into a prosperous business. As his business grew, so did his influence upon the community. By the 1880s he was a powerful member of both the board of selectman and the overseers of the poor. Two members of the committee were Harvard-trained lawyers. One of the lawyers, Alfred Chandler, also served several terms on the town's board of selectman and was a founding member of the Boston-area Immigration Restriction League. Two women sat on the committee. One was the wife of a well-known local businessman, and the other, Martha Edgerly, seems to have been a wealthy unmarried woman.[37]

The committee members were definitive New England Victorians, which explains their administration of the pool. Victorians valued order and self-restraint above all else.[38] The natatorium rules forbidding yelling, running, pushing in the water, and other "boisterous" practices were clearly designed to ensure that order prevailed at the pool and that swimmers exercised self-control. Victorians also distinguished themselves by their seriousness, which, according to one scholar, "meant not doing anything for its own sake; Victorians believed that every task ultimately served a moral purpose."[39] The committee members valued exercise and swimming instruction precisely because these activities improved the individual. According to them, swimming, diving, and water polo rejuvenated the mind, hardened the body, instilled discipline, and "engender[ed] self-respect."[40] The bath committee also ascribed broad social functions to the pool. Channing and the others claimed it would "have an educative influence on the life of the community" and serve as "one of the most potent moral forces in [the] community."[41] Dr. D. E. Hartwell, director of physical education for Boston's public schools, even claimed that the facility would curb alcohol consumption among the town's poor. In a speech before the Brookline Swimming Club, Hartwell explained that the pool would be "conducive to temperance" because the "sense of life and virility" it provided would diminish the workingman's need for "three fingers of whisky."[42] In all these ways, the swimming pool was a quintessentially Victorian institution.

Despite their social prominence and public authority, the committee members could not control the young swimmers who used the pool on free days. In its 1897 annual report, the committee blamed the boys for causing "disorder that had constantly to be suppressed."[43] Channing also wrote an article in the local newspaper complaining that the boys were "with some difficulty kept in order by the officials and an efficient police officer." But his subsequent statement acknowledged that bath officials and the policeman stationed at the pool could not in fact control the "rude and boisterous" boys: "It soon became quite evident that no bath-house would be big enough or strong enough to stand the rush put upon it, unless some means were found to regulate both the number of bathers and the use they were in some cases inclined to make of the bath-house."[44]

When the bath committee concluded that it could not reform or restrain the boys, it chose to exclude them. The committee instituted a new, far more socially restrictive, fee schedule just a month after the pool opened. On Tuesday and Saturday afternoons, admission to the pool was five cents, but at all other times it was ten, fifteen, or fifty cents depending on the day and time. During most swim periods, admission cost fifteen cents.[45] At no time was admission free. Shortly thereafter, Channing declared the new fee system a success: "This plan worked like a charm. The police officer was dismissed, and since the change was made discipline has been at all time maintained with practically no difficulty. . . . there is a much greater degree of decorum and good behavior." Displaying once again his Victorian sensibilities, Channing attributed the improved order and decorum to the educative force of the fee, not to its effect of excluding the rowdy boys. According to him, the price of admission taught patrons to respect the utility of swimming: "The small actual payment seemed to lead some of the too careless bathers to realize that [a swim] was good for something in itself, and to be taken seriously." It did not, Channing claimed, deny working-class residents access to the pool. "A few boys may have been dropped out, but . . . the poorest boy is usually able to obtain his five cents from some source."[46]

Despite Channing's assertion to the contrary, evidence suggests that the new fee structure drastically curtailed working-class boys' use of the pool. Channing was probably correct in claiming that even Brookline's poor had a nickel in their pockets, but was it a spare nickel? Could they afford to spend five cents on a thirty-minute swim, when they could buy a quart of milk, a pound of sugar, or almost a yard of shirting with it?[47] The sporadic and seasonal nature of unskilled and semiskilled labor during this period made domestic economy decisions difficult for working-class families. They frequently experienced times when the primary wage earner was out of work. These families had to save all the nickels they could in order to survive the lean periods. Even when working-class families chose to spend some of their limited resources on swimming, five cents gave them a limited window of time to use the pool. Previously, they had three free days each week. Now, they had to squeeze their pool time into two short afternoons, unless of course they could afford to pay fifteen cents. This time reduction meant that even if poor boys could scrape together five cents, as the wealthy Channing assumed, they were still much more limited in their access to the pool than before.

Attendance figures and receipt totals confirm that few working-class residents used the pool after free-swim periods were eliminated. In its first full year, swimmers entered the pool 33,332 times, while the total receipts for the same period were $4,109.40.[48] The average fee per swim was thus about twelve and a half cents. In 1900 the average fee per swim was almost fifteen cents.[49] Such a high fee per swim suggests that comparatively few patrons swam for only five cents. Considering that the fifty-cent fee applied to only four hours each week, the numbers indicate that the vast majority of swimmers paid fifteen cents each time they entered the pool. This was a prosperous crowd. Unlike the original fee schedule that separated the classes in their use of the facility, this new fee schedule segregated the town's poor out of the pool entirely.

After the fee increase, the pool served the constructive ends the bath committee envisioned. The local high school and grammar school used it throughout the school year to teach students how to swim.[50] Young women from Wellesley College who intended to become schoolteachers also had weekly swim lessons. The Brookline Swimming Club, which counted more than 200 members, used the pool to prepare for swimming, diving, and water polo contests against private athletic clubs.[51] During open swim periods, adults swam in the pool more than children and men more than women.[52] So many adult swimmers—especially ones who could afford to pay fifteen cents—suggests that the pool culture was indeed "quiet and gentlemanly." Had members of the bath committee come to observe the swim lessons, club practices, and even open swim periods, they no doubt would have been pleased with what they saw—orderly, constructive, and athletic use of the pool.

The bath committee's exclusion of working-class swimmers was a paradoxical victory. It demonstrated political power but not cultural authority. In fact, the need to exclude the boys exemplified the crumbling of the Victorian cultural order. When the bath committee changed the fee schedule, it abandoned the didacticism that was the cornerstone of Victorian reform. If the working classes could not afford to use the pool, how would it "educate" them to the virtues of cleanliness, self-discipline, and sobriety? The committee did not at first realize its loss. It claimed that the fee system had "enabled them

Brookline Pool, Brookline, Massachusetts, circa late 1890s. After the bath committee effectively excluded the town's working classes by eliminating free days, the pool served mainly as a sport and exercise facility for middle-class males. U.S. Department of Commerce and Labor, *Bulletin of the Bureau of Labor*, September 1904.

to exercise a proper control over those who have taken baths."[53] In reality, the fee did not allow the committee members to control the swimmers but only to control who swam. The fee actually deprived them control over the working-class men, women, and children they intended to reform.

Seven years after the Brookline bath committee excluded working-class swimmers from the town's pool, it welcomed them back by reinstating free days. In its 1904 annual report, the committee acknowledged that the fee system had diminished its control over working-class youths and contributed to their delinquency. "In the very hot weather, when the poorest class of boys and girls of the town have nothing to do, and free baths may be the means of occupying them and keeping them out of mischief, it seems to be the part of wisdom to attract them to the Bath House, even if they pay nothing."[54] The committee decided that it would rather have local youths roughhousing in the pool than betting craps, hanging around saloons and gambling dens, playing stickball in the street, fighting, and vandalizing property.[55]

When the bath committee reopened the pool doors to working-class boys and girls, it gained greater oversight of them, but it also capitulated to their definition of what the swimming pool was. A swim was no longer something "to be taken seriously," as Walter Channing insisted back in 1897. Rather, the pool became a place for children to play their idle time away. As the committee itself acknowledged, swimming was now a means of "occupying" children and a substitute for "nothing to do." The usage pattern that working-class boys first brought to the pool in 1897 had, by 1904, come to define its function.

The Brookline bath committee's reevaluation of the pool's function exemplified a second redefinition of municipal pools. During the first decade of the twentieth century, a new generation of reformers and city officials identified municipal pools as wholesome recreation centers that could ameliorate life in industrial slums, quell social conflict, and keep working-class children out of trouble and away from commercial amusements. Chapter 3 details this Progressive Era redefinition and examines the social divisions that accompanied it.

CHAPTER 3

"A GOOD INVESTMENT IN HEALTH, CHARACTER, AND CITIZENSHIP"

MUNICIPAL SWIMMING POOLS IN THE PROGRESSIVE ERA

On any Saturday afternoon, a few years ago, the streets of the West Side of Chicago were a battle ground for rough and tumble fights between Italian and Slav boys. National Characteristics and international misunderstandings were fertile causes for combat. In any case a fight was the cheapest and most convenient excitement the locality afforded. . . . Now on any Saturday after-noon long lines of Italians and Slavs, as well as Hungarians, Scandinavians, Irish and Germans, may be seen at the door of the swimming pool, awaiting their turn—with the peace restored. . . . Here play has become a deep, whole-some Americanizing force." —Playground Association of Philadelphia (1908)

In January 1912 the Philadelphia Bureau of City Property assigned one of its inspectors to assess the condition of the city's twenty swimming pools. The unnamed inspector visited the establishments 585 times over the next ten months. He found the pools in a dilapidated state. All the tanks "need[ed] to be strengthened by asphalt, cement or calcium silicates." The plumbing at all the pools needed repair, and most of the bathhouse roofs were "worthless." All but one needed extensive carpentry work "to put in condition the doors, windows, transoms, lockers and benches." Finally, they all needed to be repainted. The city had clearly done little over the years to maintain its municipal pools.[1]

While the inspector's assessment of their physical condition was bleak, he was sanguine about the social utility of the pools. He encouraged his superiors at the Bureau of City Property and at city hall to make the needed repairs on existing pools and build new ones "in the congested districts." The inspector did not justify the repairs and new pools by pointing to their virtues as baths or fitness facilities. Rather, the pools were "a public necessity," he claimed, because they would socialize immigrant and working-class children into healthy, happy, and patriotic Americans. "Public bath house swimming pools are undoubtedly a good investment in health, character, and citizenship," the inspector concluded, "as they stand for body, and character building, and produce better boys and girls, homes, morals, as well as greater love for their home city."[2]

This unnamed city employee encapsulated the Progressive redefinition of municipal swimming pools. After the turn of the century, public officials and reformers in several large northern cities reconceived municipal pools as centers for working-class recreation and intended them to serve a variety of purposes. On the one hand, these social Progressives believed that swimming pools would improve the lives of poor and working-class youths by providing them a safe and pleasurable refuge away from the sweltering streets, cramped tenements, and industrial landscapes that surrounded them. Proponents also emphasized the broader social function of municipal pools, claiming they would curb juvenile delinquency, alleviate urban social tensions, and "Americanize" immigrants. They championed pools as wholesome alternatives to saloons, gambling dens, and the ominous "street-corner," where, many commentators asserted, a generation of working-class youths was being schooled in vice and subversion. In short, Progressive social reformers viewed municipal swimming pools as antidotes to many of the problems they believed plagued American cities at the time.

Progressive Era pools did not, however, diminish the social divisions that existed in northern cities. Rather, they reinforced the physical distance separating the classes and the social distance separating the sexes by perpetuating class and gender segregation. As the Philadelphia building inspector advised, cities once again built pools within residential slums, where they attracted only immigrant and working-class residents. Cities also continued to gender-segregate municipal pools. Males and females either swam in separate pools or used the same pools on different days. Municipal pools were not, however, segregated along racial or ethnic lines. Blacks and working-class whites of various ethnicities swam together throughout the Progressive Era. Conflicts sometimes arose, but the disputes did not lead to racial segregation or exclusion.

The class segregation that characterized the use of municipal pools during this period was not simply a coincidental result of locating pools within working-class neighborhoods. Rather, it was an intentional public policy meant to protect the social and cultural geography of northern cities. Proposals to build outdoor pools in central locations—where working-class youths and their swimming culture would be exposed to the larger public—aroused vehement opposition from urban elites, newspaper editors, and even Progressive play reformers. Social elites believed that swimming pools located in parks or on city commons would degrade public culture and transform their traditional recreation spaces into Coney Island–like amusement centers. Middle-class critics were more concerned about social geography. They feared that centrally located pools would upset the social segregation that existed in early twentieth-century cities by attracting hordes of supposedly dirty and delinquent youths into their residential and commercial neighborhoods. By locating municipal pools within the slums, cities purposefully encouraged the working classes to stay within in their own neighborhoods.

~~~ At the same time that Chicago and Brookline redefined their municipal pools as fitness facilities, Boston's mayor Josiah Quincy attempted a more radical redefinition. In 1898, Quincy opened two municipal pools and justified them, in part, as public amusements for working-class children. Quincy located the pools within Roxbury's slums and emphasized the pleasure they would bring young swimmers. When the city's middle and upper classes learned that the pools were intended to function as public amusements, not simply baths or fitness facilities, they opposed them. Well-to-do citizen groups condemned the pools as "public philanthropy," and city councilmen who represented affluent wards withheld additional funding. While the middle and upper classes were eager for the city to promote cleanliness and even physical fitness among the poor, they were not willing, in 1898, to fund working-class amusement.

Josiah Quincy entered the mayor's office in 1896. Although he came from a Brahmin family that had already given two of its sons to serve the city as mayor, this Josiah Quincy was a reforming Democrat. He began his political career in the Massachusetts State Legislature, where he successfully sponsored bills that strengthened child labor restrictions and granted labor unions expanded rights.[3] Due largely to his efforts, Massachusetts had arguably the most complete set of labor laws in the country by 1890.[4] As mayor, Quincy looked to improve the lives of Boston's working classes beyond the factory and shop floor. In an 1897 *Arena* magazine article entitled "The Development of American Cities," Quincy articulated a new paradigm of municipal function modeled on the administration of European cities. He argued that city governments in America should expand the range of social services offered to the "average citizen." He emphasized recreation in particular: "The duty of a city is to promote the civilization, in the fullest sense of the word, of all its citizens. No true civilization can exist without the provision of some reasonable opportunities for exercising the physical and mental faculties, of experiencing something of the variety and of the healthful pleasure of life."[5]

The following year, Quincy decided to expand the city's provision of recreation by transforming the old Frog Pond on Boston's Common into a large outdoor swimming pool. He proposed to clean the pond, deepen it to a uniform four-foot depth, and build a bathhouse along its shore. Quincy viewed the Frog Pond as an ideal spot for a pool because it would cost very little money and yet, because of its size and location, could accommodate many people. "The area of the Frog Pond is about 38,500 square feet, or about six-sevenths of an acre," Quincy explained, "and an opportunity for bathing and swimming for a large number of persons would therefore be afforded. The location is of course a very central one, and a very large population resides within easy reach of it."[6]

The proposal provoked immediate opposition, especially from Boston's elite. Critics objected to the pool for the same reasons Quincy lauded it. They did not want hordes of scantily clad paupers making regular pilgrimages to such a central spot in the city. The well-to-do residents of Beacon Hill sent a petition to Quincy and the Boston City Council complaining that the pool would offend their sense of public decency: "His [the workingman's] use of an exposed and public section of our Common for bathing purposes would degrade the general public."[7] The Frog Pond was indeed an exposed area of the Common. It was clearly visible from busy Beacon Street and the expensive row houses that lined it, as well as from several walking paths within the Common. When the Beacon Hill residents used the word "exposed," they also had something else in mind—the bodies of the bathers. As one member of the board of aldermen explained, the citizens who live and work near the Common feared that "children might go there lightly clad."[8] These well-to-do citizens did not want near-naked urchins running amuck through the park.

Quincy attempted to assuage these concerns by elaborating upon the design and administration of the pool. He assured the public that "a suitable canvas screen 12 feet in height" would surround the pool. By describing it as a "screen" rather than a fence, Quincy emphasized that its purpose was to hide the pool and bathers from outside viewers. He also proposed to build a bathhouse next to the pool, so bathers could change their clothing in an enclosed private space rather than travel to and from the pool in their bathing costumes. Quincy further assured that "suitable bathing dresses would be required." This assurance was necessary because boys and young men swam naked in the city's river baths as well as at unauthorized swimming spots around the city. Finally, Quincy indicated that only "school-age boys" would be allowed to enter the pool during the daytime. Men would have to wait for the cloak of darkness before they could enter. Through these regulations Quincy attempted to convince the city's elite that a municipal pool on the Common would not expose them to offensive sights.[9]

Quincy, however, misinterpreted the full extent of their criticism. Visual propriety was an obvious concern, but it was only part of the much larger issue of public culture. Beacon Hill residents wanted to maintain their control over this most central public space in Boston. They viewed the Common, "our Common" they called it in the petition, as their civic space and assumed the prerogative to regulate its use. They welcomed the masses so long as they engaged in genteel pursuits such as taking a Sunday stroll or resting quietly by the water's edge. "We hold the best sentiment of our community," the petition stated, "is for the elevation of the masses, through preserving all that is beautiful and historic in nature and art."[10] This did not include swimming and playing in the Frog Pond. Furthermore, elite critics realized that a municipal pool on the Common would challenge their cultural authority. It would transform the Common into a culturally contested space by providing the city's working classes a very public stage on which to exhibit their values and sensibilities, as well as their bodies.

Franklin Codman echoed the concerns of Beacon Hill residents when he attacked the pool proposal during a board of aldermen meeting. He repeatedly referred to the pool as a "public bath tub," which he no doubt intended to evoke images of dirty, naked boys splashing about in a state of disorder. He then contrasted this frightful spectacle with what he considered the proper function of the Common. "The Frog Pond should be preserved for the class of people who have used it in years past" to escape the noise and bustle of city life. Municipal pools, he advised, belonged within the slums, hidden away from the larger public.[11] Quincy eventually capitulated to the powerful opposition. After receiving additional complaints from the patrician Puritan Club and the Somerset Club, he sent a short note to the board of alderman withdrawing the request for funds.[12]

Despite the Frog Pond failure, Quincy continued to advocate municipal pools. Two weeks later, in June 1898, he requested funding for two pools to be located in Roxbury, a working-class neighborhood far from Beacon Hill and its genteel residents. He proposed to reopen the old Cabot Street Bath with an enlarged tank and build a new outdoor pool in Orchard Park. These proposals stirred no controversy and were unanimously approved by the city council because the pools were buried in the slums, just as Codman had advised, and council members assumed the pools would function primarily as cleanliness baths.[13]

For council members, the showers attached to the proposed pools were the most important feature of each facility. The need to shower before entering the tank meant that municipal pools were still serving, at least indirectly, their traditional function of promoting cleanliness among the urban poor. James Watson, a representative from Roxbury, emphasized this point in supporting the Cabot Street Pool: "We have practically no bathing facilities whatsoever— in fact, I might say that a large proportion of the houses in the tenement district have no bathrooms, and the improvement asked for by His Honor the mayor is very much needed."[14] Similarly, the city's bath department, which administered the pools, justified them as baths. "The swimming-pools were established," the department noted in its annual report, "to supply summer baths to the sections of the city without water frontage."[15] In the minds of city councilmen and bath department officials, municipal pools located within working-class slums still functioned primarily as public baths.

Quincy, on the other hand, intimated that the pools might serve purposes beyond cleanliness. In proposing the Orchard Park Pool, he speculated that it "might prove useful in connection with swimming" and that it would "be considerably used, especially by boys." The mayor surely realized that boys in Roxbury would be seeking something other than clean skin if they used it as frequently as he predicted. These were just suppositions, though. Quincy was ultimately unsure what function the pools would serve. He repeatedly referred to the Orchard Park Pool as an "experiment."[16] He would wait to see what use people actually made of the pools before assigning them a specific function. This was the opposite approach taken by Brookline's Walter Channing, who knew exactly what function he wanted the town's pool to serve and went to great lengths to ensure that it served that and only that function.

Orchard Park Pool opened early in July 1898, and the remodeled Cabot Street Pool opened in August. Quincy personally visited both pools shortly after they opened in order to observe his experiment firsthand.[17] In many ways, he saw what he had expected to see. Boys swam in the pools most often. During that first summer, boys visited Orchard Park Pool 37,574 times, girls 8,062, men 5,873, while women dipped in the water only 37 times.[18] Boys and girls, who swam on separate days, accounted for nearly nine out of every ten swimmers. The city also offered swimming lessons at the pools, just as Quincy had envisioned.[19] What seemed to impress him the most, however, was the pleasure expressed by the boys and girls while in the water. According to the bath department, Orchard Park Pool was "the especial delight of children, who crowd to it in hundreds."[20] Similarly, the local Roxbury newspaper described both pools as sources of great "entertainment" for local children.[21]

Shortly after visiting the pools, Quincy reconceived the social function of municipal swimming pools. He came to see them as institutions for bringing pleasure into the lives of working-class children as well as institutions for improving their health and fitness. Quincy elaborated upon his expanded view of municipal pools in a speech before the Social Science Association on August 31, 1898, just days after he visited the Roxbury pools. First, he affirmed the connection between municipal pools and bodily cleanliness. Pools were actually better than other types of baths, he argued, because dirty children flocked to pools, whereas they had "to be driven into the bathtub or under the shower." While the pool was no longer the instrument of cleaning, the children "eagerly" showered in order to plunge into the water. Quincy also identified swimming pools as valuable institutions for promoting physical fitness and health among the urban poor.[22] In these ways, he viewed pools similarly to city officials in Brookline and Chicago at the time. But Quincy also identified pools as public amusements. He told the academicians and reformers gathered at the convention that, "while the swimming pool and gymnasium are not intended purely for amusement, the recreation which accompanies their use, and the pleasant occupation which they provide are by no means to be overlooked." Quincy concluded by claiming that municipal pools "should in my opinion rank as one of the most important municipal agencies for the improvement of the condition of the people."[23] Municipal pools fulfilled Quincy's promise of democratized recreation articulated in the *Arena* magazine article. They were the best means for providing the city's working classes with an opportunity for "experiencing something of the variety and healthful pleasures of life."[24]

When Quincy justified municipal pools as public amusements, he transcended the limits of nineteenth-century municipal function and established a new basis for it as well. He assigned city governments the responsibility for promoting the pleasure and happiness of individual citizens. Previously, American cities provided a limited and well-defined range of services that were assumed to benefit all citizens. They built roads, waterworks, and sewers; inspected food; regulated commercial activity; and operated police departments, fire departments, hospitals, and public baths. Cities provided these services because they were essential for the maintenance of order, the protection of public health, and the promotion of commerce.[25] Some cities, including Boston, also provided municipal playgrounds by the late nineteenth century, but public officials and playground advocates explicitly justified them as serving the public good by deterring crime and combating disease.[26] Advocates did not justify playgrounds as public amusements intended to brighten the lives of individual children. As Dominic Cavallo has written, playgrounds were "not so much a reform undertaken on the child's behalf . . . but a medium created to reconstruct and control his moral values."[27]

Precisely because Quincy did justify municipal pools by pointing to the pleasure they brought individual swimmers, many well-to-do citizens and their representatives in the city council suddenly opposed them. Early in the summer of 1898, when city council members viewed pools as cleanliness baths, they voted unanimously to build two of them amid the Roxbury tenements. After Quincy's speech before the Social Science Association, however, municipal pools became controversial. Council members from wealthier wards began questioning their social utility and public necessity. If pools were not primarily serving their traditional function of protecting the public's health, many believed they should not be funded.

The city council debated the value of municipal pools late in the summer of 1898. The bath department had run out of money and Quincy requested $13,700 to keep the Orchard Park and Cabot Street pools, along with a few river baths, open through September. The council convened a special meeting to vote on the emergency appropriation. Like Quincy, members of the council who represented immigrant and working-class wards had come to see the pools as summer resorts, not just public baths. During the meeting, North End Councilman Samuel Borofsky hailed municipal pools as the poor man's alternative to Cape Cod. He pointed out to representatives from wealthier sections of the city that "while a certain number of your citizens may have all the comforts of life and be able to go to the beaches," the "plain people" relied upon the public pools and river baths for summer recreation.[28] Critics rose from their chairs to question the value and necessity of public institutions that offered amusement to the working classes. George Holden Tinkham, who lived along fashionable Commonwealth Avenue and represented the affluent Back Bay, led the opposition. He called municipal pools "fads" and described them as "a wasting of money." He argued that more traditional municipal services, such as streets, schools, and sewers deserved the money because they "benefited the rich, the poor, and the stranger," whereas swimming pools only satisfied individual want.[29] Tinkham had supported municipal pools earlier in the summer because his notion of their function—bathing—fit within the scope of nineteenth-century municipal policy. A clean working class, he assumed, served the interests of all Bostonians. Now that Quincy had defined swimming pools as public amusements, he and several other council members rejected them as frivolous and unnecessary.

Tinkham swung enough votes to defeat the emergency appropriation. The vote split along party lines with Democrats voting in favor and Republicans against. This political partisanship reflected class divisions in the city. Republican councilmen generally represented affluent wards, while Democrats represented working-class sections of the city. Quincy needed fifty out of seventy-five council members to vote in favor of the appropriation but only got forty-two votes. Twelve members of the council voted against the bill outright. Eleven of them represented well-to-do wards in the Back Bay, the South End, and along the Dorchester Bay coastline. Twenty-one council members abstained from voting or were absent. The forty-two members that voted in favor of the bill mostly represented the poorer, immigrant areas of the city, including Roxbury, East Boston, South Boston, and the North End.[30]

The pool controversy extended beyond the halls of city government and divided the public along the same class lines as the council vote. Boston's Central Labor Union, which represented artisans and mechanics, strongly supported the appropriation and swimming pools in general. It publicly denounced the council members who voted against the bill and urged the city to spend $200,000 to build even more pools and river baths the following year.[31] The city's middle and upper classes disagreed. An editorial in the *Boston Evening Transcript* identified growing opposition to municipal pools after Quincy's speech before the Social Science Association. "It is a far cry from Saratoga [the site of the conference] to Boston," the editorial began. According to the paper, few Bostonians objected to municipal pools when their function was to promote cleanliness among the poor: "Cleanliness is one of the fundamental conditions of a high civilization, and when the means are afforded of making it convenient and popular the effect upon the mixed life of the city is undeniably good." Now that Quincy had defined pools as public amusements, however, the paper doubted whether anyone but the working classes would support the mayor's plan: "It goes without saying that those who pay the taxes are hardly yet prepared to back such a broad scheme of public philanthropy."[32] Another local paper editorialized about the controversy. The *Roxbury Gazette* praised Quincy for opening the Orchard Park and Cabot Street pools and claimed that the council vote exemplified elites' cultural bias. Representatives from Beacon Hill and the Back Bay regularly supported public expenditures for recreation that involved "an object lesson in art," the paper noted, but opposed public recreation that brought "entertainment" to common people.[33]

In the years following the 1898 controversy, Quincy left office and support for municipal pools waned among public officials. In 1902 the Boston School Committee requested money to construct an indoor pool adjoining a Charlestown high school. The school committee described swimming as an essential component of secondary education, citing health, fitness, and lifesaving benefits. Boston's Democratic mayor Patrick Collins vetoed the proposal, however, claiming that the "whole subject [of swimming pools] requires more consideration than we have time to give it during the early months of the present year." That same year, a councilman from Roxbury requested that the city fill-in Orchard Park Pool and plant grass over the top of it. The mayor and the city council refused the request, but it aptly symbolized the death and burial of municipal pools in Boston.[34] Even Democrats representing tenement districts no longer supported them.

Quincy doomed municipal pools in Boston during the summer of 1898 by publicly promoting them as amusement centers for working-class children. Boston historian Andrew J. Peters no doubt had Quincy's zeal for pools in mind when he eulogized the mayor's tenure in office: "It was almost a fetish with him that the poor should have as ample facilities for recreation as the rich. . . . His expenditures of unusual sums to better the condition of less fortunate citizens proved the fallacy of philanthropic administration."[35] When Quincy left office in 1901, Boston operated two municipal pools. Seventeen years later, at the end of the Progressive Era, the city had added only one more.[36] Quincy's vision of swimming pools throughout the city filled with laughing and splashing children turned out to be a mirage.

≈≈≈ Quincy's mirage became a reality, however, on Chicago's South Side. From 1903 to 1908, the city's South Park Board opened eleven municipal swimming pools within working-class slums.[37] The pools were outdoors and typically measured 50 by 100 feet. They were clearly designed as children's play spaces. The main tanks were shallow, so children could stand in the water to splash and roughhouse, and many were bordered by sand boxes, where young swimmers dug holes and buried their limbs. Each pool was part of a larger recreation center that also included sports fields, a running track, a gymnasium, playground apparatus, and a community hall. These "small parks" were the most elaborate municipal athletic and play facilities in the country at the time. Local reformers and park officials intended them

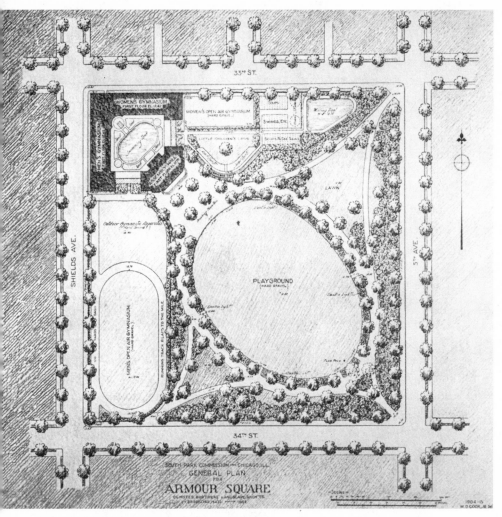

Plan of Armour Square Recreation Center, Chicago, 1903. The design of Armour Square and its facilities were typical of Chicago's Progressive Era recreation centers. Courtesy of Frances Loeb Library, Harvard Design School, Cambridge, Massachusetts, neg. 117371.

to brighten the lives of working-class youngsters, curb juvenile delinquency, weaken social antagonisms, and inspire patriotism. They were definitive Progressive institutions.

The South Park Board located the swimming pool recreation centers within the city's poorest residential slums. Six of them surrounded the stockyards and slaughterhouses in southwest Chicago. The giant Union Stock Yard, which opened Christmas Day, 1865, shaped the geography and demography of the area. Ramshackle clusters of homes grew into expansive slums as waves of migrants from foreign shores and the American countryside crashed upon the yards district in search of work. The Irish, Germans, and Scandinavians came first, then Poles, Italians, Bohemians, Lithuanians, and other eastern Europeans. Expediency rather than thoughtful planning directed the area's development. Families packed into narrow wooden "two-flat" homes and three story tenements along mostly unpaved streets. When housing in a particular neighborhood reached capacity, owners or tenants erected makeshift rear tenements. When those filled, they simply crammed one more family into the structure.[38]

The neighborhoods around the stockyards were dirty, malodorous, and unhealthy. A stagnant open sewer called Bubbly Creek crept through the area on its way to the South Branch of the Chicago River. Some homes actually stood in pools of sewage. Despite the close proximity of the city dump, trash piled up in the streets and alleys throughout the district.[39] The stench from the trash and the outdoor privies drove residents indoors, especially on hot days. The meatpacking plants contributed to the oppressive environment by emitting belches of smoke and a continuous foul odor. The living conditions in Back of the Yards were so bad, that investigator Robert Hunter chose not to include his findings on this district in his 1901 report on tenement conditions throughout Chicago for fear that they might mislead readers into thinking conditions throughout the city were worse than they actually were.[40]

The park board grouped three other swimming pool recreation centers around the South Chicago steel mills. Much like the stockyards district, this area was a stereotypical industrial slum. In 1905 it was populated predominately by eastern European immigrants, especially Poles, who worked as unskilled and semiskilled laborers. Multiple families shared small wooden tenements that crowded up against the mills. The district as a whole was virtually barren of trees and grass.[41] The tenements, mills, warehouses, and railroad tracks were packed so close together that children had few open spaces in which to play, except the dirty and dangerous streets.[42] Nor could youngsters escape the shadows of smokestacks, cranes, and other industrial silhouettes, which were darkened by the black cloud of soot that enveloped the area.[43] Given these conditions, it is no wonder that children living in Chicago's slums had only a fifty-fifty chance of living past the age of three.[44] By locating eight of the eleven swimming pools near the steel mills and stockyards, the South Park Board clearly reached the city's neediest working-class children and adolescents.

City officials and local reformers intended the swimming pools and play-

Stanford Park Swimming Pool, Chicago, 1916. Chicago's Progressive Era swimming pools were located within residential slums and typically had an urban appearance. Notice the boy peering over the brick wall in order to catch a glimpse of the female swimmers. Chicago Historical Society, neg. DN-0066566.

fields to ameliorate living in such an oppressive environment. The recreation centers exemplified the recent awareness among Progressive Era social reformers that children and youths required pleasurable recreation in order to grow into healthy and well-adjusted adults. This view was not generally accepted in 1898, when Josiah Quincy identified municipal pools as public amusements, but became so during the first decade of the twentieth century.[45] "Play is not something incidental," the Playgrounds Association of America claimed in 1908, "not a luxury, but as necessary as light and air, without which a child can grow up, if at all, but stunted and perverted."[46] J. Frank Foster, superintendent of the South Park system, echoed this sentiment when he explained that Chicago's swimming pool recreation centers were designed to provide an oasis for "the little bare-footed girls and boys about Archer Avenue and 25th street, the curly-headed blacks in rags and filth in the Black Belt, the vicious youths at the doors of the saloons in the Stock Yards districts, and the many-tongued foreign children in South Chicago [who] appeal to us to be saved from their apparent destiny of ill health, viciousness and crime."[47] For several hours each day, these children could escape their cramped homes and trash-laden streets for the pleasure of baseball, swings, and swimming. The swimming pools were the most popular facility at the recreation centers. Each one consistently attracted 1,000 swimmers a day. In 1909 the park board recorded more than 750,000 total swims at its eleven pools.[48] As Foster intended, the pools clearly appealed to the city's ragamuffin youths.

The recreation centers also embodied environmental social theories popular at the time that emphasized the role surroundings played in determining an individual's behavior, values, and material condition. Strands of environmental determinism ran through nineteenth-century thought, but Victorian reformers, such as the directors of the New York Association for Improving the Condition of the Poor (AICP), generally blamed the people themselves for their misfortune.[49] The AICP only provided aid to a clearly defined group of people whose poverty, in its view, resulted not from their own doing. This included widows, deserted wives, abandoned children, and the physically feeble. The association denied aid to the rest of New York City's poor because it believed their poverty resulted from personal failings such as intractable shiftlessness and intemperance.[50] Until such people had an internal moral reawakening, the AICP had no hope for them. Progressive reformers, on the other hand, believed in human pliability. They assumed that virtually anyone could become productive, law abiding, and sociable if provided the proper environment.[51]

Armed with these environmental social assumptions, park officials believed the recreation centers would help solve several pressing urban problems by providing a healthy and wholesome place for working-class youths to play. One problem was juvenile crime. Progressives were acutely concerned about the activities of working-class adolescents, especially boys. They believed that the social environment of saloons, gambling dens, and the street corner encouraged juvenile delinquency. Graham Taylor, who headed the Chicago Commons Settlement and was a professor of sociology at Chicago Theological Seminary, wrote: "It is significant that in our juvenile courts a large proportion of the delinquents received are between ages 14 and 16, the very period when the small playground begins to lose its grip and appeal."[52]

Chicago reformers believed that swimming pools would combat petty crime and juvenile delinquency by attracting teenagers off the street and out of the saloon. "We cannot imagine," Jane Addams wrote in 1907, "a boy who by walking three blocks can secure for himself the delicious sensation to be found in a swimming pool preferring to play craps in a foul and stuffy alley."[53] A study conducted by the Chicago School of Civics and Philanthropy a couple of years after the recreation centers opened seemed to confirm reformers' assumption that swimming pools and playfields would reduce crime. The study found that the number of juvenile delinquency cases dropped an average of 28 percent in neighborhoods where recreation centers were established.[54]

Park officials also intended the recreation centers to alleviate social antagonisms within immigrant, working-class neighborhoods. The pool, athletic fields, and meeting hall provided a common ground for the South Side's ethnically diverse population to come together to exercise and play. Waiting in line together, changing side by side, and interacting in the pool, park officials predicted, would break down ethnic divisions and foster a more vibrant community life by promoting dialogue, understanding, and even friendships. B. A. Eckhart, president of the West Chicago Parks Commission, claimed that, "In these [recreation centers] and in their work lie the beginning of the social redemption of the people in large cities. They furnish the spectacle of a 'city saving itself,' of the people of a great city finding nature and God by finding their neighbors and themselves."[55]

Chicago officials and reformers also envisioned the recreation centers as institutions for assimilating foreign immigrants into American culture, although they differed on what they thought American culture should be. Some hoped that the pools would "Americanize" immigrants by washing away ethnic particularities.[56] Other reformers, however, believed the recreation centers would strengthen immigrants' attachment to their adopted country by promoting an appreciation and respect for diversity. "There is no doubt," Jane Addams wrote in 1912, "that the future patriotism of America must depend not so much upon conformity as upon respect for variety, and nowhere can this be inculcated as it can in the public recreation centers."[57] In both cases, though, the purpose was to make the immigrants more "American" and less menacing by instilling them with a new outlook and set of values.

Some historians argue that Progressive Era play reform destroyed immigrant and working-class children's vibrant "street-play" culture by pulling them off the streets and forcing them to play at organized games under direct supervision.[58] This was not the case at Chicago's municipal swimming pools. Park officials did not attempt to control or organize what children did in the pools, and the young swimmers behaved much as they would have in Lake Michigan or the Chicago River. J. Frank Foster recognized that "direction . . . is to the children the most offensive thing that can be introduced." Consequently, he gave swimmers "plenty of room to play at any game they wish, without any restraint."[59] Foster believed that the best way to attract kids off the street and foster a sense of patriotism in them was to let them develop their own patterns of play in the pool.[60]

Photographs offer the best extant evidence as to what occurred at the Chicago pools. The most common swimmers, by far, were boys and girls. They came on separate days—two days a week for females and four for males—and often stood in long lines waiting for a bathing suit and towel. The boys' suits consisted of white trunks with gray vertical stripes. Their torsos were left bare. The girls' bathing suits covered much more of their bodies. They were essentially short-sleeved navy blue jumpsuits, with pant-legs extending down to the knee and high collars fastened around the base of the neck. A police officer patrolled the entrance area and the changing rooms on the boy days, while a matron performed the same function when girls used the pools. On their way from the changing rooms to the pool, swimmers passed through a shower room, where an attendant inspected their bodies, making sure they had given themselves "a thorough wash before entering the pool."[61]

While the process of getting to the pool was structured and orderly, the activities in and around it were not. Swimmers had considerable autonomy to play as they pleased. A series of photographs, titled "Typical Swimming Day," show young swimmers splashing, laughing, and wrestling in the water. The girls were as frolicsome as the boys. The activities in and around the pool were social and interactive. When not in the water, the adolescent youngsters sat on the side of the pool chatting with friends, huddled around the drinking fountain slurping water, or buried themselves in the nearby sand boxes. Poolside attendants did not organize games or otherwise direct the activities of the swimmers. What stands out in the pictures is the ubiquity of broad smiles and laughter. Chicago park officials may have intended the pools to curb juvenile delinquency and promote patriotism, but that did not seem to detract from the fun.[62]

The social composition of the swimmers reflected the social geography of the city. The recreation centers drew exclusively from the poor but ethnically diverse people that lived nearby. Local reformer Marian Lorena Osborn found that 75 to 80 percent of the people who frequented the Davis Square recreation center (located in Back of the Yards) came from within three blocks and

"Typical Swimming Day" at Armour Square Swimming Pool, Chicago, 1909. Courtesy of Frances Loeb Library, Harvard Design School, Cambridge, Massachusetts, neg. 117372.

were primarily children of Lithuanian, Polish, and Russian immigrants.[63] A group of reformers from Philadelphia who studied Chicago's recreation centers in 1908 found the same ethnic diversity: "[O]n any Saturday afternoon long lines of Italians and Slavs, as well as Hungarians, Scandinavians, Irish and Germans, may be seen at the door of the swimming pool, awaiting their turn."[64]

The ethnically diverse, working-class crowd that swam at Chicago's Progressive Era pools included black citizens. Blacks could and did play ball on the fields, read in the libraries, and swim in the pools, although they did not play, read, and swim in numbers proportional to their percentage of the population. Part of the reason for this underuse was that the park board did not locate any of the swimming pool recreation centers within Chicago's "black belt," which in 1910 stretched from 22nd Street to 51st Street, between State

"Typical Swimming Day" at Davis Square Swimming Pool, Chicago, 1909. Courtesy of Frances Loeb Library, Harvard Design School, Cambridge, Massachusetts, neg. 118106.

and LaSalle.[65] The absence of recreation centers in this area is conspicuous considering the abundant provision of such facilities in other working-class areas of the South Side.[66]

Although the city did not build any pools within the "black belt," three South Side recreation centers and one municipal pool on the city's West Side were located near to black neighborhoods. Black Chicagoans used most of the facilities at each center without unusual incidence, but swimming pools were the exception.[67] Blacks and whites swam together, but fights and disputes did occur. White swimmers sometimes abused blacks in an attempt to discourage them from using the pools. A playground director told the Chicago Commission on Race Relations that he had frequently seen white boys maliciously dunk black boys under the water and hold them down until they were close to drowning. The director of Ogden Park reported a curious incident where a trio of black girls got shuffled to the back of the line while waiting to enter the pool. Eventually they left. The director wondered "whether there was some threat or whether the girls were naturally timid about going into the pool."[68]

Park officials and park policeman did little to punish or otherwise deter incidents such as these. Many were sympathetic with the whites who harassed black swimmers. The directors of several recreation centers preferred blacks not to use their facilities. An Armour Square official reasoned that since whites had traditionally made the fullest use of the pools, the presence of black swimmers caused "ill feeling and trouble." Several park policemen agreed. An officer at Armour Square reportedly told a group of young black men, "niggers [sic] ought to stay in Beutner Park [a playground used predominately by blacks]." An officer at Hardin Square recreation center boasted that he could summon countless young men in the neighborhood to "procure arms and fight shoulder to shoulder with me if a Negro should say one word back to me or should say one word to a white woman."[69]

Racial conflict, however, was not the rule at Chicago pools. The Union Park Pool, located adjacent to the largest black neighborhood on the city's West Side, was frequented by large numbers of blacks and whites. The park director made a concerted effort to attract black swimmers. He "advertised among the colored people" and did "everything [he] could to get them to use the swimming pool." His efforts succeeded. Blacks accounted for 40 percent of the total attendance during the 1910s. The pattern of interaction in the pool varied with the age of the swimmers. Young children "mingled freely," while adolescents and adults generally "kept separate." The director emphasized that there was no trouble between black and white swimmers, "but they stayed in separate groups."[70] With strong leadership from public officials, blacks and whites could not only swim together in the same pool but do so peacefully during the Progressive Era.

～～～ The same social divisions that existed at Chicago's Progressive Era pools were true in other cities as well. New York City opened its first municipal pool in 1906 at West 60th Street right between an Irish immigrant neighborhood and an African American enclave. The second pool opened in 1908 and was located on East 23rd Street, within the infamous East Side slums. Both pools were local institutions that drew swimmers from the surrounding immigrant, working-class neighborhoods.[71] The pools were also gender-segregated. Females had "exclusive use" of the pools three days a week and men and boys the other four.[72] Pool use did not, however, divide along racial lines. The pools were racially integrated and attracted both black and white swimmers. As in Chicago, minor disputes did occur. Black and Irish swimmers, for example, contested the use of the West 60th Street pool. One cynical commentator surmised that it was a fallacy for the city to think it could "wash out the race problem in a swimming pool."[73]

While the social use was the same, the New York City pools differed significantly in design and function from Chicago's quintessential Progressive pools. They were buried inside bathhouse basements, measured only thirty feet by sixty feet, and were encircled by a metal railing that permitted swimmers to enter and exit only from narrow stairs jutting into the water from each corner.[74] New York officials intended the bathhouse pools to promote cleanliness, although in an indirect way. The pools were used to lure recalcitrant tenement dwellers—who, according to one commentator, had "instincts for . . . recreation" but not for bathing—into the bathhouses, where they would have to shower before being able to swim.[75] But because the "recreation" offered by the West 60th and East 23rd pools was limited by their small size, drab environment, and lack of pleasurable accoutrements, the pools attracted relatively few swimmers.

Many more boys and young men plunged into the natural waters around Manhattan. From June to September, they lined the banks of the Hudson, East, and Harlem Rivers, perpetuating the same swimming culture developed by earlier generations. The *New York Times* provided a social portrait of this seasonal ritual as it occurred early in the twentieth century:

> [H]ow enthusiastically the juvenile New Yorker takes to the water. Along the water front of the lower part of the city, built up with wharves and warehouses and crowded with shipping, venturesome youngsters are seen swimming about between the piers, clambering upon vessels to dive from their sides, shouting a shrill defiance to watchmen and longshoremen, always with one eye watchful for the appearance of the police. As one follows the river up town, and the water front becomes more open and less crowded, the number of bathers increases until in Harlem the occasional vacant strips of rocky bank are so lined with them that one wonders whence they all come. Along the Hudson and even the Muddy Harlem River the same groups of naked or lightly clad urchins are seen, happy in their enjoyment of water.[76]

Swimming in the rivers was a central part of adolescent, working-class life early in the twentieth century. Ludwig Kottl recalled his childhood days in New York's Upper East Side: "We'd play hooky, buy cigarettes and sneak into the Yorkville Casino by climbing down the drainpipe into the toilet. If it was summertime, we'd go down to the dock and go swimmin'. We used to sit by the dock, just sittin' there talkin', makin' up stories. There might be forty or fifty of us."[77] Sidney Kingsley immortalized this swimming-in-the-river adolescent culture in his 1937 play *Dead End*.

The rivers around New York were filled with more than just naked boys. Refuse and debris of all variety floated in the Hudson, East, and Harlem Rivers. Oral histories from New Yorkers who grew up during the early twentieth century describe in graphic detail the filth they waded through while swimming in the city's rivers. Bill Bailey, who grew up in Hell's Kitchen, recalled: "We did quite a bit of swimmin' in the Hudson. That was the only place we could go. . . . When I think about it now, the sweat goes runnin' down my neck. We swam among the condoms, the garbage, and the filth, everything the Hudson was noted for. As a matter of fact, the first intestines I ever seen came floatin' down there once."[78] Pete Pascale remembered the East River being equally as filthy: "At 114th Street they had the sewer that went right out there when we were swimmin'. . . . Every once in a while the sewer stuff would come out. Gheeegh! Everything came out. Goddamn, we had to push that crap away when we went in there, otherwise ya caught it in the face. That stuff hit us left and right, but that was the only place we coulda swam, because in the other place there was a fence. The other thing we hadda watch were the water rats. They were swimmin' round there. They were big son of a guns."[79]

The trash floating in the rivers and the strong currents made swimming quite treacherous. On one warm Sunday in 1910, nine people drowned in the waters around New York City, and many more had "narrow escapes from death," according to the *New York Herald*.[80] Unfortunately, this was not an unusual day. Drowning reports filled New York newspapers throughout the summer. The threat of death, however, did not deter many swimmers. Bill Bailey and his friends witnessed a boy drown in the Hudson after getting his head stuck in a milk can. "That stopped everyone from swimming for a couple of weeks," Bill remembered, "but then everyone went back."[81]

The dangers involved in river swimming and the increasingly polluted condition of the waters around Manhattan prompted city officials to look into developing alternative swimming sites. In 1907 the city considered purchasing a 365-acre tract of land near Rockaway Point in Brooklyn and transforming it into a public beach park. The city eventually abandoned the plan, however, in part because most denizens of Manhattan could not afford the time and expense of getting to and from the site on a regular basis.[82] Three years later, John Purroy Mitchel, the recently elected president of the board of aldermen, identified a more convenient place for the city's working classes to swim and recreate. He proposed building a large, outdoor swimming pool and athletic complex in Central Park, modeled on the Chicago recreation centers. The proposal provoked intense opposition. Middle- and upper-class New Yorkers objected to the swimming pool in particular, because they believed it would degrade the park and upset the city's class-divided social geography.

Mitchel, grandson of Irish patriot John Mitchel, was an unlikely champion of municipal swimming pools. He was a good-government reformer dedicated to making the administration of New York City efficient and honest; he was not a social reformer. Mitchel was a lawyer by training and began his public career at the age of twenty-eight investigating municipal corruption. He led probes into the affairs of Manhattan Borough president John Ahearn in 1907 and Bronx Borough president Louis Haffen in 1908. His investigations convinced the New York State Legislature to remove both men from office. The public notoriety Mitchel received catapulted him into elected office. In 1909 the city elected him president of the board of alderman as an anti-Tammany fusion candidate. Mitchel also served on the board of estimate, which meant his were two of the few hands that tied and untied the city's purse strings. As president of the board of aldermen and later as mayor of New York City, Mitchel made efficiency and parsimony his personal crusades. According to his biographer, "Mitchel made a vice of his virtues. In his zeal for efficiency and economy, he too often ignored the real needs of the people of New York."[83] This was not the case in 1910.

Mitchel unintentionally stumbled onto the swimming pool idea while investigating Haffen. One of the three principal charges he leveled against the Bronx Borough president was that Haffen had recommended the purchase of a public beach that was grossly unsuitable for swimming or bathing.[84] While investigating the affair, Mitchel became acutely aware that working-class children had limited opportunity for summer recreation, except to play in the increasingly dangerous streets, swim in polluted rivers, or frequent morally questionable commercial amusements. Because Mitchel was not a social reformer, he approached this problem from outside the established paradigm of Progressive play reform. Play reformers, such as those in Chicago, preferred many facilities located within working-class residential neighborhoods rather than a few centrally located recreation complexes.[85] Mitchel's exquisitely rational and economical mind, however, concluded that a large central facility would serve the city's poor more efficiently. He unconsciously applied the tenets of Taylorism to recreation provision and, by so doing, challenged the assumptions of mainstream play reformers.

Mitchel unveiled his plan before the city's board of estimate just months after taking office. He proposed installing a 100 by 200 foot outdoor swimming pool, a wading pool, a playground, and several sports fields in the northeast corner of Central Park, adjacent to 100th Street, in a large field commonly known as the North Meadow.[86] Mitchel justified the park "improvements" as an attempt to make the city's provision of recreation more democratic. Central Park provided "almost every conceivable convenience" for wealthy horsemen, carriage riders, and automobile owners, Mitchel asserted, but disregarded the interests of common people. This troubled the new board of aldermen president because, according to him, Central Park afforded many poor denizens of Manhattan "their only summer vacation ground." Furthermore, Mitchel recognized that poor and working-class New Yorkers had recreation interests different from people higher on the social ladder. The masses did not want "open space with trees, grass, highways, and benches," but a pool in which to swim and developed fields for sports and games. "The purpose of my resolution," Mitchel explained, "is to popularize the uses of Central Park."[87] The board of estimate agreed that the park should be popularized and voted unanimously to appropriate $225,000 for the project.[88]

Mitchel's plan provoked vehement opposition from social and cultural elites precisely because they did not want Central Park to become a Mecca for popular recreation. Shortly after Mitchel unveiled his plan, a group of the city's richest and most prominent men formed the Central Park Protective Association (CPPA). William Gibson, a well-connected lawyer who resided at the Hotel Gotham, organized the group and directed its activities. The other members were "men of real influence in the city's affairs," according to the *New York Times*, and included university presidents, lawyers, financiers, industrialists, and one world-renown sculptor.[89] Jacob Henry Schiff was typical of the association's membership. He headed the banking firm of Kuhn, Loeb, and Company and sat on the board of directors of several other corporations, including Western Union Telegraph and Union Pacific Railroad. He had been vice president of the New York Chamber of Commerce and was a member of the Metropolitan Museum of Art and the American Museum of Natural History.[90] As his membership in these two Manhattan institutions indicated, Schiff's taste in recreation tended toward the artistic and intellectual. The group's other members were equally prominent.[91]

These elite critics were primarily concerned with protecting the cultural landscape of Central Park and the cultural geography of New York City. They wanted the park reserved for the genteel uses Frederick Law Olmsted and

Calvert Vaux intended when they designed it back in the 1850s. "The proper use of Central Park is as a promenade and driving place," proclaimed former congressman John De Witt Warner.[92] The CPPA viewed Mitchel's plan as an attempt to introduce working-class culture into their oasis of genteel recreation. They feared that the swimming pool and athletic fields would transform the park into a popular amusement center. "We want no swimming pools, wading pools, children's nurseries, or anything of that kind there," one critic clamored. "No Coney Island, if you please, in that Park."[93] Elites focused their attacks on the swimming pool in particular. George McAneny, president of the Borough of Brooklyn, marveled that "mere mention" of the swimming pool "alarmed so many people."[94] Similarly, Mitchel lamented that the pool had "come in for the greatest amount of criticism."[95] The pool provoked impassioned opposition from the city's social and cultural elites because they believed it would institutionalize rowdy and boisterous play in the park. As one critic complained, a swimming pool would transform Central Park into a "cheap pleasure grounds, and license destruction, as if boisterous pleasure seeking were the fundamental principle of progress and development."[96]

The CPPA did not only object to a swimming pool in Central Park; it opposed outdoor pools anywhere in the city. At a press conference announcing the formation of the association, Gibson pointed out that the city already had several waterfront parks and contended that it was at these "natural spots where swimming should be indulged in," not artificial pools.[97] Gibson rejected municipal pools in general and favored natural swimming venues because he hoped to confine the "boisterous pleasure seeking" of working-class swimmers to Manhattan's periphery. While naked, rowdy boys swimming in the Hudson and East Rivers no doubt offended Gibson, he at least did not have to see or hear them. What made artificial pools so threatening to Gibson and other elites was that these institutions could transport the boys' swimming culture into any and all areas of the city, even Central Park.

Even though Central Park did not contain facilities dedicated to popular recreation, the masses had nonetheless already appropriated sections of it for their own uses. The North Meadow in particular attracted a large number of children and adolescents from the expanding Upper East Side slum.[98] They poured onto the north lawns, trampling the grass and greenery and eroding the genteel character of the park. Eugene Philbin, president of the New York Parks and Playground Association, described the pedestrian traffic that walked back and forth between the densely packed tenements and the park: "Most of those who use Central Park for their sports come from the streets east of Third Avenue. The population of the upper east side has increased very greatly in recent years, and along the street leading to one of the park entrances there is a continual stream of people coming and going."[99] "A Good Citizen Mother" complained in a letter to the *New York Times* that these working-class park-goers were destroying the tranquillity and beauty that Central Park was intended to provide: "Going into the Park at the 100th Street entrance, on the west side, there is no place I know of where I can be comfortable. Everyone is herded together on the big meadow. Already it is overcrowded, and as the weather gets warmer the crowd becomes denser. There are many groups playing tennis, boys playing with heavy balls, and dozens of dear but very dirty small children that are crowded up to my baby." Another New Yorker wrote to the *Times* that same day complaining that Mitchel's proposed park changes would exacerbate the problem by attracting many more urchins and rowdy youths. Palmer Langdon claimed that it was far more "reasonable" to build swimming pools and playgrounds "in the congested parts of the city . . . before invading Central Park."[100]

The city's leading play reformers shared Langdon's view. They also wanted to keep the athletic fields, playground, and most especially the swimming pool out of Central Park. Charles Stover served the city as parks commissioner at the time of the controversy. Mitchel probably expected him to be a staunch ally in his fight to popularize Central Park, because Stover was a pioneering play reformer. In 1890 he founded the New York Society for Parks and Playgrounds, which opened the city's first playground in the heart of the Upper East Side slums. Then, in 1898, he helped organize the Outdoor Recreation League, which lobbied for the city's first municipally operated playground and outdoor gymnasium. Stover also directed the recreation and playground program at the University Settlement on and off from 1890 to 1910. When Mayor William Gaynor appointed him parks commissioner in 1910, Stover was widely recognized as the leading play reformer in the city.[101]

Stover and other local play reformers opposed Mitchel's plan, in large part, because they desired to maintain class segregation in the city. Philbin publicly opposed the Central Park swimming pool and playfields on the grounds that they would attract working-class children "into a part of the city where they are not wanted." He preferred to keep them playing in the shadows of their East Side tenements.[102] Unlike Philbin, Stover did not oppose all aspects of Mitchel's plan. He indicated that perhaps a few play apparatuses and a covered shelter on the North Meadow would be appropriate. Stover supported these minor modifications because he believed that a small playground in the northeast corner of the park would actually reinforce class seg-regation. "Now if we are to control the people who swarm in on us," he told the *New York Times*, "and if we are to keep them in the places where we would like them to be, we must provide proper accommodation for them."[103] Stover determined that the best way to cope with working-class children flocking to Central Park was to confine them to one isolated area of it.

Although Stover favored a small playground in Central Park, he vehe-mently opposed the swimming pool. "I have never been in favor of putting a swimming pool in Central Park," declared the parks commissioner. "I should consider it disastrous if the only swimming pool belonging to the city was put there. It would attract all sorts of undesirable people."[104] The pool, he ex-plained, would serve "only to draw thousands of children from the East Side to the Park and add to the congestion."[105] Whereas the playground would give city officials greater control over the stream of children who already came to the park, the swimming pool would exacerbate the problem. It would open the floodgates and attract such a deluge of urchins and working-class adoles-cents that city officials could not hope to control them.

During the midst of the controversy, Stover proposed a compromise. As an alternative to the Central Park pool, he suggested that New York build a few outdoor pools in other areas of the city. The first, he proposed, should be located "under the approaches to the Manhattan Bridge."[106] A day later, the *New York Times* published an editorial praising Stover's idea and offered its own suggestion as to where the pools should be located. "Swimming and wading pools may be made elsewhere [not in Central Park]," the paper agreed, "perhaps under the broad arches of the Queensboro Bridge."[107]

Both Stover and the *Times* proposed such dismal locations for outdoor mu-nicipal pools in order to protect the city's segregated social geography and se-clude its working-class swimmers. The Manhattan and Queensboro Bridges rose out of Manhattan from within two large, working-class sections of the city. The Manhattan Bridge extended out from the Lower East Side slums, near the Bowery. A pool underneath this bridge would draw the children who lived in the crowded tenements radiating out from the waterfront deeper into the slums. Similarly, an outdoor pool underneath the Queensboro Bridge, which departed Manhattan at East 60th Street, would attract children living in the Upper East Side tenements away from Central Park. When the boys and girls from this neighborhood trekked west to Central Park, they passed through several long blocks of increasingly well-to-do homes before arriving at the mansions along Fifth Avenue. A pool under the Queensboro Bridge would draw the children in the opposite direction, toward the riverfront and deeper into the slums. The pool would thus reinforce the socially segregated character of the city by curbing the stream of visitors that came to the park from east of Third Avenue.[108] Furthermore, pools located underneath bridges would thoroughly seclude swimmers so few others would ever see or hear them.

While most of the debate over Mitchel's plan swirled around issues of social and cultural geography, the proposed swimming pool also aroused concerns about public health. Throughout most of the controversy, New York City mayor William Gaynor remained conspicuously quiet. Eventually, he made a much-publicized visit to the proposed pool site in Central Park before declaring his views on the matter. The mayor concluded that the pool would not mar the park's natural beauty and would not offend other park visitors because it would be "on a ledge of rocks removed from the public gaze." Gaynor did, however, express concern about the sanitary condition of such a large pool, fearing it might threaten public health.[109] The *New York Times* echoed this concern. In several editorials criticizing Mitchel's proposal, the paper referred to swimming pools as "disease breeders" and argued that even "under the best conditions possible," a Central Park pool would still be "unsanitary."[110] To support its claim, the *Times* tweaked class prejudices. It implied that the pool would become a public health hazard precisely because the working classes would swim in it. "If [the pool] becomes popular and is used by all classes it will become foul in a very short time."[111]

Gaynor and the *Times* expressed concerns about swimming pools that were common at the time. As far back as the 1890s, reformers and city officials worried that pools were unsanitary, but their fears were based mostly on speculation and anecdote. Between 1908 and 1915, however, a spate of scientific studies confirmed that swimming pools posed a real threat to public health. Wallace Manheimer, a bacteriologist at Columbia University, conducted several studies that were subsequently published in scientific journals and popular periodicals.[112] He found that typhoid fever, ear and eye infections, dysentery, and gonorrhea were easily transmitted in pools. Municipal pools posed the greatest threat to public health, Manheimer asserted, because of the poorer "class of patron" that swam in them.[113] Like the *New York Times*, Manheimer assumed that the poor and working classes were generally dirty and most likely to be infected by communicable diseases. To ensure proper sanitation, he recommended that pool water be circulated through a filter and regularly treated with either calcium hypochlorite or anhydrous chlorine, which were first available for use in swimming pools around 1910. Filtration worked best to remove suspended matter from the pool, while chemical treatment effectively sterilized the water. He found that simply emptying and refilling pools regularly, as most cities did, was not an effective means of keeping the water sanitary.[114]

Mayor Gaynor eventually concluded that the city could not afford to keep such a large pool sanitary and rejected Mitchel's plan. When the controversy ended, Parks Commissioner Stover abandoned the idea of opening alternative outdoor pools in other areas of the city. Over the next five years, New York opened two more indoor bathhouse pools but no outdoor pools.[115] At the time, Philadelphia operated twenty outdoor pools and Chicago nineteen. New York, on the other hand, operated none.

Stover and other leading New York play reformers never advocated outdoor municipal pools because the way children used swimming pools contradicted their rationale for providing play facilities. New York reformers lobbied for playgrounds, baseball fields, and gymnastic equipment because these facilities promoted organized and "directed" play, which they assumed would socialize children into disciplined workers and moral citizens. Swimming pools, on the other hand, encouraged unrestrained and disorderly play, which they believed led to crime and self-abandon.[116] In this way, New York play reformers differed from their counterparts in Chicago. Chicago park officials prioritized addressing immediate urban problems, such as juvenile crime and social conflict. They intended recreation facilities to help solve these problems by attracting potentially delinquent kids off the streets and bringing ethnically and even racially diverse residents together to play. Swimming pools served these functions well precisely because they appealed to the working classes. New York play reformers, on the other hand, prioritized individual socializing. They appreciated the immediate social benefits of pulling kids off the streets, but they also intended the play experience to instill habits of discipline, cooperation, and obedience. Swimming pools did not suit their purpose because pool play tended to be boisterous, rowdy, and unorganized.

The differences between play reformers in Chicago and New York resulted in large part from the differing influence of Luther Gulick in both cities. Gulick was the play movement's chief theorist and a strident advocate of directed play. As president of the Playground Association of America (PAA), which was based in New York City, and head of the association's New York branch, he profoundly influenced the city's approach to play and recreation.[117] He was less influential in Chicago, which had its own homegrown play movement. Even though they participated in the PAA, Chicago play reformers such as Jane Addams, Graham Romeyn Taylor, and J. Frank Foster advocated a more eclectic and open approach to play and recreation that included unorganized (but still supervised) activities, such as playing in a pool.[118]

Although New York City did not open an outdoor pool during the Progressive Era, it did develop an outdoor swimming facility in 1911 on a strip of Coney Island. Working-class New Yorkers finally had a beach and swimming spot intended for their use, but like the other Coney Island attractions, it was a destination they could only visit a few times each summer.[119] Furthermore, the Coney Island location marginalized public swimming. It banished swimmers to the extreme periphery of the city and linked swimming, both geographically and culturally, with the amusement parks and sideshows that dominated Coney Island and people's perception of it. The location also separated swimming from the everyday life of the city. The physical distance a fifteen-year-old boy traveled from his Lower East Side tenement to Coney Island represented how far public swimming existed outside the city's social and cultural norms. As John Kasson astutely points out in *Amusing the Million*, Coney Island was "a special place on the map" where social conventions and cultural standards were temporarily suspended.[120] By providing an outlet for unrestrained behavior and concentrating it at a destination location, Coney Island actually protected the established social and cultural order back in the city. Visitors understood that they were on a "moral holiday," to borrow Kasson's phrase, while at the amusement parks or lounging on the beach. When they left, life returned to normal.

Municipal swimming pools highlight the diversity and internal tensions within Progressive Era social reform. In some cities, most notably Chicago, municipal pools became quintessential Progressive institutions. With broad public support, middle-class reformers assigned them a central role in their effort to improve the lives of poor and working-class youths and solve a variety of urban "problems," including juvenile delinquency and social conflict. In other cities, however, most notably Boston and New York, municipal pools languished during the Progressive Era. The poor and working classes in both cities supported recreation-oriented municipal pools, but the middle and upper classes generally did not. Play reformers in New York, Republican city councilmen in Boston, social elites in both cities, and the *New York Times* all opposed outdoor municipal pools, in large part, because the working classes had determined the culture and patterns of use that prevailed at these public institutions. As Michael McGerr argues in *A Fierce Discontent*, the primary goal of much Progressive social reform was to remake the poor and working classes in the image of the middle class.[121] Municipal swimming pools did just the opposite. They legitimated working-class culture by providing it with an institutional outlet. Critics recognized that public officials could not control what occurred at swimming pools and that centrally located facilities would infect public culture with working-class values and sensibilities.

The social divisions evident at Progressive Era municipal pools reveal much about middle-class assumptions about class, ethnicity, and race at the time. Pool use divided along class lines—but not ethnic or racial lines—because city officials, reformers, and the middle-class public viewed the working classes en masse as the "great unwashed." Recall Daniel Kearns's description of the black and white "street gamins" who swam in the Philadelphia pools, Wallace Manheimer's conclusion that public pools were particularly unsanitary because of the "class of patron" that used them, and the assertion in the *New York Times* that a municipal pool in Central Park would be a "disease breeder" because it would be used "by all classes." All these views reflect an inclusive class prejudice. Middle-class Americans at the time perceived immigrants, laborers, and blacks as equally dirty and prone to carry communicable diseases. As a result, they avoided swimming in the same pool with the working classes no matter their race or ethnicity.

Progressive Era pools also reinforced the sexual division of urban space. Girls and young women were not excluded from the public realm but rather segregated within it at municipal pools. Public officials did not explain or justify the persistence of gender segregation even after municipal pools were redefined as recreation institutions, but a few explanations seem likely. Even though pools were no longer viewed as baths, they still necessitated more bodily exposure than was acceptable in public. And, pools facilitated physical contact. They provided a fluid environment that dissolved boundaries of personal space. Grabbing limbs, wrestling, and dunking all seemed like natural acts in a pool. Public officials were acutely concerned at the time about promiscuous contact between males and females at dance halls and amusement parks; they certainly did not want the same to occur at municipal pools. Finally, the surface of the water provided a screen that obscured what occurred below. Swimmers could touch and grab one another without the lifeguard or poolside police officer noticing. Because of this combination of factors—bodily exposure, physical contact, and difficulty of surveillance— public officials mandated that males and females swim separately.

The pervasive gender segregation at municipal pools contrasts with the mixed-gender socializing that occurred at commercial amusements early in the twentieth century. The historiographical literature on dance halls and amusement parks emphasizes that these new urban spaces broke down sexual divisions of urban space. As Kathy Peiss writes, "commercialized recreation fostered a youth-oriented, mixed-sex world of pleasure, where female participation was profitable and encouraged."[122] The history of municipal pools locates the limits of the heterosocial urban world developing around the turn of the twentieth century. Entrepreneurs may have capitalized on the desire of young men and women to interact socially beyond the observation of parents and chaperones, but public officials reinforced the sexual division of urban space at swimming pools. Furthermore, other urban spaces remained gendered or gender segregated throughout the early twentieth century as well, including workplaces, department stores, and saloons.[123] Commercial amusements were harbingers of changing public relations between males and females but were more the exception than the rule during the Progressive Era. In many urban contexts, including swimming pools, gender divisions still prevailed.

THE TRAUMATIC EARLY
HISTORY OF FAIRGROUNDS
PARK POOL

Before the Progressive Era ended, city officials in St. Louis further reconceived municipal swimming pools and reshuffled the social composition of swimmers. In 1913 the city opened an enormous circular swimming pool in Fairgrounds Park and promoted it as a leisure resort for almost all citizens. The city permitted both sexes to swim together, and the pool's resortlike character attracted virtually all levels of St. Louis society and many adults. While working class and middle class, males and females, and children and adults now swam together in this gigantic pool, blacks and whites did not. City officials barred black Americans from the pool even though blacks and whites swam together at an earlier municipal pool. Fairgrounds Pool was the first gender-integrated municipal pool in the northern United States and also the first one officially segregated along racial lines.[1] The simultaneous occurrence of these two social transformations was not coincidental. City officials excluded blacks because most whites did not want black men interacting with white women at such an intimate and crowded public space. Although an anomaly when it opened in 1913, Fairgrounds Pool foreshadowed what would occur at municipal pools throughout the northern United States during the 1920s. It represents one point of origin of the mixed-gender, racially segregated leisure society that came to predominate during the twentieth century.

Prior to the opening of Fairgrounds Pool, the social composition of municipal-pool swimmers in St. Louis was the same as in New York, Chicago, and Philadelphia. Working-class blacks and whites swam together, whereas men and women and prosperous and poor did not. St. Louis opened its first public bath in 1907 on 10th Street between Carr and Biddle. The facility was located in the midst of what one newspaper called a "ghetto district" and contained only showers and tubs. The bath accommodated men and women, but the facilities for each were completely separate, even to the point of having the two groups enter through different doors.[2] The facility attracted a racially and ethnically diverse crowd of working-class residents. According to a local newspaper, "Greek, Italian, negro [sic], Irish, German, French, American—they were all there, sweating, grinning, and scolding at one another in strange tongues."[3] Official attendance statistics confirm the racial diversity of the bathers. During the bath's first four years of operation, the number of black bathers increased steadily: 517 the first year, then 1,209, 3,448, and 4,352 in 1911.[4] This steady increase suggests that city officials actively encouraged blacks to use the facility or, at the very least, did not discriminate against them.

The social composition of swimmers at the city's first municipal pool was the same. Bath House No. 2, which contained a twenty-nine by eighty-nine foot pool, opened in 1909 in another working-class section of the city. City officials intended the indoor pool to lure working-class residents into the facility's showers and also promote physical fitness. As at the first bath, men and women were kept separate, but blacks and whites were not. In its first year of operation, 337 blacks used the facility.[5] A small number, granted, but understandable considering the pool was located within an overwhelmingly white neighborhood. The important point is that this municipal pool intended to function as a bath and fitness facility for the city's working classes was gender segregated and racially integrated.

By the early 1910s, St. Louis officials recognized the need for a municipal pool that promoted recreation and even leisure. Unlike other major American cities, St. Louis was not located close to a body of water that residents could conveniently frequent as a summer resort. While some daring youths swam in the Mississippi River, it was too muddy for most residents and lacked a beach. The city's elite traveled great distances in order to vacation near pleasurable shores. In 1909 the *St. Louis Post-Dispatch* reported that "almost a third of St. Louis society" was spending the summer along "that delightful stretch of the Atlantic seaboard on the Massachusetts, New Hampshire, and Maine coasts."[6] The vast majority of the city's residents, however, could not afford to escape the city to Magnolia, Massachusetts. They were left to sweat out the torrid days of summer in hot discomfort.

Because the masses could not get to a beach, city officials decided to bring the sea and the sand to them. The means they chose was a giant swimming pool. Under the direction of the Public Recreation Commission, the city built an innovative swimming pool in Fairgrounds Park that resembled a seaside resort. It was by far the largest public swimming pool in the country at the time and probably the world. The pool measured 440 feet in diameter and accommodated thousands of swimmers at a time. The pool was circular, which meant that it could not easily host swim meets or permit lap swimming for exercise. Rather, city officials intended the pool to promote leisurely use. They installed an artificial sand beach around the exterior of the pool, which provided swimmers and even nonswimmers the physical space necessary to lounge by the water. Sections of the pool also had a zero-depth entry, so swimmers could wade out into the water. The recreation commission contemplated making the pool even more like an ocean resort by installing a "huge paddle device for making waves." Swimmers would have been able to frolic in waves as though they were at the New Jersey Shore. The commission liked the idea but concluded that the device was too expensive. Even without the wave machine, locals still referred to Fairgrounds Pool as "the St. Louis Coney Island."[7]

The pool did not just resemble a resort; in many ways, it functioned like one. The facility attracted thousands of swimmers each day. Some came from as far away as fifteen miles.[8] Families that traveled especially far often turned their visit into a short vacation. They camped in the park at night and spent their days swimming and playing in the sand.[9] Unlike earlier municipal pools that served a particular neighborhood, Fairgrounds Pool served as a destination resort for the whole city and surrounding countryside.

By designing Fairgrounds Pool as a leisure resort, St. Louis officials redefined the accepted social function of public recreation. During the late nineteenth and early twentieth centuries, cities provided public recreation facilities because officials and reformers assumed they served the public good. Similarly, middle-class Americans justified their own participation in sports and active recreation by pointing to "the social benefits they supposedly gained from their efforts."[10] St. Louis officials made vague and halfhearted allusions to "healthful exercise" and "innocent use of leisure time" when justifying Fairgrounds Pool, but they really emphasized the pleasure it brought the people of St. Louis. The facility was a "valuable civic asset," the recreation commission claimed, because it made "life bearable to thousands during the excessively hot summer."[11] Shortly after the pool opened, the commission announced that it would not build any more indoor pools because "the greatest enjoyment for the greatest number" was achieved with outdoor pools.[12] St. Louis officials had come to view public recreation as a source of "personal pleasure and fulfillment," to borrow Donald Mrozek's language, "that needed

Fairgrounds Park Pool, St. Louis, 1933. Fairgrounds Pool was an early resort pool in the United States. It was bordered by a sand beach, had a zero-depth entry, and attracted a diverse crowd. From the St. Louis Globe-Democrat Archives of the St. Louis Mercantile Library at the University of Missouri—St. Louis.

little, if any, external justification."[13] In short, they equated recreation with leisure, not personal or social improvement. While this shift in attitude triumphed generally during the 1920s and 1930s, it began, in part, with Fairgrounds Pool. Even in 1914, however, this pleasure-centered justification of public recreation was not as novel as it would seem. Fairgrounds Pool merely legitimated what had been the usage pattern at municipal pools all along. City officials and the middle-class public had finally appropriated the working-class sensibility that one could partake in recreation activities merely for the pleasure they afforded.

Fairgrounds Pool was also socially innovative. It dissolved the class divisions that characterized the use of earlier municipal pools. Because of its beachlike character and its location in an accessible park rather than a residential slum, the pool attracted virtually all levels of St. Louis society. City officials indeed intended the pool to serve a broad cross section of the community. In his dedicatory address, St. Louis mayor Henry Kiel emphasized that the pool was "for rich and poor alike."[14] St. Louisians did not disappoint the mayor. Local newspapers marveled at the social diversity of the swimmers. The city's working classes and recent immigrants, including children and adults, flocked to the pool.[15] They were the most numerous swimmers. And yet, the city's fashionable set—"West End belles and beaux, and many a prosperous looking man from downtown"—also came to the pool in large numbers.[16] The social intermingling that occurred was unique and astonishing. Well-to-do and poor rubbed shoulders in line, changed next to one another in the dressing rooms, swam past one another in the water, and all sat out on the same sandy beach. The class-divided urban world characteristic of industrial America was beginning to give way to a society in which Americans from different social classes recreated together.

An even more novel social innovation took place at Fairgrounds Pool—men and women, boys and girls also all swam together. City officials permitted mixed-gender swimming because they viewed the pool as a beachlike resort rather than a bath, fitness facility, or playground. Whereas bathing, fitness, and children's play were generally single-sex activities, beach activities were not. Even during the height of American Victorianism, men and women played in the surf together and sat side by side in the sand at beach resorts along the Atlantic coast. Because Fairgrounds Pool was so disassociated from bathing, fitness, and child's play, city officials applied the social standard of the seashore to it.

The opening of the pool in July 1913 created a cultural crisis in St. Louis. The community had to sort out new standards of public decency and visual propriety to govern this unique public space. These were not minor civic issues. Thousands of people flooded into the pool each day to swim, and thousands more came to watch. On one Sunday shortly after the pool opened, a local newspaper reported that 25,000 men, women, and children swam in the pool, and another 25,000 watched from the periphery.[17] The pool and swimmers had quickly become a public spectacle. As a result, several contentious issues arose over bathing suit styles and the boundaries of male-female interaction.

One concern was how swimmers should dress, both at the pool and on their way to it. In their eagerness to plunge into the water, male and female swimmers often ignored traditional conventions of proper dress in public.

They rode on streetcars and walked down sidewalks wearing nothing but their bathing suits.[18] Swimmers also tried to expedite their entry into the pool by changing behind trees and shrubs in the park rather than waiting for a dressing room. A reporter for the *St. Louis Post-Dispatch* described the levels of indiscretion she witnessed while strolling through Fairgrounds Park one morning: "It isn't exactly comfortable to know as you are making your way across the park that behind every large tree or bush as many men as it will shelter are likely to be discovered in various stages of dishabille. . . . It isn't always comfortable to the innocent bystander, still you can laugh at their greater discomfiture. It is when you come across happy little family parties, disrobing in the open that you really feel like taking to cover. You don't know which way to run though. If you get on a street car you are likely to encounter bare-limbed men and women."[19]

Another contentious issue was what bathing suit styles were appropriate for a mixed-gender pool. Many young women wore what one newspaper described as "loud" and "fancy" costumes designed to draw attention to their bodies. Other women wore garments unsuited for swimming, such as flimsy sundresses that clung to their bodies when wet. Some of the dresses were also light in color, so they revealed patches of skin underneath when wet. Many female swimmers also chose to shed the stockings and sleeves that were traditionally part of women's bathing suits.[20] Lifeguards and pool attendants ejected the most immodest swimmers, but others at the pool, especially older women, demanded explicit regulations and rigid enforcement. According to one newspaper report, several ladies were so offended at the sight of some female swimmers that they marched down to city hall to complain in person about the "shocking disarray in which some of our little citizens, some of them hardly Americanized, went about."[21] As this complaint suggests, the conflict over swimsuits split along ethnic, class, and generational lines.

In response to the complaints, the Recreation Commission designated Charlotte Rumbold the "censor of [bathing] costumes." Miss Rumbold established fixed regulations, yet they were not as restrictive as St. Louis's self-appointed guardians of propriety would have liked. Women would not have to wear stockings at the pool but would be required to wear swimsuits that were dark in color and made of thick material. Women's suits also had to cover the shoulders and arms down to the elbow but could be hemmed just above the knee. Women older than fourteen were required to wear skirts over their trunks in order to hide their developed or just developing hips. These regulations ensured that the mixed crowd of swimmers and spectators would not be able to see the shape of a woman's body. The only stipulations for men were that their suits cover their torso and pelvic area and not be white.[22]

As for the young men and women who traveled to the pool in their swimsuits or changed in the park, Miss Rumbold encouraged them to cover themselves with coats but intimated that she had little power to control them.[23] The guardians of public morality who complained about the "hardly Americanized" little swimmers could influence policies inside the pool, but the tendencies of the masses would define public decency on the streets surrounding it. The willingness of so many swimmers to flagrantly cast aside the traditional standards of propriety indicates the extent to which those standards were a public veneer obscuring the social reality of most Americans.

Miss Rumbold also established guidelines concerning permissible interaction between males and females at the pool. "We can't prevent men from speaking with women," she acknowledged, "but any girl who is offended at being addressed by a stranger has only to call one of the guards. They will escort the man from the pool—it has already been done several times." She also instructed lifeguards to remove any man and woman petting one another or otherwise having too much physical contact while in the water or on the beach. Miss Rumbold made clear that the city would not let the pool become like a "dance hall," where, as she put it, young men try to "pick-up" women.[24]

Like dance halls, amusement parks, and other commercial amusements at the time, Fairgrounds Pool marked an important step in the emergence of a mixed-gender public. It brought men and women together to play and relax, whereas leisure activities during the nineteenth century generally separated the sexes.[25] The pool also provided young men and women a place to chat and flirt beyond the eyes and ears of parents and chaperones. My maternal grandparents, John V. Egan and Helen Brueckner, grew up near Fairgrounds Park and took advantage of the freedom it offered young people by going there for their first date in the early 1920s. They played tennis rather than go swimming in the pool, however, because my grandmother was afraid of the water. In other ways, though, the pool was an antidote to the heterosocial culture developing at commercial amusements rather than a perpetuation of it. Whereas the owners of dance halls and amusement parks intentionally created situations where young men and women could touch and press up against one another, St. Louis officials did their best to prevent such contact.[26]

The bathing suit and swimmer interaction regulations nevertheless underscored the sexualized character of the pool. City officials clearly intended the policies to dampen the sexual charge sparked by partially dressed males and females observing one another and interacting in public. By requiring women's thighs, arms, and shoulders to be covered up and the curves of their bodies obscured, officials attempted to make voyeurism less titillating. Also, recall Rumbold's comment that she did not want the pool to take on the character of a dance hall. Implicit in this statement is her understanding that the pool could very easily become like a dance hall. As historian Catherine Horwood eloquently points out in her examination of women and bathing in England, mixed-gender swimming "inevitably stirred up the murky waters of sexuality, both in terms of arousal and contact—or lack of it—with the opposite sex."[27]

It was precisely because city officials viewed the pool as a sexually charged public space that they excluded black Americans. A week before it opened, the city's chief of police ordered the officers stationed at Fairgrounds Park to bar all blacks from entering the pool. After he issued the order, Chief Young checked with the city counselor to verify the legality of his edict. Because blacks were not excluded from other public facilities, including the city's first municipal pool, he was not sure this policy was legal. The counselor affirmed the city's right to exclude black citizens, and the pool became officially and explicitly for whites only.[28]

Black residents of St. Louis resisted their exclusion. Two weeks after the pool opened, a group of young black men plotted to make a rush past the pool attendants and police guards and jump into the water. Unfortunately for the protesters, Police Chief Young found out about the planned "negro [sic] invasion" and stationed ten additional officers at the pool to repel the attack. The city also hurried construction of a ten-foot-high fence around the perimeter of the facility. Whether it was the increased police force or the tall fence that deterred them, the protest never occurred.[29] Black residents of St. Louis would have to wait thirty-six years before they could plunge into the expansive waters of Fairgrounds Pool.

Although no public official or local commentator explicitly explained why the city excluded blacks from Fairgrounds Pool, a comparison with the city's admission policy at the earlier pool offers strong evidence that gender integration was the primary reason. It was not merely a coincidence, in other words, that gender integration and racial segregation occurred simultaneously. As we have seen, city officials were extremely concerned about physical contact between men and women at the pool and unwanted romantic advances. Popular prejudices among whites at the time stigmatized black men in general as sexually undisciplined and, in some cases, prone to uncontrollable sexual desire for white women.[30] The thought of black men interacting with white women at a municipal pool—where erotic voyeurism, physical contact, and making a date were all possible—heightened these fears and compelled city officials to officially exclude black swimmers. Recall the attitude of the police officer at Chicago's Hardin Square recreation center, who was eager to pummel any black man who said even "one word to a white woman." The concerns that underlay this attitude were certainly heightened at swimming pools. Gender integration, in short, necessitated racial segregation.

≈≈≈≈≈ Fairgrounds Pool was an anomaly when it opened in 1913 and remained so until the 1920s. Throughout the Progressive Era, swimming pools in the rest of the northern United States remained much smaller; they continued to divide swimmers along gender and class lines but not racial lines; and they attracted mostly children and adolescents. Fairgrounds Pool was, however, a harbinger. After 1920, cities across the northern United States built large resort pools that dissolved the earlier gender and class divisions and attracted large numbers of adults. Just as in St. Louis, this general social integration was accompanied by the exclusion of black Americans. As a result, race became the overwhelming social division in the use of municipal swimming pools. Whites swam together regardless of their class and gender, while blacks were either denied the opportunity entirely or provided a separate facility. Chapter 4 details the nationwide redesign of municipal pools as leisure resorts during the 1920s and 1930s and the accompanying democratization of swimming. The simultaneous onset of racial segregation is taken up in chapter 5.

CHAPTER 4

THE "SWIMMING POOL AGE"
1920 TO 1940

A wonderful neighborhood and fraternal spirit, however, seems to have gripped the entire section and the guards stationed about the pool seem almost an unnecessary adjunct to the enterprise. Everybody seemed imbued with the community spirit and bent on having a thoroughly good time. Men, women, children of the Ninth ward section are getting acquainted with each other and cementing bonds of community friendship such as can only be gained through intimacy in acquatic [sic] sports. —Wilmington Evening Journal *(1925)*

On Labor Day 1934, tiny Avalon, Pennsylvania, held its first annual Water Carnival at the town's municipal swimming pool. The pool, which opened earlier in the summer, was an ideal place to hold a community celebration. Many of the town's 5,000 residents could fit in the large pool and the remainder could lounge along the broad concrete deck surrounding it. The Water Carnival included swim races and water stunts, but the main attraction was the "bathing beauty contest." In the days before the event, local newspapermen visited the Avalon pool to take pictures of the contestants preparing for the contest. One photo showed Gladys Korman sitting on a diving board, wearing a low-cut one-piece suit, provocatively dipping her toes in the water. Another photo showed four other contestants applying makeup as they sat beside the pool. The caption read: "Sisters Mary Jane and Peggy Aland, Left, and Martha and Gertrude Hacher show how they prepare for the beauty contest." These photos advertised who and what spectators could expect to see. During the contest, twenty teenage girls paraded before the large mixed-gender crowd wearing lots of makeup and fashionable, tight-fitting swimsuits that exposed their legs, arms, and shoulders and revealed the outlines of their hips and breasts. The hundreds in attendance stared at the girls, evaluated their appearance, and cheered for the most alluring.[1]

Avalon's swimming pool and Water Carnival exemplify several historic changes that occurred in the history of municipal swimming pools between 1920 and 1940. That a town with 5,000 residents had a municipal pool was quite novel and shows the astounding proliferation of swimming pools at the time. Previously, most municipal pools were located in a few large northern cities. During the 1920s and 1930s, however, over a thousand cities and towns throughout the country opened swimming pools. The building occurred in two distinct phases. The first phase lasted from 1920 to 1929. During this period of relative prosperity, cities built pools to meet Americans' increasing demand for outdoor recreation and leisure activities. With the onset of the Great Depression, municipal pool construction slowed. The federal government, however, initiated a second wave of pool building in 1934 that lasted until the end of the decade. The New Deal swimming pools were as phenomenal a public works endeavor as the much-touted Grand Coulee Dam and the Tennessee Valley Authority. They provided leisure and recreation for millions of Americans who desperately needed relief from the heat and hard times.

Municipal pools were also completely redesigned during the 1920s and 1930s. Like Avalon's pool, they were typically quite large. Some were bigger than football fields and capable of accommodating thousands of swimmers at a time. The pools of the interwar years came in a variety of shapes—circular, semicircular, foot-shaped, kidney-shaped, and the traditional rectangular. The pools also provided considerable leisure space—sandy beaches, grassy lawns, and broad concrete decks. As a result, lounging, sunbathing, and socializing became quintessential pool activities. Cities typically located these resort pools in large parks that were easily accessible to most residents. Whereas earlier pools had a distinctly urban appearance and setting, these new pools looked quite natural, surrounded as they were by sand and grass and situated in the sylvan beauty of a park.

The resort pools of the interwar years democratized swimming in America and transformed the social composition of swimmers. Millions of new swimmers—including large numbers of females, adults, and middle-class Americans—flocked to them. Gone were the days when working-class boys dominated these public spaces. Most critically, the social divisions that characterized pool use during the Industrial Age largely evaporated during the 1920s and 1930s. Working class and middle class, men and women, and children and adults all swam together. The social integration resulted from several factors. For one, the redesign and relocation of pools made them appealing to adults and the middle class. Adults enjoyed lying out on the sand beaches and socializing on the pool decks. Middle-class Americans felt comfortable accessing pools located in large parks rather than buried in residential slums. At the same time, the prejudices that had deterred the middle class from swimming with the working classes during the Progressive Era weakened during the 1920s. Working-class whites did not seem quite as poor, dirty, and foreign as before. Gender integration resulted mainly from changes in public policy. Across the nation, public officials permitted males and females to swim together beginning in the 1920s because they intended the new resort pools to promote family and community sociability. They looked to swimming pools to bring diverse members of the community together, not keep them apart, as was the case earlier. The result was a complete social reconstruction of these public spaces.

As public officials intended, the municipal pools of the interwar years functioned as centers of community life. They attracted thousands of people at a time and, unlike at most public spaces, the social contact was sustained and interactive. Swimmers spent hours, often the entire day, at pools—playing games, sunbathing, and chatting. As the *Wilmington Evening Journal* noted in the epigraph, municipal pools provided a unique public space, where diverse Americans came together and reestablished community bonds eroded by modern city life. And, as with Avalon's Water Carnival, municipal pools became preferred venues for summertime community events. Cities and towns often celebrated Memorial Day, the Fourth of July, and Labor Day at the local pool. Despite the obvious social schisms of the era, community life thrived in the water and on the beaches of municipal pools.

Avalon's Water Carnival—especially the "bathing beauty contest"—most evocatively reveals changes in swimming pool culture. Gender integration and the subsequent downsizing of swimsuits transformed municipal pools into erotic public spaces. Males and females shared the same water, rubbed shoulders on sandy beaches, and viewed one another mostly unclothed. Public officials mandated conservative swimsuits early in the 1920s in an attempt to ensure modesty and dampen the sexual charge. After the mid-1920s, however, the acceptable size of swimsuits gradually shrank until, by 1940, men wore nothing but tight trunks and many women wore two-piece brassiere suits. Swimmers and spectators at municipal pools could gaze upon the legs, hips, back, bust line, and shoulders of women and almost the entirety of men's bodies. As a result, municipal pools became public stages for putting oneself on display and public venues for visually consuming others. This exhibitionism and voyeurism eroticized municipal pools and contributed to a fundamental shift in American culture. Public objectification of female and male bodies became acceptable, and public decency came to mean exhibiting an attractive appearance rather than protecting one's modesty.

〜〜〜 Looking back from the vantage point of 1940, the *New York Times* viewed swimming pools as iconic institutions of the 1920s and 1930s. In an editorial assessing the state of "American civilization," the paper marveled at the number of swimming pools constructed since the end of World War I, describing the building spree as one of "the two outstanding sport developments of the quarter century since the World War." The editorial went on to claim that the popularity of swimming pools demonstrated the vitality of American life: "In this matter of swimming pools . . . [Americans have] good reason for doubting that our civilization is in the same pass as ancient Rome before its fall." With war raging in Europe and tensions mounting with Japan, however, the paper wondered if the America that had recently become defined by its swimming pools might be coming to an end. "If our civilization is doomed to destruction and temporary oblivion the scientists of the future may wonder at the purpose of the great number of shallow, rectangular depressions in our extinct cities. They would be our swimming pools."[2] Fortunately, this did not come to pass. But, how is it that the *New York Times* came to see swimming pools as emblematic of this era in American history?

Prior to 1920, northern metropolises operated the vast majority of municipal pools in the United States. Philadelphia and Chicago alone accounted for nearly 25 percent of them.[3] These cities continued to build pools in the 1920s, but the more noteworthy development was the proliferation of municipal pools into other regions of the country. Cities in the West and South provided few swimming pools before 1920, even in large metropolises. The municipal pools that did exist were typically indoors, which is something of a paradox considering the climate in both regions.[4] As late as 1925, Los Angeles operated fifteen indoor and only three outdoor pools. Over the next five years, however, the city built eight more outdoor pools for its expanding citizenry. Spokane, Washington, operated no municipal pools before 1919 but then opened three outdoor facilities during the 1920s. This same pattern was true in the South. Like Spokane, Fort Worth, Texas, operated no municipal pools before 1920 but opened four between 1921 and 1927, including a Jim Crow pool for the city's black residents. Nashville operated one indoor pool in 1925 but built nine outdoor facilities over the next five years. Dallas opened three outdoor pools during the 1920s, including the 160 by 400 foot Lake Cliff Pool, which, despite its name, was a concrete-bottom artificial pool. City officials designated one of the three new pools for black residents. At only 50 by 100 feet, however, the Hall Street Pool was not nearly as resort-like as the whites-only Lake Cliff Pool. Like Fort Worth and Dallas, several other southern cities, including Atlanta and New Orleans, opened segregated pools for black citizens in the 1920s. As a result, many urban blacks in the South had public pools in which to swim, just not the same ones as whites.[5]

Municipal-pool building in small cities and rural towns was even more novel. Before 1920, few communities with a population less than 30,000 operated a swimming pool.[6] During the 1920s, however, hundreds of small cities and towns built pools. The pools constructed early in the decade tended to be makeshift and inexpensive. In 1922 Pendleton, Indiana, simply dug a large sand-bottom hole next to a creek that ran through the town and diverted the water into it. The town then constructed two bathhouses nearby and hung lights overhead. The whole project cost $3,000.[7] Later in the decade, small towns devoted considerably more public money to pools, in some cases building elaborate pool complexes. In 1930 Clairton, Pennsylvania, finished work on a $100,000 pool that contained two large tanks, several diving platforms, a 15 by 130 foot "sand beach," and a 12-foot wide "promenade." It was an elaborate facility for a city of 15,000.[8] By the end of the decade, small communities as diverse as Sheldon, Iowa; Rutland, Vermont; Florence, South Carolina; and Havre, Montana all operated municipal pools.[9]

The pool-building spree of the 1920s was fueled by expanding economic prosperity, increased leisure time, and a general trend toward communities devoting public resources to recreation facilities. Historian William Leuchtenburg has described United States economic development during this period as "the second industrial revolution." New assembly-line production methods enabled manufacturers to produce more goods for less money. American companies earned unprecedented profits that trickled down to employees in the form of higher wages. At the same time, the price of goods declined significantly. According to Leuchtenburg, "the real earnings of workers—what their income actually would buy at the store—shot up at an astonishing rate in the 1920s." The prosperity of the decade and the general liquidity of the American economy led to increased spending by individuals, corporations, and the government. More Americans than ever before could afford—often through credit—to purchase cars, household products, and other consumer goods. The thriving economy also led to a general construction boom. Corporations and developers erected skyscrapers, state governments paved thousands of miles of roads, and municipal governments spent unprecedented amounts of money on public libraries and community hospitals. If the previous two decades were unique for the breadth and fervor of reform, the 1920s stand out as a period of prosperity and spending.[10]

While American workers earned more during the 1920s, they also worked less. Generalizations are difficult because work schedules differed from industry to industry and even factory to factory, but overall the length of the average workweek and workday shrank significantly from the late nineteenth century through the 1920s. During the 1890s, a typical workweek for manual laborers consisted of six ten-hour days. In some industries, such as steel, employees worked twelve-hour shifts seven days a week. So many hours on the job left little time for recreation. During the next thirty years, however, strikes, worker agitation, and reforms gradually chipped time off the standard work schedule. By 1910 most factory jobs entailed about fifty-five hours of work a week. By 1920 the average time spent on the job had dropped to forty-eight hours. According to historian Daniel T. Rodgers, "[t]he result of this 25 percent shortening of the 'normal' industrial workweek was a rapid rise in explicit leisure-time activities: bicycling, picnicking, camping, vaudeville, movies, amusement parks, dance halls, and a host of new participant and spectator sports."[11] Or, put another way, the shortened workday and workweek created greater demand for recreation and leisure facilities.

New and bigger movie theaters, sport stadiums, and department stores met part of this demand. The expansion of commercial recreation during the 1920s is a well-documented story.[12] Not as well documented is the role municipal governments played in meeting the increased demand for recreation. Cities built new parks, zoos, and athletic fields; they also built lots of swimming pools. In 1916, 49 U.S. cities operated a total of 117 outdoor pools, while 15 cities operated 61 indoor pools. By 1929, the number of cities with municipal pools and the total number of municipal pools had increased almost sixfold: 308 cities now operated a total of 700 outdoor pools and 122 cities operated 310 indoor pools.[13]

Pool building during the 1920s was so robust that it gave rise to a whole new sector of private enterprise. Entrepreneurs started an array of new businesses that specialized in pool construction and the manufacture of pool equipment. William Scaife and Sons manufactured specialty pool filters, Wallace & Tiernan produced chlorinators, and Fairbanks-Morse built pumps designed especially for pools.[14] Architect Wesley Bintz was perhaps the best-known pool specialist at the time. He created and patented an innovative aboveground pool design adopted by Pana, Illinois; Elizabeth, New Jersey; Beaumont, Texas; and many other cities.[15]

This nascent pool industry sponsored a monthly trade publication optimistically titled *Swimming Pool Age*. The magazine first appeared in 1927 and was marketed to municipal parks and recreation officials and managers of private clubs. Its articles touted the social and economic virtues of swimming pools and instructed readers on proper chlorinating procedures, pool management, and novel marketing strategies. The magazine was also filled with advertisements from the myriad small companies that manufactured and sold pool products. The appearance of *Swimming Pool Age* and the burgeoning pool industry that supported it testified to the dramatic proliferation of swimming pools during the 1920s. This was indeed the era when swimming pools came of age.

A few years after the appearance of *Swimming Pool Age*, its epochal title seemed quite fanciful. The construction of swimming pools slowed when prosperity came suddenly, it seemed, to an end in 1929. Yet, beginning in late 1933, a massive second wave of pool building commenced. Like much else in American life, the pool building of the 1930s was directed and financed by the federal government. One of President Franklin Delano Roosevelt's strategies for coping with the Great Depression was finding constructive work for unemployed Americans. Beginning in 1933 with the Civil Works Administration (CWA) and continuing in 1935 with the Works Progress Administration (WPA), the federal government spent billions of dollars employing millions of Americans on thousands of public works projects. Under the direction of Harry Hopkins, the CWA and WPA built and reconstructed roads, hospitals, schools, airports, parks, and swimming pools. These projects served many purposes: they put unemployed men to work, stimulated the local economy, improved the nation's infrastructure, and expanded recreation opportunities.[16]

Pool construction was particularly impressive. Between 1933 and 1938, the federal government built nearly 750 swimming pools and remodeled hundreds more. The CWA was responsible for 351 new pools and improvements to 226 others. The WPA built 387 pools and remodeled 128 more. These figures do not include the 1,681 "wading pools" built by the WPA and Public Works Administration (PWA) during the same period.[17] The construction projects were spread across the country so their benefits would be somewhat evenly distributed. A small sampling of the pools completed just in 1936 included ten in Connecticut, seven in Alabama, nine in Indiana, fourteen in Kansas, five in Louisiana, four in New Hampshire, thirteen in Washington, and twenty-seven in Texas. Most of these pools were built in small cities and towns. Of the fourteen pools opened in Kansas in 1936, twelve were in cities with populations fewer than 10,000, and seven of those were in cities with fewer than 3,000 people.[18] This tidal wave of federally funded pool construction was so comprehensive that the WPA guidebook to Kansas proclaimed in 1939 that "there is scarcely a town with a population of more than 1,500 that lacks . . . a [municipal] swimming pool."[19]

Big cities also benefited from the federal largesse, but none so much as New York City. In the summer of 1936, Parks Commissioner Robert Moses opened eleven gigantic pool complexes funded entirely by the federal government through the WPA. Each of these state-of-the-art facilities cost more than $1 million to build and contained three separate pools—a large swimming tank typically 120 by 300 feet, a 60 by 100 foot diving tank, and a shallow wading pool 50 by 100 feet. The pools were scattered throughout the city in neighborhoods such as the Lower East Side, Astoria, Greenpoint, Harlem, and Red Hook.[20] New York City mayor Fiorello LaGuardia took special interest in the pool projects. During construction of the Thomas Jefferson Pool in Harlem, the mayor drove to the site to check on the progress. Finding the gate locked, he pulled his chin up over the fence and peered in like an excited schoolboy.[21] LaGuardia and Moses organized extravagant opening ceremonies for the pools. Each ceremony started with an afternoon parade through the local neighborhood that ended at the pool. With thousands in attendance, a local priest blessed the water, and Olympic stars and circus clowns performed swimming exhibitions. The climactic event occurred at nightfall, when LaGuardia flipped the switch to the innovative underwater lights and declared "Okay, kids, it's all yours!" The sudden illumination never failed to mesmerize the crowd. Some of these dedication ceremonies attracted as many as 40,000 people and were described as "the most memorable event in the history of the neighborhood."[22]

The New Deal swimming pools had special meaning for many Americans. They stood as tangible reminders that the federal government was helping them and their communities cope with the economic and social hardships of the depression. This was especially true in the Midwest, a region also suffering severe drought. The pools served as symbolic antidotes to the dust storms and dry soil. They were psychological and social oases. Throughout the country, New Deal pools offered millions of Americans immediate relief from the heat, boredom, and anxiety of the depression years. They also brought communities together in recreation and fellowship. For these reasons, Reverend C. L. Rush predicted that the New Deal pool in Warren, Ohio, would become an enduring local symbol of the times: "When we look back some years hence we will look upon the swimming pool as one of the bless-

Astoria Pool with Hell Gate Bridge in the Background, Queens, New York, 1936. Astoria Pool was one of the eleven wpa pools opened in New York in 1936. Long Island State Parks Region Photo Archives / New York City Parks Photo Archive, neg. Q-4, 10776.2.

ings that came to the people of Warren during the times of stress and it will remind us of the crisis that was faced."[23] He proved remarkably prescient. For many who lived through the depression, especially in small communities, swimming pools remain as emblematic of the times as the National Recovery Administration Eagle.[24]

The nearly 2,000 municipal pools built between 1920 and 1940 democratized swimming in America. Municipal pools were immensely popular during this period, attracting tens of millions of swimmers each year. In 1937, for example, Philadelphia counted 4.3 million swims in its municipal pools; St. Louis, 1.4 million; Allentown, Pennsylvania, 359,000; and Oklahoma City, Oklahoma, 106,000.[25] Individual pools amassed astonishing single-day attendance totals. Pittsburgh officials counted 25,000 swimmers and spectators one day in 1932 at Highland Park Pool. Packard Park Pool in Warren, Ohio, attracted 2,500 swimmers one Saturday in 1934 and more than 2,000 the following Saturday.[26] In a 1934 article titled "Swimming . . . the New Great American Sport," *Fortune* magazine estimated that upwards of 30 million Americans swam in pools a total of 350 million times each year.[27]

The popularity of swimming pools during this period is perhaps best understood by comparing swimming with other leisure-time activities. In 1933 the National Recreation Association conducted a study of Americans' leisure pursuits. Out of 5,002 people surveyed in ten states, 2,976 (60 percent) identified themselves as swimmers. Of those, 1,602 (32 percent) indicated that they swam "frequently." Overall, swimming ranked seventh in participation out of ninety-four leisure activities, behind only reading newspapers, listening to the radio, attending the movies, visiting friends, reading fiction, and auto riding for pleasure.[28] Swimming was far more popular than any other active recreation. Twice as many people swam frequently as hiked frequently and nearly ten times as many people swam frequently as regularly rode bicycles.[29] Perhaps most surprising, the survey found that almost as many people swam frequently as went to the movies regularly, 1,602 as compared to 1,642. Although the survey did not ask respondents where they swam, their social characteristics strongly suggest that most did their swimming at municipal pools.[30]

The survey also revealed that swimming had become popular among virtually all social groups. Most of the respondents were adult women, the least common swimmers of years past.[31] The authors of the study also indicated that roughly equal numbers of working-class and middle-class Americans participated. Among married women twenty-seven to thirty-five, swimming ranked tenth in participation, one place behind sewing and millinery. Among men thirty-six to forty-five, it ranked fifth. The participation numbers, however, actually understated Americans' desire to swim. Out of all ninety-four leisure-time activities listed, swimming ranked second as the activity people "most desired" to do.[32] The nearly 750 New Deal pools constructed during the five years following the survey no doubt satisfied some of this unmet demand.

The popularity of swimming among women represented the biggest change from the Progressive Era. In 1914 an average of 300 to 500 females swam in each of Philadelphia's twenty-three outdoor pools each *week*. By 1934 the city averaged 1,200 to 1,500 female swimmers a *day* at each of its thirty-nine pools.[33] When Columbus, Ohio, opened its first pool in 1905, one local official estimated that fewer than 12 women in the whole city knew how to swim. So few women used the pool that city officials apparently bribed them into the water. "We gave the women two dollars apiece to go into the pool and stay twenty minutes," recalled one official. Whether the city actually bribed women into the water or not back in 1905, it was certainly not necessary by the late 1920s, when more women used the pool than men.[34] The case of Columbus was unusual but accurately reflects the astounding increase in the number of women swimming at municipal pools during the interwar years.

The number of adult swimmers also increased markedly. During the early twentieth century, children, especially boys, accounted for 75 to 90 percent of the swims at most municipal pools. Many cities, including San Francisco, Wilmington, and Peoria, permitted only school-age children to swim in their municipal pools. During the 1920s and 1930s, however, the number of adults at pools nearly equaled the number of children. A study undertaken by *Beach and Pool* magazine in 1933 found that adults accounted for approximately 48 percent of the total attendance at swimming pools nationwide. Noting the change from earlier patterns of use, the magazine quipped that "[t]he pool has become 'grown up.'"[35] At some municipal pools, including San Francisco's Fleishhacker Pool and Washington, D.C.'s Banneker Pool, the number of adults far exceeded the number of children.[36] Swimming pools had indeed grown up.

Several factors contributed to the popularity of swimming pools during the interwar years. Advances in pool sanitation—especially the widespread use of chlorine—relieved many Americans' fear that they might contract a communicable disease while swimming in a public pool.[37] New swimsuit designs—especially the "one-piece" suit for women—made it less arduous and more enjoyable to enter pools. Earlier women's suits could weigh as much as fifteen pounds when wet.[38] The new streamlined suits also made pools popular for people watching. Many of the millions of Americans who frequented pools were attracted by the bare limbs and shapely curves of other swimmers. Gertrude Ederle and Olympic stars such as Annette Kellerman and Johnny Weissmuller also contributed to the popularity of swimming pools during the 1920s by popularizing swimming. Ederle's crossing of the English Channel in 1926 focused considerable media attention onto swimming and sparked widespread interest. According to *Fortune* magazine, "Ederle had much the same effect on swimming that Lindbergh had on aviation. She boomed it. She made it a tremendous vogue."[39]

The most critical factor in popularizing municipal pools, however, was their redesign as leisure resorts. Whereas earlier pools were typically small, rectangular, and austere, the pools of the interwar years were typically enor-

Cameron Pool, Cameron, West Virginia, circa late 1930s. With its sandy beach, nonrectangular shape, and water slide, Cameron's WPA pool typifies the resort pools constructed during the interwar years. Cameron Public Library Collection, West Virginia State Archives, Charleston.

mous, constructed in a variety of shapes, and offered considerable leisure space. Wilmington, Delaware, built a "foot-shaped" pool in Price Run Park that measured 480 feet long and varied between 120 and 180 feet wide. In 1931, Pittsburgh opened a large pool complex in Highland Park. The facility had two large pools—a main tank 220 feet long and 90 feet wide and a 220 by 220 foot wading pool. A waterfall cascaded over one side of the main pool and a large sandy beach bordered the other.[40] San Francisco constructed the largest pool of the era. Fleishhacker Pool measured 1,000 feet long and 150 feet wide, held 6 million gallons of water, and could accommodate 10,000 swimmers at a time. It was so large that lifeguards sometimes patrolled the water in rowboats. Fleishhacker Pool also included a large sandy beach, a "promenade" patio, two concession stands stocked with soda and ice cream, and a cafeteria.[41] Even small cities and towns built enormous pools. In 1925 Flint, Michigan, opened a 250-foot circular pool that contained a sand beach, pool deck, and second-story "veranda."[42] At the end of the swimming pool age, in 1940, Montpelier, Vermont, finished work on a "saucer-shaped" pool with a surface area larger than an acre.[43]

These new designs revolutionized the use of municipal pools. The circular, oval, and irregular-shaped tanks were not well suited for lap swimming or aquatic competition. Rather, they promoted a casual almost aimless use. Swimmers meandered and socialized in the water as much as they played and certainly more than they exercised. Americans also gathered at the resort pools of the interwar years to lounge on the grassy lawns, sunbathe on the sandy beaches, and stroll along the "promenade" patios. Lounging, sunbathing, and socializing defined pool use during this period. In a 1930 article on the opening of Rahway, New Jersey's new swimming pool, the *Elizabeth Daily Journal* reported that hundreds of people "lolled about in comfort on its superb sand beach."[44] In 1937 a New Yorker similarly described the scene at one of that city's municipal pools: "innumerable half-clothed bodies of sprawling, sweltering humans lolling in the sun."[45] Their common choice of the verb "loll" to describe what people were doing at pools is revealing. Municipal pools had become less a site of physical activity and more a public place to relax, recline, and meander in the water.

Photographs taken at swimming pools vividly capture this new pool culture. A 1925 photo of San Francisco's Fleishhacker Pool shows hundreds of swimmers casually lying about a grassy hill overlooking the pool, lounging upon a sandy beach, and strolling along the pool deck. There are far more people relaxing around the gigantic pool than swimming in it. Many small groups converse intimately, while others contentedly absorb the sun. A photo taken in the late 1930s at the Glen Echo Amusement Park swimming pool in Maryland shows a similar scene. Dozens of young adults lounge on the beach next to the pool. One man lies on his back with his head nestled in a woman's lap. Others are sprawled about on their stomachs, backs, and sides absorbing the sun. Several patrons sit in wood chairs underneath colorful umbrellas. Many small groups of three and four people huddle together chatting among themselves. These scenes epitomize the leisurely use Americans made of swimming pools during the interwar years.

As these photos show, sunbathing was a particularly popular pool activity. Before 1920 most Americans assiduously avoided tanned skin because of long-standing prejudices that associated it with outdoor field labor. Also, cultural standards of beauty valued white skin. During the mid-1920s, however, a tanning craze swept the country after Coco Chanel appeared in tabloids with sun-drenched skin. Chanel sparked the trend but certainly did not cause

Fleishhacker Pool, San Francisco, 1925.
California Historical Society, San Francisco, neg. FN-19552.

it. The cultural shift had much deeper roots. The increasing popularity of outdoor recreation, as well as the reality that most laborers now worked indoors rather than in the fields, led many Americans to reassociate tanned skin with youth, health, and beauty.[46] The swimming pools of the interwar years, with their sandy beaches and pool decks, were ideally suited for sun worship. For many, sunbathing became a primary reason for visiting a pool. In 1935 twelve-year-old Charlie Stebbins wrote a letter to President Roosevelt requesting additional public pools in Washington, D.C. Charlie wanted a pool closer to his home not because it afforded him a fun place to splash and play, but because pools were the best place to lie out in the sun. "Each year I have gotten most of my sun tan at the municipal pool," he informed the president.[47]

The history of residential swimming pools followed the same trajectory as municipal pools. They too were redesigned as leisure spaces during the 1920s. The earliest at-home pools, installed around the turn of the twentieth century, were typically indoors and served as exercise facilities. George Vanderbilt commissioned perhaps the first residential pool in 1895 at his Biltmore mansion near Asheville, North Carolina. He located the pool in the basement as part of a larger fitness area that included a rowing machine and dumbbells. The pool's design was quite austere. It was completely floored

Swimming Pool and Beach at Glen Echo Amusement Park, Montgomery County, Maryland, circa late 1930s. Suntanning and lounging became quintessential pool activities during the interwar years. Theodor Horydoczak Collection, Prints and Photographs Division, Library of Congress, Washington, D.C., neg. LC-H814-T01-1690-13.

in white tile, which gave it "a clinical, anxiously hygienic character."[48] Such an atmosphere encouraged the Spartan exercise for which it was intended. After the turn of the century, other industrialists added similar exercise-oriented pools to their mansions. Singer Sewing president Frederick Bourne equipped his Oakdale, Long Island, mansion, Indian Neck Hall, with a basement pool, right next to his skating rink, bowling alley, and Turkish bath. John Hay Whitney housed his indoor pool in the same building as his clay tennis court and wildlife trophy room.[49] While these early indoor pools were certainly status symbols, they symbolized the sporting life glorified by Theodore Roosevelt, not ostentatious wealth or glamorous repose.

The design and function of residential pools began to change in the late

1910s, when America's mega-rich adorned their estates with ornate outdoor pools. According to architectural historian Thomas van Leeuwen, the pools "were designed to play a theatrical and monumental role more than to provide mere athletic facilities. Their principal purpose was to embellish the garden and to enliven parties." F. Scott Fitzgerald provides an accurate social portrait of outdoor estate pools in his classic novel *The Great Gatsby*. The pool at Jay Gatsby's fictitious Long Island mansion served as the backdrop to a series of spectacular evening parties, where tuxedo-clad men and slinkily dressed women lingered around the pool sipping cocktails with jazz syncopating in the background. James Deering, heir to the International Harvester fortune, created something akin to this glamorous pool culture in real life. Although not much of a swimmer himself, Deering built an elaborate pool at his Florida Villa Vizcaya in 1916. He hosted countless parties along the shore of the pool and even had stars from Ziegfeld's Follies perform swimming shows for him and his wealthy friends. William Randolph Hearst first met Marion Davies, the woman with whom he had a long infatuation, at a Deering pool party.[50] These early outdoor estate pools served as showcases of wealth, style, and popularity.

During the 1920s, the locus of residential pool construction moved west to southern California. The region's Mediterranean climate, the concentration of new money, and Hollywood's desire to glamorize its stars made outdoor pools a logical fit. As movie stars and film producers built mansions into the Hollywood hills, they invariably included a swimming pool in the construction plans. Douglas Fairbanks and Mary Pickford added an innovative outdoor pool to the grounds of their Pickfair Mansion in 1920 that was different in both design and function from most East Coast estate pools. The large pool measured 55 by 100 feet and was shaped like a banana rather than the usual square design. A sandy beach bordered one side of the pool while a grassy lawn grew along the other shore. The lawn was covered with reclining chairs, tables, and a large umbrella. The ample leisure space encouraged swimmers to lay prostrate around the pool, soaking up the warm California sun. A few years later, William Randolph Hearst built a house and swimming pool for Marion Davies right on Santa Monica Beach. The pool was long and narrow with plenty of open deck space for lounge chairs and tables. The pool's location linked its function with beach culture. According to Leeuwen, it was "a center for worshipping the sun" and "a seaside fun palace." During the 1920s and 1930s, countless more movie stars and producers adorned their Los Angeles–area homes with outdoor swimming pools dedicated to hedonistic leisure.[51] Southern California was well on its way to becoming the aqua-studded landscape one sees now while flying overhead.

By the 1930s, swimming pools—both residential and municipal—had taken on a distinct cultural identity. They became emblematic of a new set of values and a new vision of life focused on pleasure, leisure, and physical beauty. Although presented in caricatured form, this cultural identity is most clearly apparent in media portrayals of swimming pools. During the 1930s, magazines and movies inundated Americans with images of pools. The June 1934 cover of *Beach and Pool* magazine showed four gorgeous young women relaxing out in the sun. They lay prostrate with their arms folded behind their heads, accentuating the repose. One of the girls elegantly held a cigarette, portraying a very chic image.[52] A 1937 ad for Ry-Krisp cereal that appeared in *Life* magazine showed actress Marion Talley leaning back along a diving board with a pool shimmering in the foreground. The ad told readers that Talley was "lovelier" and "youthful looking" in part because she ate Ry-Krisp. The ad was set at a swimming pool because it evoked these qualities much better than a breakfast table.[53] In the suggestively titled movie, *Palmy Days* (1931), a score of beautiful women lounged around a penthouse pool and frolicked in the water. The pool was not integral to the movie's story line but was simply the most appropriate setting to depict the characters' sensuous and fun-filled lives. In the 1933 film *Dancing Lady*, Joan Crawford and Franchot Tone spent considerable time poolside. In one scene, Tone reclined on the pool deck holding a drink, while Crawford, who was leaning against the pool ladder dipping her toes in the water, gazed at him flirtatiously.[54] These images reflected and reinforced the cultural meaning that Americans attached to swimming pools at the time. They represented a life-style of sun, sensuality, and repose.

〰〰〰 In addition to democratizing swimming and leisure, the municipal pools of the interwar years also dissolved the social divisions that characterized pool use during the Progressive Era. Across the northern United States, swimming pools became social melting pots into which males and females, young and old, and working class and middle class all plunged together. Public officials were largely responsible for this widespread social reconstruction of municipal pools. They permitted males and females to swim together because they intended the new resort pools to promote family and community sociability. Public officials also purposefully contributed to the class integration of municipal pools by building facilities that appealed to middle-class Americans and by locating them in open and accessible parks rather than residential slums. In short, public officials intended swimming pools to bring families together and foster a community life that transcended the social lines of gender and class. "Let's build bigger, better and finer pools," exhorted Nathan Kaufman, Recreation Director for Allegheny County, "that's real democracy. Take away the sham and hypocrisy of clothes, don a swim suit, and we're all the same."[55] But class integration required more than just the redesign and relocation of municipal pools. It also necessitated a weakening of class prejudice. Middle-class Americans generally became willing to frequent the same municipal pools as working-class Americans during the 1920s and 1930s because laborers and immigrants did not seem as unhealthy and poor as they had a generation earlier.

The municipal pools in Wilmington, Delaware, exemplify the widespread social integration that occurred between 1920 and 1940. Wilmington operated four pools prior to the 1920s. As was typical, working-class boys constituted the vast majority of swimmers and use split along class, gender, and generational lines.[56] These social divisions evaporated in 1925, however, when the city opened an enormous pool in Price Run Park. The pool measured 400 feet long and between 120 and 180 feet wide, was surrounded by a sand beach, and was located in an attractive and easily accessible park.[57] It was a definitive pool of the swimming pool age.

Shortly before Price Run Pool opened, the city announced that, "men and women will be allowed to bathe at the same time and no restrictions will be placed on children's bathing."[58] City officials permitted children and adults and both sexes to swim together because they intended the pool to promote family sociability. A parks department official explained that the city built such a "large modern outdoor pool" so "young folks can swim together and dads can bring their families."[59] This intention arose out of new ideals of family life popular at the time, known as the "companionate family." Encouraged by psychologists, educators, and popular writers, Americans reconceived the family as the wellspring of social and emotional fulfillment, in which, according to historians Steven Mintz and Susan Kellogg, "husbands and wives would be 'friends and lovers' and parents and children would be 'pals.'"[60] Gender-integrated swimming pools were supposed to help foster these closer familial relationships by providing a recreation space where husbands, wives, and children could all play and relax together.

The design and location of Price Run Pool made it practical and acceptable for males and females to swim together. In an editorial praising the new pool, the *Wilmington Every Evening* explained that, "[b]eing open to public view, and being as large as a small lake, it is possible for men, women, and children to bathe there at the same time." By contrast, the paper continued, the city's other pools were "small and enclosed" and thus only appropriate for "women to use . . . on certain days and men on other days."[61] City officials agreed. The four Progressive Era pools remained gender segregated for years after Price Run Pool opened.[62] The city sanctioned mixed-gender swimming, but only at a pool set in a highly visible space and large enough so that women would not feel crowded by male swimmers.

Price Run Pool also dissolved the class divisions that characterized the use of earlier pools. Although the class makeup of swimmers is difficult to reconstruct conclusively, newspaper reports provide clues that the pool attracted a socially diverse crowd. Not surprisingly, laborers and their families flocked to the pool. Local newspapers noted that the pool was particularly popular with Ninth Ward residents, a nearby working-class neighborhood inhabited largely by railroad workers.[63] Members of Wilmington's Central Labor Union enjoyed the pool so much that they petitioned city officials to open it on Sundays, so they could spend an entire day there with their wives and children.[64] Many middle-class residents also frequented Price Run Pool. The large number of cars regularly parked outside offers the best evidence of a considerable middle-class presence. One day, the *Morning News* reported that "many" swimmers came "by automobile from distant sections of the city."[65] The "distant sections" no doubt included many middle-class suburbs. On another occasion, a reporter counted "hundreds of automobiles . . . parked about the pool."[66] The variety of swimsuits at the pool further indicated a diverse crowd. Some swimmers wore makeshift garments of "any kind," whereas others were adorned with "color bathing suits and parasols."[67] Consumer items such as cars and fashionable swimsuits were not infallible indicators of middle-class status, but they do strongly suggest the presence of well-to-do residents. Even though the standard of living improved for Americans during the 1920s, automobiles in particular remained too expensive in 1925 for most in the working classes.[68] As the *Every Evening* claimed, Price Run Pool was "a mecca for people throughout Wilmington."[69]

Officials in other cities explicitly intended their large, centrally located pools to diminish the social and physical distance between rich and poor. In Bethlehem, Pennsylvania, an industrial city with easily recognizable class lines, Mayor Archibald Johnston announced in 1918 his intention to develop a large park and swimming pool to be used "by *all the people* without distinction as to class or residence."[70] Johnston hoped the commingling in the park and pool would bridge the city's social divisions and help alleviate class antagonisms. When Saucon Park opened a year later, newspaper reports marveled at the diversity of people it attracted. The "laboring men of the shops and foundries" were there "in goodly numbers," reported the *Bethlehem Globe*, as were "the banker and business men." The article concluded that the park represented "true democracy in its broadest sense."[71] Mayor Johnston similarly touted the class diversity of swimmers and park-goers, claiming that both facilities had brought about a "thorough intermingling of our citizens" and "a fuller understanding of, and the better co-operation of, all classes."[72] In 1925 Bethlehem opened an even larger, gender-integrated pool in Saucon Park. The *Globe* described the new pool as a "rendezvous" for all residents. It was, according to the paper, the "most popular place" in the city.[73] One Sunday during its first summer of operation, the pool attracted between 8,000 and 10,000 people, which represented about 15 percent of the city's entire population.[74]

The class integration of municipal pools reflected a significant shift in social values, namely a weakening of class prejudice. During the Progressive Era, middle-class northerners avoided swimming in the same pools as the working classes largely because they viewed them as poor, dirty, and foreign. Beginning in the late 1910s, however, several factors mitigated these prejudices. First, the decline in European immigration to the United States made the urban working class seem less poor and less foreign than it had previously. The millions and millions of European peasants who flooded into northern cities before 1915 had constantly reinforced middle-class prejudices about the working classes. After 1915, however, European immigration declined significantly due to World War I and then the Immigration Acts of 1921 and 1924. Whereas an average of 800,000 European immigrants arrived each year between 1900 and 1915, an average of 200,000 arrived annually between 1916 and 1930. During the 1930s, European immigration plummeted even further, to less than 50,000 a year. Over the same period, earlier arrivals acculturated, their children assimilated, and family fortunes often improved. As a result of both declining immigration and accelerated acculturation, the face of the working class seemed more "American" during the 1920s and 1930s than it had during the Gilded Age and Progressive Era.[75]

At the same time, the material conditions for working-class northerners generally improved. Many moved out of urban slums and into working-class suburbs, and most participated in the consumerism of the 1920s. As a result, the northern working class began to live and look more middle class. As historian Gary Cross notes, consumption "blurred ethnic and class divisions."[76]

Furthermore, public health campaigns and declining rates of disease among working-class whites made them appear less unhealthy in the 1920s than they had previously.[77] At the same time, advances in pool sanitation—namely the widespread use of chlorine—made the contraction of diseases in a pool seem unlikely. Public officials and newspapers aggressively publicized pool sanitation measures in order to counteract long-standing fears.[78] They largely succeeded.

Finally, the Great Black Migration between 1915 and 1930 heightened perceptions of racial difference in the North, which helped whites of all social classes forge a common identity out of their shared whiteness. As numerous scholars have pointed out, the presence of black racial "others" helped create a heterogeneous white society—what David Nasaw calls "a sort of 'herrenvolk' democracy"—in the North.[79] While Nasaw finds evidence of this in the late nineteenth and early twentieth centuries at commercial amusements, a mixed-class, white crowd did not appear at municipal pools in the North until the 1920s, after large-scale black in-migration had commenced and, as Matthew Pratt Guterl contends, black-white racial difference became the overriding social distinction in the North.[80] In short, the intense emphasis on "race" during the 1920s and 1930s made class and ethnic differences among northern, urban "whites" seem less salient and significant than they had previously. Because of all these changes—the end of large-scale European immigration, improving material conditions among the working classes, advances in pool sanitation, and the emergence of race as the predominant social division in the North—middle-class whites generally became willing to swim in the same pools as working-class whites.

〰〰 The large, heterogeneous white crowds that gathered at municipal pools during the interwar years transformed pools into centers of community life. This was particularly true in small cities and towns, where recreation opportunities were limited and a large pool could accommodate much of the population at one time. When Ellsworth, Kansas, population 2,100, opened an outdoor pool in 1924, it quickly became the town's principal gathering spot during the summer. "The new swimming pool is the most popular place in town," noted city clerk Elden Shaw. "Auto loads from surrounding towns drive here, eat their supper in the grove and swim. Old people who do not swim go there to look on and visit."[81] Kunkle's Grove Pool in Palmerton, Pennsylvania, similarly served as a summertime social center for this small industrial city tucked amid the Blue Mountains. When the pool opened in 1929, the *Palmerton Press* emphasized that it was "free" and open to "everyone." Longtime resident Joseph Plechavy recalled that the pool did indeed attract just about everyone in town. "It didn't matter who you were, you swam at the pool." Plechavy recalled spending countless afternoons and weekends at the pool "yakking with whoever was there." The pool also hosted summertime community events, including the American Legion "Community Picnic," the Fourth of July Celebration, and the annual Palmerton Picnic. These events brought the whole town together at the pool, where neighbors swam, chatted, devoured ice cream, and celebrated their shared identity as Americans and Palmertons.[82]

Big-city pools also fostered a vibrant community life. The *Wilmington Evening Journal* described the social effect Price Run Pool had upon the city: "A wonderful neighborhood and fraternal spirit, however, seems to have gripped the entire section. . . . Everybody seemed imbued with the community spirit and bent on having a thoroughly good time. Men, women, children of the Ninth ward section are getting acquainted with each other and cementing bonds of community friendship such as can only be gained through intimacy in acquatic [sic] sports."[83] The large WPA pool opened in the Greenpoint section of Brooklyn similarly served as a center of community life. "From the day it opened [in 1936]," the *New York Times* wrote in 1990, "it became a resort for people who could not afford vacations and the hub of the working-class neighborhood's summertime social life."[84] A study commissioned by the New York City Department of Parks concluded that the city's WPA pools "provided a special sense of community identity."[85] The pools were shared social spaces; in using them, local residents developed attachments to the neighborhood and to one another.

Municipal pools became such vital community institutions in large part because they were uniquely intimate and sociable places. Hundreds and often thousands of people gathered together at municipal pools. They changed clothes next to one another, showered together, negotiated crowded spaces, and lay out side by side on sandy beaches. These activities necessitated interaction and dialogue. The conversations and contact that occurred at swimming pools were not fleeting as at most public spaces. People spent hours, sometimes the entire day at municipal pools—swimming, chatting, sunbathing, and picnicking. Furthermore, the visual and physical intimacy at pools gave rise to thorny issues that often necessitated community dialogue to resolve. What swimsuit styles were appropriate? What should the boundaries of male-female interaction be? Should any social group be prohibited from using the pool? In short, a meaningful public discourse occurred at municipal pools that enabled Americans to foster, monitor, and even dispute community life.

Snapshots of swimmers at municipal pools during the 1920s and 1930s present a very different picture of community life than appears in most scholarly works on the period. In arguably the best general history of American society and culture in the 1920s, Lynn Dumenil posits that a "dominant theme is the erosion of community and personal autonomy in the face of an increasingly nationalized and organized society."[86] Robert and Helen Lynd made a similar claim in their 1929 seminal sociological work *Middletown*. "In the main," they concluded, "the cleavages which break up Middletown into its myriad sub-groups appear to have become somewhat more rigid in the last generation."[87] The popularity of municipal swimming pools is one example where just the opposite occurred. Nativism, the revival of the Ku Klux Klan, and labor strife all testify to the schisms of the period. Yet, in the realm of recreation, social groups that had previously been separated—males and females, children and adults, working class and middle class—came together in large numbers at municipal pools and, in the words of one observer, got "acquainted with each other."[88] Swimming pools provided a public space for neighbors and family members to reestablish the bonds eroded by urbanization and industrialization.

~~~ Gender integration combined with the downsizing of swimsuits between 1920 and 1940 eroticized municipal pools. When cities first permitted mixed-gender swimming, they typically required swimmers to wear modest swimsuits in order to dampen the sexual charge sparked by males and females interacting at such intimate public spaces. During the late 1920s and throughout the 1930s, however, swimsuits shrank, revealing more curves and more skin. As a result, swimming pools became erotic public spaces where scantily clad males and females displayed themselves and visually consumed others.

In the late 1910s bathing suits covered most of a person's body, especially if the person was a woman. Fabric shielded all but a woman's neck, face, and forearms from public view. A female swimmer wore stockings on her legs and a puffy skirt that extended down to her knees. On top, she wore a loose, thick blouse, cut high around the neck, with elbow-length sleeves. She also typically bundled her hair under a swimming cap. A proper male swimmer was not quite this clothed, but almost. He wore loose-fitting trunks that extended down to the knee and a loose top that was cut high on the neckline. The top did not have sleeves, but the armholes were snug.[89] These suits were designed to protect a swimmer's modesty, not facilitate ease of movement. As historian Claudia Kidwell put it, their purpose was "to cover, conceal, and obscure" the body.[90]

Few cities regulated bathing suit styles before 1920 because the weight of public opinion kept most swimmers in line with cultural standards. As one Chicago recreation official put it, cities left the choice of suits "to the conscience of the wearer."[91] This policy worked so long as the traditional dictates of public decency remained strong enough to influence the conscience of swimmers. In the early 1920s, female swimmers began to flout the old standards. Inspired by the example of Olympic swimmer Annette Kellerman, many young women dared to wear the controversial "one-piece suit" at municipal pools and public beaches. The suit became so identified with the famous swimmer that it was popularly called "the Annette Kellerman." The one-piece suit was a particular style, not simply a generic name for any suit with the top and bottom sewn together. It was far more streamlined and tight fitting than the old blouse and skirt variety, especially around the hips. The suit appealed to women in part because it allowed more freedom of movement in the water. It was no coincidence that the old suits were called "bathing suits" and the new variety "swim suits." The one-piece suit actually permitted women to swim.[92]

Ease of movement, however, was not the sole appeal of the new style. Young women in particular thought that their bodies looked more fetching in the close-fitting costume. According to *Harper's Bazaar*, the Kellerman suits were "distinguished by an incomparable, daring beauty of fit."[93] The *New York Times* explained more directly in 1921 that young women wore the suits because they "regard them as rather frisky."[94] This sleek, sexy suit fit the "new woman" of the 1920s well. It revealed the curves of her body as well as her disregard for tradition.[95]

The burgeoning popularity of the Kellerman suits early in the 1920s caused many cities to forbid the close-fitting style at gender-integrated pools. Washington, D.C., banned "Annette Kellerman bathing suits" in 1921 at its pools, but only during the month of May, when mixed-gender swimming was permitted. During the rest of the summer, when women swimmers would not be observed by men, the suits were acceptable.[96] Similarly, Wilmington permitted women to wear one-piece suits at its four gender-segregated pools, but not at Price Run Pool, where, city officials announced, "boldness in dress will not be tolerated." If a female swimmer wore an inappropriate suit, lifeguards forced her to cover herself with a long, baggy over shirt.[97] In both cities, officials required women to cover their limbs and hide their curves at mixed-gender pools because they did not want the female form to spark a sexual charge or become a public spectacle.

Over the next twenty years, however, the size of acceptable swimsuits gradually shrank and the female body did indeed become an arousing spectacle at municipal pools. During the mid-1920s, most cities permitted female swimmers to take off their stockings and skirts as long as they wore loose bloomers down close to their knees.[98] A modified version of the one-piece suit became acceptable at most gender-integrated pools by the late 1920s. It had a lower neckline than the original "Annette Kellerman" and a shorter skirt. By the 1930s, short trunks replaced skirts. These bottoms revealed the shape of hips and exposed almost the entire thigh. The tops of these suits were more form fitting as well, revealing the outline of breasts. Women started wearing open-backed swimsuits in the mid-1930s. The two-piece brassiere suit, which exposed a woman's midsection, was the last major design change of the era. These suits appeared as early as the mid-1930s but did not become common until the end of the decade.[99] In total, a woman's thighs, hip line, shoulders, stomach, back, and breast line all became publicly exposed between 1920 and 1940. Whereas ten yards of material was necessary to make a woman's bathing suit early in the century, one yard was enough by the end of the era.[100] The evolution of men's swimsuits was not nearly so incremental. The major change occurred in the mid- to late 1930s, when male swimmers shed their loose-fitting tops and exposed their chest, back, and belly to the public. At the same time, swimsuit bottoms became shorter and more form-fitting.[101] Whereas the function of earlier swimsuits had been to cover and conceal, the latter suits served to expose and showcase the human body.

A combination of factors contributed to the downsizing of swimsuits. For one, young women pressured city officials to liberalize swimsuit regulations by continually wearing forbidden styles. This grass-roots resistance occurred mostly at public beaches, which were more difficult for public officials to regulate than swimming pools.[102] One controversy occurred in Somers Point, New Jersey, during the summer of 1921, when many young women came to the beach wearing "Annette Kellerman suits." Instead of hiring a full-time bathing suit censor and dragging the women before the local magistrate—as the city had done in previous years—Mayor Albert Crissey permitted one-piece suits on the beach "so long as bathers wear them and conduct themselves with propriety."[103] The liberal policy attracted a flood of young women to the beach as well as an army of male voyeurs. The *New York Times* described the scene: "The response today turned the bay front into a scene of flashing limbs and display of shapely forms. A fringe of trees lining the beach and the Ocean City–Somers Point Bridge were turned into bleachers from which motorists enjoyed the scenery." Several local women's groups complained to Crissey about the daily parade of human flesh. The Women's Republican League sent the mayor a petition demanding he revoke the policy. The men in town disagreed. A local Rotarian Club voted unanimously to support the new policy. According to a newspaper report, "[p]hotographs of bathing girls on parade in Venice, Calif., with all of the girls wearing one-piece costumes were circulated during the discussion." After viewing the pictures, the Rotarians concluded the suits were not at all indecent.[104]

Several years later, young women pushed the boundary of acceptable swimsuits even further by wearing "abbreviated one-piece suits" at Bradley Beach, New Jersey. Beach censors continually arrested the women, but city recorder Joseph Megill eventually stopped fining them. With so many women wearing the skimpy suits, he concluded, they must be "the trend of the times," and who was he to defy "popular demand for such bathing suits."[105]

The brazenness of young women was not solely responsible for the shrinking size of swimsuits between 1920 and 1940. Swimsuit manufacturers and Hollywood producers spurred the market for skimpy suits through advertising campaigns and movies. In 1921, an obscure knitting mill named Jantzen began mass-producing swimsuits and initiated a national advertising campaign to boost sales. Jantzen marketed its swimsuits as fashion garments, encouraging women in particular to buy a new suit each summer rather than wear "last year's style." For this strategy to work, the company had to create new styles each season. Sometimes it introduced new colors or added a frill, but most often it trimmed the suit down so that it covered less of the body.[106] The mass production of increasingly skimpier suits and the advertising campaigns telling Americans that skimpy suits were in style helped reshape the accepted standards of pool and beach modesty.[107]

Hollywood movies also influenced swimsuit trends and cultural attitudes about proper dress. The swimsuits actresses wore onscreen in such movies as *The Kid from Spain* (1932) and *Dancing Lady* (1933) inspired considerable imitation. Young Americans in particular copied the appearance of their favorite stars by, among other things, wearing the same clothing styles. As historian Jeanine Basinger points out, "fashion and glamour were the elements of . . . film that women could actually get their hands on."[108] When Dolores Del Rio wore a bare-midriff brassiere suit in *Birds of Paradise* (1932), many young women wanted to wear the same. To promote this imitation, swimsuit manufacturers collaborated with Hollywood studios to ensure that swimsuit styles worn in a particular movie were simultaneously available to consumers. A 1937 ad for BVD swimsuits, for example, featured photos of several Hollywood stars taken at the swimming pool set of the soon-to-be-released movie *Vogues of 1938*. The advertisement showed women what style would be popular next summer and how to dress like a star, "from $3.95 up."[109] Movies also helped refashion cultural attitudes about proper dress by exposing millions of Americans to swimsuits that pushed the boundaries of existing standards. The nymphs lounging around the penthouse swimming pool in *Palmy Days* (1931)—wearing ultra-tight-fitting, low-cut suits—conditioned Americans to seeing these sexy and revealing swimsuits. Having already been revealed on screen, the suits seemed more conventional when they appeared at the local pool.[110]

The downsizing of swimsuits marked a profound transformation in the meaning of public decency in America. Since at least the mid-nineteenth century, prevailing standards of dress were intended to prevent a person's body from becoming a public spectacle. Victorian etiquette adviser Mrs. Oliver Bell Bunce reminded readers in 1892 that "[a] lady or gentleman should conduct herself or himself on the street so as to escape all observation."[111] Conservative dress ensured that a person's appearance did not attract attention.[112] The same underlying value influenced bathing suit styles. As late as 1922, a women's group in St. Petersburg, Florida, asked the mayor to enforce local bathing suit regulations strictly so that "married men" would be protected from "the wiles of the sea vamp."[113] The skimpy suits worn by young women violated established standards of public decency precisely because they attracted men's attention to their bodies.

Over the next decade, however, Americans flipped the meaning of public decency on its head. In 1925 C. A. Chader complained to the *Wilmington Every Evening* about the skimpy suits women wore at Price Run Pool. The focus of his complaint was not young women with sultry bodies, but rather large women with unattractive bodies. "Many unsightly conditions prevail [at the pool], and if I dare say, the most is the appearance of stout women in one-piece bathing suits."[114] Similarly, in describing the trend toward men shedding the tops of their suits a decade later, journalist Paul Heudepohl noted the absence of protest from other swimmers, with one exception. "[W]hile there are certain types of men that can wear trunks and look perfectly decent, there are still a number of persons that do not have the Adonis-like figure that can parade on the beaches and not cause or create some protest from a certain group of the populace."[115] The public was no longer offended by the sight of a seductive body but by the sight of an unattractive body. It was now "decent" to expose your chest, stomach, and back, but only if you had "an

Beauty Contest Winners, Glen Oak Pool, Peoria, Illinois, circa early 1930s. Municipal swimming pools frequently hosted bathing beauty contests during the late 1920s and the 1930s. Courtesy of Peoria Public Library.

Adonis-like figure." Public decency had come to mean presenting an attractive, even eye-catching, appearance rather than protecting one's modesty.

The new definition of public decency was constantly on display at municipal pools. The most conspicuous display of bodies occurred during the many beauty contests held at municipal pools beginning in the late 1920s. Peoria, Illinois, for example, held its first "Bathing Beauty Revue" in 1929 at the Glen Oak Municipal Pool. The annual contest quickly became one of the Park Department's most popular "special events," attracting a large number of contestants and spectators.[116] The annual beauty contest at the Avalon, Pennsylvania, municipal pool began in 1934, the same year the pool opened.[117] At these events, young women paraded before crowds of ogling spectators, displaying their bare limbs and sultry figures.

Beauty Contest, Salisbury, Maryland, 1940. Beauty contests enabled mixed-gender crowds to stare at the bare limbs and shapely forms of teenage girls. FSA-OWI Collection, Prints and Photographs Division, Library of Congress, Washington, D.C., neg. LC-USF33-020635. .

Similar exhibitionism also became integral to everyday pool culture. In 1932 a reporter for the *Philadelphia Evening Bulletin* visited the city's Tenth and Mifflin pool and found young women "being bathing beauties." The "gay, sleek, and handsome" girls were quite attentive to their appearance. Nineteen-year-old Anne Brown "wore a turquoise blue backless camisole top suit" and "carried around a small comb which she uses constantly with a dreamy look." Seventeen-year-old Suzie Porter applied makeup, concentrating "on her dark eyes." When not enhancing their appearance, the girls lay in the sun and flirted with the "stunning" male lifeguards. The reporter concluded that this pool in downtown Philadelphia was a particularly good place for young women to put themselves on display: "The pool is an outdoor one and the bright light is flattering to the youthful beauty."[118] A 1937 photo taken at a municipal pool in Caldwell, Idaho, captured a similar scene. Several teenage girls lounged about the grassy lawn bordering the pool. One combed her hair, while three others lathered their bodies with olive oil. Just like the pool

Sunbathers at Municipal Pool, Caldwell, Idaho, 1941. Female swimmers frequently beautified themselves and put themselves on display at swimming pools. FSA-OWI Collection, Prints and Photographs Division, Library of Congress, Washington, D.C., neg. LC-USF33-013102-M3.

in downtown Philadelphia, this pool in small-town Idaho served as a public stage on which to display beauty, act stylish, and exude sexuality.

As a result of the exhibitionism, municipal pools became popular venues for visually consuming attractive bodies. Pools were a voyeur's delight. Many Americans frequented pools not to swim or even sunbathe but to stare at scantily clad males and females. Of the almost 10,000 people who crowded into Bethlehem's Saucon Park Pool one Saturday in 1925, the local newspaper estimated that more than half spent their time "watching the swimmers."[119] So many voyeurs frequented Price Run Pool in Wilmington that city officials implemented a five-cent "spectator" fee and considered constructing "bleachers" at the pool to "accommodate [the] thousands of spectators who visit the pool to see the bathers enjoying themselves."[120] In 1934 *Fortune* magazine concluded that swimming pools had become so popular in part because the skimpy suits swimmers and sunbathers wore sparked "the full voltage of cosmic urge."[121]

Newspapers also recognized the visual eroticism at pools and filled their pages each summer with gratuitous photos from local swimming pools. In virtually every instance, the photos showed svelte and attractive young women in and around the pool. During one three-day period in July 1932, the *Pittsburgh Press* printed four pictures taken at local pools. One showed two teenage girls descending into the water from a pool ladder, another showed a particularly attractive girl laying seductively atop an inner tube, while the other two pictures showed groups of young women propped up on the side of the pool staring into the camera.[122] During the same three-day period, another Pittsburgh daily printed its own montage of swimming pool photos. One photo showed three young women reclining in and around South Park Pool, while another showed two teenage girls, already in their one-piece suits, giving their admission tickets to a male attendant.[123] In the six pictures that appeared in both papers those three days, the fully clothed attendant was the only male pictured, while all of the women were young, attractive, and in their revealing swimsuits. Furthermore, the bare-limbed girls had nothing to do with the news, as evidenced by the absence of an accompanying news article. The pictures simply captured the voyeurism and visual eroticism that were now integral to the swimming pool experience.

In her excellent study of youth culture during the 1920s, *The Damned and the Beautiful*, Paula Fass characterizes the decade as a time during which Americans adjusted themselves to social and cultural change. Throughout this period, she wrote, "personal adjustments, cultural accommodation, and social reconstruction were taking place everywhere in society."[124] Municipal swimming pools clearly reflected—and contributed to—much of the social restructuring and cultural accommodation that defined the era: the gender and class integration of public space, the sexualization of public culture, and the triumph of a therapeutic ethos.

Not as apparent were the ways that swimming pools contributed to some of the personal adjustments of the era. The sexual climate at swimming pools, for example, heightened the public and personal importance of physical appearance. Scholars have noticed that gender ideals became defined more thoroughly in physical terms during the 1920s and 1930s. To be an ideal woman required a svelte body and a pretty face. To be a masculine man required a powerful and muscular physique.[125] At the same time, physical appearance became a primary source and expression of individual identity. Americans' perception of themselves and others became increasingly tied to how they looked.[126] The swimming pools of the interwar years encouraged both of these developments by putting Americans' physical appearance on public display. Previously, bodies were not publicly visible. Even at swimming pools and beaches, bathing suits revealed little flesh and no curves. All this changed during the interwar years at swimming pools and beaches. People could now see who possessed slender and muscular physiques and who did not. The experience of being at a pool pressured individuals to realize the ideal. Movies and advertisements may have shown Americans what the ideal body looked like, but swimming pools made it an imperative to actually possess that body.

The swimming pools of the interwar years also recast women into a new public role. Previously, cultural standards demanded that women be inconspicuous while in public and that women's bodies remain strictly private. Gender-integrated pools and skimpy swimsuits, however, transformed women and their bodies into visual objects. Although both men and women publicly displayed themselves at pools and were observed by others, women were clearly the primary spectacle. Only women participated in the swimming pool beauty contests, and newspapers almost always published swimming pool photos that featured only women. Many young women embraced and internalized this new public role, viewing it as a sign of liberation and a means of self-expression. As historian Joan Jacobs Brumberg writes, young women of the 1920s "intuited that modern femininity required some degree of exhibitionism or, at least, a willingness to display oneself as a decorative object."[127] This was certainly the case at swimming pools, where young women applied makeup, combed their hair "with a dreamy look in [their] eyes," and wore tight-fitting and revealing swimsuits because "they regard them as rather frisky." And yet, as Brumberg astutely points out, accepting the public role of visual object may not have been as liberating as some women assumed. It diminished the public importance of other personal qualities, such as intelligence and character, and markedly increased women's anxiety about the size and shape of their bodies.

The swimming pools of the interwar years also show how easily Americans combined consumerism with non-consumption-oriented cultural forms. Municipal-pool swimmers certainly displayed consumer goods. Fashion-conscious swimmers donned Jantzen and BVD swimsuits "from $3.95 up," women conspicuously applied makeup at pools, and many swimmers smoked cigarettes while lounging poolside. In these ways, swimming pools reflected the maturation of consumer culture that occurred during the 1920s. However, consumption was not central to the swimming pool experience. Americans flocked to municipal pools in order to cool off in the water, relax out in the sun, socialize with neighbors, and see and be seen. Cultural historians largely ignore the vibrancy of non-consumption-oriented cultural forms during this period in their effort to interpret the rise of consumer culture. In their introduction to *The Culture of Consumption*, for example, Richard Fox and Jackson Lears claim that "consumption became a cultural ideal, a hegemonic 'way of seeing' in twentieth-century America."[128] Not exactly. A vision of the "good life" developed at swimming pools that was not primarily focused on buying or consuming material goods. This is not to claim that the culture that developed at swimming pools conflicted with the increasing consumption that also characterized the era. Rather, they complemented one another, and both were integral to the type of life so many Americans desired at the time—a life filled with material abundance, comfort, pleasure, and leisure.

Swimming pools also demonstrate the continued vitality and popularity of noncommercial recreation. Historians have focused so much attention on commercial recreations and attributed so much social and cultural significance to them that a student of U.S. history might wonder if public forms of recreation disappeared sometime early in the twentieth century or, at the very least, became socially and culturally irrelevant. The history of municipal swimming pools shows otherwise. Swimming pools, for the most part, resisted commercialization. Entrepreneurs opened some for-profit pools during the interwar years, but they struggled to compete against the ubiquitous publicly owned pool, and many went out of business.[129] As *Fortune* magazine pointed out in 1934, "swimming presents an anomaly [in our modern industrial world]. Despite the 30,000,000 people who practice it, few entrepreneurs have been able to commercialize it. . . . [Swimming remains] the one sport-for-sport's sake in which everyone can indulge." Swimming pools may have been an anomaly as *Fortune* claims, but they were not an insignificant countercurrent to the trend toward commercialization. Rather, they were a national tidal wave. Swimming was by far the most popular form of active recreation in the country at the time. *Fortune* estimated that upwards of 30 million Americans swam in pools 350 million times each year.[130] The National Recreation Association survey conducted in 1934 found that almost four times as many Americans swam regularly as frequented amusement parks and about five times as many swam regularly as frequented dance halls. Furthermore, the municipal pools of the interwar years were not holdover institutions from a bygone era that struggled to hold on to their constituency. They were innovative, and their growth was explosive during this period. In other words, public recreation did not just survive during the interwar years; it expanded and flourished. Furthermore, if John Kasson, Kathy Peiss, and Lewis Erenberg are correct that Americans' experiences at amusement parks and dance halls altered American society and culture in profound ways, then what occurred at swimming pools certainly had social and cultural import as well.[131]

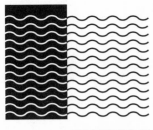

CHAPTER 5

"ONE FOR THE WHITE RACE AND THE OTHER FOR THE COLORED RACE"

THE ONSET OF RACIAL DISCRIMINATION, 1920 TO 1940

In one of the largest parks in Pittsburgh, the city—with public funds—erected a swimming pool. . . . Negroes, of course, have a right to go there and swim. Some of them did. They were set upon by a group of white hoodlums and severely beaten. This was last year. Recently two Negroes went to the pool to swim and they too were clubbed by white hoodlums. I forgot to mention the very important fact that white women swim in this pool also with the men.—Ernest McKinney, **Pittsburgh Courier** *(1932)*

When New York City opened its eleven WPA pools in 1936, the Department of Parks started an annual "Learn to Swim" campaign. A publicity poster for the campaign reflected the social integration that had occurred at the city's pools. It indicated that the swim classes were available "for all ages" and showed a cartoonlike drawing of males and females standing next to one another in the background. The composition of the poster did suggest, however, at least one social division at the pools. All the swimmers clustered on the left side were white, while all those on the right side were black. The poster implied that blacks and whites would not be learning to swim together.

The racial segregation depicted on the "Learn to Swim" poster reflected the actual use of municipal pools in New York and other cities throughout the northern United States at the time. The social melting pot that municipal pools became during the 1920s and 1930s was accompanied by the exclusion and segregation of black Americans. The pattern of discrimination varied with the size and culture of the city. Large metropolises, which oper-

WPA Learn to Swim Poster, New York Department of Parks, 1940. The racial separation depicted in the poster reflected the actual use of municipal pools in New York and other northern cities at the time. By the People, For the People: Posters from the WPA, 1936–1943 Collection, Prints and Photographs Division, Library of Congress, Washington, D.C., neg. LC-USZC2-5399.

ated many pools, generally segregated black swimmers at Jim Crow pools. In cities with a southern heritage such as St. Louis and Washington, D.C., segregation was officially mandated. Public officials explicitly assigned certain pools for black residents and others for whites. Further north, in cities such as New York and Chicago, city officials encouraged de facto segregation by locating pools within racially homogeneous neighborhoods. They built one or two pools within black residential neighborhoods and the rest in thoroughly white neighborhoods. When blacks sought admission to pools earmarked for whites, attendants discouraged them from entering but did not outright deny them admission. Enforcement then fell to white swimmers who often harassed and assaulted black Americans who transgressed this new racial boundary. In this way, segregation was frequently achieved through violence. In smaller communities with only one pool, racial discrimination took the form of outright exclusion. Access to these pools was intensely contested because there was no other pool to which city officials could relegate black swimmers.

Several factors contributed to the onset of racial segregation and exclusion at municipal pools in the North. The most significant were the Great Black Migration, the emergence of race-based sanitation and health fears, and gender integration. The influx of approximately 1.5 million southern blacks between 1916 and 1930 reshaped the social geography of northern cities in ways that facilitated de facto segregation at pools. During the migration, urban neighborhoods became more rigidly divided along racial lines. Black residents of Chicago, Cleveland, New York, Detroit, and other northern cities became concentrated within one or two well-defined "black belts."[1] As a result, public activities such as shopping and recreation tended to split along racial lines. Blacks generally frequented the pools nearest to their homes, and whites did the same. Furthermore, the influx of southern migrants heightened racial antagonism in northern cities by increasing competition between blacks and working-class whites for jobs, housing, and public services. The antagonism led to race riots as well as countless isolated episodes of violence. Ethnic whites, for example, frequently attacked blacks who entered "their" neighborhoods.[2] While these attacks were not specifically directed at would-be swimmers, the threat of assault did deter black swimmers from venturing to pools in white neighborhoods. The 1919 Chicago Riot best exemplifies the rising racial tensions of the migration years and, in particular, highlights the increasing sensitivity among northern whites to sharing the same water with blacks. The riot began after white bathers threw rocks at several black teenagers who had floated into water fronting a "white" beach along Lake Michigan.

One of the teenagers drowned and "a seven-day orgy of shootings, arsons, and beatings" followed.[3]

The Great Migration further contributed to the onset of racial discrimination at swimming pools by heightening northern whites' concerns about the cleanliness and health of northern blacks. During the Gilded Age and Progressive Era, pool use divided along class lines—but not racial lines—in large part because middle-class Americans viewed the urban poor en masse as the "great unwashed." They perceived working-class whites and blacks as equally dirty and prone to carry communicable diseases. This class-based prejudice was constantly reinforced by the waves of poor immigrants entering the United States from southern and eastern Europe.[4] When European immigration declined after 1914, black migrants from the South replaced European immigrants as the most conspicuous poor in northern cities. The vast majority settled in trash-laden, rundown slums, while many first- and second-generation European immigrants moved to slightly better neighborhoods. Furthermore, northerners generally viewed the southern migrants as dirty, crude, and likely to be infected by communicable diseases.[5] This stereotype was reinforced by public health reports that indicated rising rates of tuberculosis, smallpox, and venereal diseases among northern blacks as a result of the migration.[6] The combined effect was that Progressive Era class-based sanitation fears gradually gave way to more thoroughly race-based fears. Just as the urban middle class had previously avoided swimming with the working classes, northern whites of all social classes now objected to swimming with blacks, in part, because they feared contracting a communicable disease and becoming contaminated by their supposed dirtiness.

Gender integration and the eroticization of swimming pools, however, were the most direct and crucial causes of racial exclusion and segregation at municipal pools in the North. When cities permitted males and females to swim together, white swimmers and public officials suddenly attempted to separate blacks from whites. Although the rationale remained mostly unspoken, northern whites in general objected to black men having the opportunity to interact with white women at such intimate and erotic public spaces. They feared that black men would act upon their supposedly untamed sexual desire for white women by touching them in the water and assaulting them with romantic advances.[7] Racial segregation also enabled communities to restrict white women's social and sexual choices by limiting their opportunities to meet and form relationships with black men. Finally, the importance of the exposed male body as a sign of masculinity also likely contributed to the onset of racial segregation and exclusion at municipal pools. As Gail Bederman has shown, justifications of racial superiority were based in part on assumptions and assertions of white men's superior manliness. "Turn of the century manhood," writes Bederman, "constructed bodily strength and social authority as identical."[8] If black men were permitted to frequent the resort pools of the interwar years, some of them would have displayed powerful and muscular physiques and thereby conspicuously challenged white supremacy. That challenge could be avoided by keeping blacks separate from whites at public spaces where men's bodies would be exposed. For these mostly unacknowledged reasons, gender integration and the eroticization of swimming pools necessitated racial segregation.

The onset of racial segregation at municipal swimming pools was part of a larger social and intellectual transformation that occurred in the urban North between the two world wars. Matthew Guterl argues in *The Color of Race in America* that northerners reconstructed their notions of race along rigid black-white lines during the 1920s and 1930s: "If many turn-of-the-century Americans wrestled with problems of racial classification, all that changed in the twenty years following the Great War. . . . The result was a culture of racial thinking termed 'bi-racialism' by the eugenicist Lothrop Stoddard, which encouraged Americans to focus on race-as-color and almost solely on whiteness and blackness, leaving them increasingly unable, or unwilling, to deal with national 'race questions' other than the purportedly peculiar conundrum posed by 'the Negro.'"[9] The history of swimming pools reveals that a related social reconstruction occurred at the same time. Simply put, between about 1920 and 1935, class, gender, and generational distinctions, as represented by public social divisions, became less salient in northern cities, while racial distinctions, as defined by color, became more so. Class, gender, and generational divisions certainly did not evaporate during this period nor were black-white racial distinctions suddenly invented. However, northern urban society did become fundamentally more integrated along class, gender, and generational lines, yet more segregated along racial lines. The social reconstruction of municipal pools offers one example of this larger transformation and suggests some of its causes as well.

≋ In August 1931 Pittsburgh opened a gigantic outdoor swimming pool in Highland Park that became a racial battlefield precisely because it was gender-integrated. The facility had two large pools—a main tank 220 feet long and 90 feet wide and a 220 by 220 foot wading pool. In total, the pools were the length of a football field and twice as wide. When densely packed, which they often were, the pools could accommodate 10,000 swimmers. The facility also included a large sandy beach and a broad concrete sun deck, where swimmers could indulge in the exhibitionism and voyeurism now integral to the pool experience.[10]

Thousands ventured to Highland Park Pool the day it opened, including many black Americans. They no doubt expected unencumbered access just as they had to all the other municipal pools in the city. To their surprise, attendants picked each and every identifiably black person out of the stream of people entering the pool and asked to see his or her "health certificate," even though no white swimmers had to prove that they were disease free. When prospective black swimmers could not produce the document, which none could, attendants turned them away. That evening, representatives from a local black citizens group asked Superintendent of Public Works Edward Lang, whose department administered the city's pools, to clarify the admission policy. Lang disavowed any knowledge of the health certificate requirement and assured them that no further discrimination would occur.[11]

The next day, fifty or so young black men made their way to the pool. As Superintendent Lang had promised, the attendants permitted them to enter. When the black swimmers approached the pool, some of the estimated 5,000 people already in the water began shouting threats. The young men appealed to the police officers stationed at the pool for protection but were told that once they entered the water the police could (or rather would) do nothing to help them. Frightened but undeterred, they slipped into the crowded pool. A reporter for the *Post-Gazette* described the violence that followed: "Each Negro who entered the pool yesterday was immediately surrounded by whites and slugged or held beneath the water until he gave up his attempts to swim and left the pool." The white swimmers eventually beat all fifty young men out of the water.[12]

The following day, four more young men tried to swim in the pool but never made it through the front gate. Eugene Dickerson, Hugh Davis, J. D. Williams, and Emmanuel Phillips were attacked by "a group of whites" as they approached the facility. Police officers stationed at the pool watched as the men punched and kicked the teenagers to the ground. When the barrage of fists and feet slowed, the officers finally stepped in and arrested two men for "disorderly conduct" and "inciting to riot." The two arrested were Dickerson and Davis, the young men who suffered the most severe beatings. The following morning, the local magistrate found both men guilty and fined them twenty-five dollars each.[13]

Over the next two weeks, the same pattern repeated several times. Small groups of black swimmers entered the pool and subjected themselves to potentially life-threatening attacks by white swimmers. The pool police then arrested the black swimmers for "inciting to riot." This charge was speciously apt. The presence of black swimmers did indeed incite other swimmers to riotous behavior, but surely the authors of the law envisioned behavior more antagonizing than swimming in a pool. But that is the critical point. Blacks swimming in the same pool with whites was—all of a sudden—so antagonizing that it led many white swimmers to brutally attack them. If the "inciting to riot" charge was not too farfetched, the magistrate typically found the black victims guilty and fined them between five and twenty-five dollars.[14]

The violence climaxed that first summer on August 20. A dozen teenagers ventured to the pool and made it through the gate and showers without incident. As they approached the pool, however, several men began shouting threats. The group tried to ignore the taunts and stares, perhaps trusting Mayor Charles Kline's recent public assurance that the police officers stationed at the pool would protect them. If so, their trust was misplaced. According to the *Courier*, the city's black newspaper, one of the officers actually encouraged swimmers to beat the boys out of the water. "We can't afford to let these niggers run this town," he was quoted as saying. As the black teens waded into the pool, "white bathers" started by throwing rocks at them and then swarmed them like human piranhas—punching and dunking them without mercy.[15]

After a particularly vicious blow to the head, one of the victims "gave a piercing distress call" heard by an African American church group picnicking in a nearby section of Highland Park. Several in the group rushed to the pool to investigate the cry for help. Seeing the mob beating the overmatched youths, the *Courier* reported that "one or two started as if to climb over the fence to go to the boys' aid, but, the policemen drew their guns and threatened to shoot if they tried to do this." Velma Brown, a member of the church group, screamed at the officers for not stopping the violence, so they clubbed her with a mace. Another picnicker, T. H. Lewis, stepped in to protect Brown, but the officers dragged him to a nearby cottage where, according to the *Courier*, they "beat him" and "battered him painfully about the head, face, and mouth." When the onslaught finally ended, the police arrested seven people for disorderly conduct—all seven were black. T. H. Lewis was charged with the more serious crime of assaulting a police officer with a deadly weapon. The officers who beat him claimed that he attacked patrolman Charles Scherlein with a knife. Even one of Pittsburgh's daily papers, the *Sun-Telegraph*, found it odd that the arresting officers could not produce the knife.[16]

The racial violence at Highland Park Pool was widely discussed in the local press. Newspaper commentators and city spokesmen attempted to exonerate the city and the larger white community by attributing the violence to East End Italian "hooligans." This was a local ethnic-racial clash, they implied, rather than a citywide racial problem. In a literal sense they were probably correct. Even though most reports of the violence described the attackers generically as "white men" and "white bathers," some evidence suggests that young Italian men did indeed throw most of the fists that bloodied the faces of black swimmers. In doing so, however, they were the instruments for imposing a racial segregation policy favored by city officials and the white community in general. The pool police officers—who had non-Italian names such as Walter Burns and Charles Scherlein—did not arrest the attackers or otherwise limit the violence. Rather, they encouraged the beatings. The hundreds, sometimes thousands, of other swimmers at the pool—who came from throughout the city—did not stop or deter the violence either. Rather, they implicitly condoned the violence by sometimes vacating the pool en masse as soon as black swimmers entered.[17] Top city officials were also culpable. They permitted the violence to continue by not disciplining or even transferring the police officers who oversaw the attacks. As the *Courier* recognized, the violence was "winked at by the Department of Public Safety and almost openly countenanced by city officials."[18] The events that summer show that white swimmers, police officers, local magistrates, and even top city officials all sought to exclude black Americans from Highland Park Pool.

The clear cause of this determined effort was mixed-gender use. Even as racial violence plagued Highland Park Pool, blacks and whites swam together in relative harmony at the city's other municipal pools, which, not coincidentally, remained gender-segregated. "No trouble arises [at the other pools]," reported the *Courier*, "because the boys, white and colored, and the girls, white and colored, are in the pool on days set aside for their respective sex."[19] The only pool at which trouble did arise was Highland Park Pool. "The whole trouble," the *Courier* explained, "seems to be due to the way the Highland Park Pool is operated. It is the only city pool where men and women, girls and boys swim together." According to the paper, mixed-gender swimming brought "the sex question into the pool, and trouble is bound to arise between the races."[20] As happened in St. Louis with the opening of Fairgrounds Park Pool, gender integration necessitated racial separation. Whereas St. Louis officially excluded black residents, Pittsburgh let white swimmers beat them out of the water.

Representatives from the local National Association for the Advancement of Colored People (NAACP) branch met with city officials late in the summer of 1931 in an attempt to resolve the racial conflict at the pool. Noting the harmonious use of the city's other pools, the black leaders requested that males and females be separated at Highland Park Pool as well. Gender segregation, they explained, "would take the sex and social features out of the issue" and resolve the problem. They also explained to Mayor Kline and Superintendent Lang that black women were just as concerned as white women about the intimacy involved in swimming at a mixed-gender pool. "None of the colored girls want to swim with the white boys, and the white girls do not want to swim with the colored boys."[21] In advocating gender segregation, however, black leaders were swimming against the social current of the times. They sought to maintain patterns of public social interaction characteristic of the Industrial Age. City officials refused, because by 1931 they had come to see race as a more meaningful public social division than gender. Mayor Kline proposed not to return to gender segregation but, rather, to make racial segregation official, offering black swimmers exclusive use of Highland Park Pool one or two days a week. The black leaders, however, refused to consent to such an arrangement.[22]

Even though the sexual security of women was at the heart of the conflict, the debate over pool use was a male-dominated discourse. Men did the negotiating and the fighting, all the while representing or expressing the interests of women. Black men claimed that black women did not want to swim with white men. On the other side, white men attacked black men to keep them from swimming with white women. It seems quite clear that white men and black men did not want women of their respective race swimming with men of the other. What the women themselves thought is not as clear. Despite the emergence of the "new woman" in the 1920s, exemplified in part by the increasing number of women swimming in municipal pools, the voices of women in Pittsburgh—white and black—were not heard, at least not publicly, about this conflict that supposedly centered on their interests.

Frustrated by the city's commitment to mixed-gender use and its unwillingness to protect the safety of black swimmers at Highland Park Pool, the city's black leadership organized a political protest. The local NAACP and the Twelfth Ward Civic Group hosted several community meetings late in the summer of 1931. At one meeting held at the Bethesda Presbyterian Church, "thousands jammed and packed every nook and corner of the edifice while speakers flayed discrimination and race prejudice." The message was clear and simple: punish the city's Republican administration by voting Democrat in the upcoming election.[23] Mayor Kline was not up for reelection, but several political allies were. Many black voters did indeed abandon the Republican Party and vote Democratic. The day after the election, the *Courier* reported that, "the people must have wanted a change and wanted it badly. From the way they played hopskip and jump from Republican to Democrat." The result was that black voters helped oust several Republican aldermen close to Mayor Kline.[24]

Despite the successful protest vote, racial violence returned to Highland Park Pool the following summer. A few days after it opened for the 1932 swimming season, two young black men, Clyde Crawford, twenty-eight, and August Ross, twenty-two, entered the pool unmolested but not unnoticed. All 200 white swimmers in the water quickly got out. Many of the men changed their clothes and gathered weapons as the two black men swam alone in the enormous pool. When Crawford and Ross climbed out, an estimated 100 of the earlier swimmers "brutally pummeled and slugged [them] with clubs." According to the *Courier*, lifeguards "made a valiant effort to protect the victims," but the police let the beatings continue. Both men sustained severe injuries that necessitated hospitalization. None of the assailants were arrested. This brutal assault effectively intimidated black swimmers from entering the pool again that summer.[25]

Shortly before the beginning of the 1933 swimming season, Mayor Kline promised to protect black swimmers and even stationed a black police officer, Louis West, at Highland Park Pool. Kline's change of heart probably had something to do with the upcoming mayoral election. If black voters abandoned the Republican Party as they did in 1931, he was sure to lose. For the first several weeks, small groups of black swimmers used the pool without incident. On July 17, however, racial violence returned. Officer West had been reassigned to the city zoo, which left black swimmers unprotected. Mrs. Henry Lindsay, the wife of a prominent undertaker, was swimming in the pool that day with her two daughters when a large man threatened that she better leave, "if she knew what was good for her health." Well aware of the mayor's promise, Lindsay reported the threat to Lieutenant Walter Burns, the ranking officer at the pool. Burns replied that the mayor's assurance of protection was nothing but political "ballyhoo" and then told Lindsay that her kind was "not wanted" at the pool. Afraid for the safety of her daughters, she gathered them and left. A few hours later, a group of male swimmers attempted to enter the pool but was attacked while showering. One of the men escaped from the bathhouse and called for the police to rescue the others, but the officers refused, explaining that they "could not get their clothes wet."[26]

The return of violence effectively resegregated the pool and prompted black leaders to once again seek justice through political protest. Shortly after the July 17 incidents, the Pittsburgh NAACP held a meeting at the Wesley Center African Methodist Episcopal Church that attracted hundreds of angry citizens. "Remember to go to the polls in September," one speaker exhorted the crowd, "and cast a vote of protest against the present administration. Every blow the victims received at the Highland Park Pool was a blow administered to the Negro as a group."[27] Most black voters followed the advice, casting a majority of votes for the Democratic challenger William McNair. "Helping materially in the destruction of the citadel of the rock-ribbed Republicans," reported the *Courier*, "went the bulk of the Negro voters in the role of determined Democrats." The migration of black voters tipped the balance of power in Pittsburgh to the Democrats. McNair's victory marked the end of a twenty-seven year Republican reign in the steel city.[28]

Despite black voters' instrumental role in McNair's election, the plight of black swimmers worsened under the new administration. Prior to the 1934 swimming season, McNair asked black leaders to accept voluntary exclusion from Highland Park Pool in exchange for exclusive use of nearby Washington Boulevard Pool, a small, dilapidated facility that had already been abandoned by white swimmers. Even though black leaders rejected the offer, the actual use of both pools reflected this arrangement. According to East End resident Olander Raymond Justice, black swimmers did not dare to swim in Highland Park Pool because they "were in grave danger of losing their lives." Instead, they crowded into Washington Boulevard Pool, where the city permitted mixed-gender swimming one-and-a-half days a week. Recreation officials further outraged the East End black community by hiring only white lifeguards to oversee Washington Boulevard Pool, even though all the swimmers were black. This was particularly insulting because jobs were so scarce at the time.[29] After the 1934 season ended, Mayor McNair ordered that black swimmers be barred from entering Highland Park Pool. Jim Crow racial segregation had become official city policy.[30]

The following summer racial violence spread to Pittsburgh's gender-segregated pools. On July 7, 1935, a group of five white youths terrorized young Frank Reynolds, nine years old, at Paulson Playground Pool. According to the *Courier*, they "beat and kicked" him in the dressing room and then held him underneath the water while in the pool. Frank's mother reported the assault to Inspector Kellie of Police Station No. 6. Instead of investigating the incident, Kellie admonished her. "Why can't you people use the Washington Boulevard pool," he told her, "I don't approve of colored and white people swimming together."[31]

Inspector Kellie's comment reveals that social assumptions that developed in one social context could quickly and easily be applied to others. For two generations prior to 1935, it was socially normal for blacks and whites of the same sex to swim together in Pittsburgh's municipal pools. At first, the assumption that blacks and whites should not swim together was narrowly applied to gender-integrated pools. As whites experienced swimming only with other whites at Highland Park Pool, however, this narrow social assumption expanded into a more general assumption that blacks and whites should not swim together regardless of the gender mix. As a result, Pittsburgh's still gender-segregated pools became racial battlefields as well. What began at Highland Park Pool altered social assumptions in ways that clearly affected other spheres. In this way, violence and segregation at municipal pools did not simply reflect general social attitudes and patterns of social interaction; what happened at pools played a role in determining them.

～～～～ It is clear from the cases of Fairgrounds Park Pool in St. Louis and Highland Park Pool in Pittsburgh that gender integration was the most direct and crucial cause of racial segregation at municipal swimming pools. But why? Why in the minds of white public officials and white swimmers did mixed-gender use necessitate racial separation? In his 1933 autobiography *Along This Way*, James Weldon Johnson observed that "in the core of the heart of the American race problem the sex factor is rooted; rooted so deeply that it is not always recognized when it shows at the surface. Other factors are obvious and are the ones we dare to deal with; but, regardless of how we deal with these, the race situation will continue to be acute as long as the sex factor persists."[32] Johnson was not specifically referring to the "race problem" at swimming pools, but he might as well have been. Black commentators openly acknowledged the inextricable link between gender integration and racial exclusion at municipal pools. Northern whites, on the other hand, were more reticent in their words if not their actions. No public official or white swimmer publicly explained why mixed-gender use necessitated racial separation, but several explanations seem likely.

The resort pools of the interwar years offered visual, social, and even physical access to other swimmers. Pool users visually consumed one another, chatted and arranged dates, and potentially touched in the crowded water. At the time, most northern whites objected to black men interacting with white women in any of these ways. For one, they feared it would lead to sexual assault and even rape. Widespread racial prejudices at the time led most whites to view black men generally as sexually aggressive and, in some cases, prone to uncontrollable sexual desire for white women. This racist stereotype originated and took on its most vitriolic form in the South, but it also shaped the thinking of northerners as well.[33] According to historian Matthew Guterl, "the southern tradition of Negrophobia became the dominant mind-set" among northern whites during the late 1910s and 1920s. The popularity of D. W. Griffith's 1915 epic *Birth of a Nation* reflected what Guterl has aptly called the "southernization of northern racial discourse."[34] *Birth of a Nation*—which, according to historian Robert Sklar, "went over well with white audiences almost everywhere"—portrayed black men as, among other things, uncontrollable brutes bent on raping white women. In one scene, Flora Cameron—the embodiment of white southern womanhood—leapt to her death to avoid the advances of a brutish-looking black man. In another, a light-skinned black man made up to look particularly devious attempted to ravish the daughter of a northern Carpetbagger. When galloping Klansmen rescued a white woman from the clutches of rapacious black men in the film's climactic scene, "every audience spontaneously applauds" reported the *New Republic*.[35] Through this powerful new media, the movie showed millions of viewers that white women must be protected from black men's sexual aggression. Widely publicized health studies reinforced the prejudice that black men were licentious. These studies reported that black Americans suffered comparatively high rates of venereal diseases, which they attributed to supposedly natural tendencies toward sexual immorality.[36] Even a northerner as progressive-minded and respectful of social difference as Jane Addams believed that, in the words of historian Ann Douglas, "black men, did, in fact, have a proclivity for raping white women."[37] This widespread belief caused northern whites to fear that black men would act on their sexual desire for white women if allowed to swim and sunbathe with them at municipal pools.

Racial segregation at mixed-gender pools also served as a means to inhibit interracial marriages and consensual relationships between black men and white women. With few exceptions, northern states did not pass laws forbidding interracial sex or interracial marriage.[38] This did not mean, however, that northern whites consented to either. Most certainly did not.[39] Rather than pass "antimiscegenation" laws, northerners relied on other means to keep black men and white women sexually apart.[40] One was preventing them from interacting in social settings where they might get to know one another. Swimming pools were just such settings. The social contact that occurred at pools was sustained and interactive. Swimmers chatted with one another, struck up friendships, flirted, and arranged dates. By racially segregating these uniquely sociable public spaces, northern communities limited the opportunities blacks and whites had to meet and form relationships that might lead to physical intimacy or marriage.

In this way, racial segregation also restricted white women's social and sexual choices by limiting their access to black men. Whether white women agreed with the policy or not—many surely did—it was nonetheless imposed upon them. Because white males determined that they did not want black men interacting with their wives, mothers, daughters, and sisters at municipal pools, male public officials and male swimmers imposed and enforced a social policy that kept them separate. While racial segregation also restricted white men's access to black women, which some black commentators applauded, it was not a restriction that was imposed on them by another social group. Furthermore, as historian Kevin Mumford shows, northern white men had social and sexual access to black women through other means— namely prostitution and "black and tan" dance halls and speakeasies. Whereas white men could and did "slum" in black social settings to access black women, black men could not similarly cross racial boundaries to access white women.[41]

Finally, racial segregation at municipal pools also likely resulted from white concerns that black men displaying their bodies at highly visible public spaces would undermine white supremacy. During the early twentieth century, the male body became an increasingly important symbol of manliness. American men came to believe that a superior man possessed a muscular and powerful physique. This, in part, explains the weight-lifting craze around the turn of the century, the emulation of Bernarr MacFadden, and the phenomenal success of Charles Atlas's mail-order body-building business during the 1920s and 1930s.[42]

The emphasis on physical markers of manliness, however, posed problems for white Americans' assertion of racial superiority. As Gail Bederman explores in *Manliness and Civilization*, white Americans justified racial discrimination and their own assumed racial superiority in part by pointing to the superior manliness of white men. When manliness was defined in economic, political, and moral terms—as it was by the middle class during the nineteenth century—white men's claim to superior manliness in relation to black men seemed secure.[43] When it became defined more in physical terms, as it did during the early decades of the twentieth century, white men's claim to superiority became more tenuous. After all, most black men worked at strenuous physical jobs that, in many cases, contributed to powerful, muscular physiques. Many white men, on the other hand, worked at sedentary white-collar jobs that did not strengthen the body. In most public settings, the physical shortcomings of some white men in comparison to some black men would not have been apparent because all were fully clothed. At the swimming pools of the interwar years, however, men exposed their bodies to the public. If blacks and whites were permitted to swim and sunbathe together at these pools, some black men could literally show themselves to be the masculine equal and in many cases superior of white men. The visual comparison would implicitly undermine one of the long-standing justifications for white supremacy. In short, it would challenge racial hierarchy as it was constructed in America at the time, much like Jack Johnson's victory over Jim Jeffries did in the 1910 heavyweight title bout.[44] One of the ways to defend the ramparts of white supremacy was to keep mostly naked black men from appearing alongside mostly naked white men at municipal swimming pools. Few, if any, public officials or white swimmers consciously reasoned all this out in their minds. Rather, they would have intuited that black men conspicuously displaying powerful physiques in front of thousands of people at local pools was objectionable.

~~~~~~~ Pittsburgh was not unique in that white swimmers imposed and enforced racial segregation through violence. The same was true in other northern cities as well, such as Elizabeth, New Jersey. When the city opened its first pool in 1930, city officials refused to admit black residents, even though blacks and whites had bathed together at the city's river bath. Unaccustomed to such blatant public forms of discrimination, local NAACP officials protested black residents' exclusion from Dowd Pool. They met with Elizabeth's Recreation Commission just days after the pool opened in order to resolve what the commission called "the bathing problem for the colored people." After a long discussion, commission president James O'Neill "informed the Colored Delegation that the Supt. will be given full instructions in the morning to allow the colored people the use of the swimming pool at all times." City officials obviously did not want blacks to swim in Dowd Pool with whites, but they would not brazenly violate New Jersey's civil rights law, which prohibited racial discrimination at public facilities.[45]

The integration order marked the end of official racial exclusion at Dowd Pool and the beginning of harassment and violence. Two days later, three teenagers tested the new policy. Allen Chase approached the ticket booth alone at about three o'clock but was arrested for disorderly conduct before passing through the gate. The admission attendant claimed that Chase had refused to pay the standard ten-cent admission fee and threatened to beat him up if not admitted for free. Chase vehemently denied the accusation,

Highland Park Pool, Pittsburgh, circa 1940s. The statue of Neptune displays the physical ideal of manliness at the time and emphasizes the significance of physical markers of masculinity at swimming pools. Copyright, Pittsburgh Post-Gazette, 2005, all rights reserved. Reprinted with permission.

claiming that he merely inquired whether it was true that blacks would be admitted to the pool and then intended to run home and get his swimming suit. The police officer stationed at the pool arrested him nonetheless.[46]

An hour later, Morgan Dickinson and Walter Gordon paid their ten cents, showered, but never made it into the water. Another attendant, Thomas Keating, stopped the two teenagers as they exited the locker room and admonished them for not taking a shower. While Dickinson and Gordon were assuring Keating that they had in fact showered, a group of white swimmers appeared atop the staircase leading up to the pool and threatened to pummel the two teenagers if they attempted to enter the water. Sensing trouble, Patrolman Newallis, the same officer that had arrested Chase, "advised the colored youths not to make use of the pool." Undeterred, the young men cited the recreation commission ruling giving them equal access to the pool and then returned to the locker room to shower again. When they finally ascended the stairway, Dickinson and Gordon encountered dozens of "menacing swimmers" standing shoulder-to-shoulder blocking their access to the pool. According to the *Elizabeth Daily Journal*, they were then "somewhat roughly handled by the crowd." Dickinson and Gordon finally managed to escape after fourteen more police officers arrived to restore order. The officers arrested one of the white assailants, thirty-four-year-old Michael Capko, and charged him with inciting to riot. The next morning, Allen Chase and Capko were both arraigned in Police Court. Chase was fined ten dollars for allegedly threatening the pool attendant, and Capko five dollars for leading the assault on Dickinson and Gordon.[47] The message to black residents was clear: if you try to swim in Dowd Pool, you will be arrested on trumped-up charges or pummeled by white swimmers. Both forms of intimidation effectively deterred black residents from using the pool for several years.

Then, on July 6, 1938, several young men approached Dowd Pool, paid their admission, showered, and actually entered the water. They were the first identifiably black people to swim in Dowd Pool, eight years after it opened. It is not clear what prompted the young men to seek entry after so many years of whites-only use. Their presence in the pool did not go unnoticed. According to a recreation department official, they were "subjected to certain petty annoyances at the hands of white bathers." The white swimmers "ducked" the youths by holding them underwater, shouted threats at them, and poured buckets of water into the lockers where they had left their clothes. The young men left the pool wet, bruised, and perhaps even short of breath. And yet this time, they would return.[48]

Over the next two weeks, ordinary black citizens—many of them teenagers and children—courageously integrated Dowd Pool. Knowing that they would be assaulted and perhaps arrested, they nonetheless returned to the pool day after day. Every black swimmer that entered the water quite literally risked his or her life. Swimming pools were inherently dangerous places even under ideal circumstances. At Dowd Pool during the summer of 1938, black swimmers also had to contend with fellow swimmers dunking and punching them. Furthermore, the safety net for endangered swimmers, the lifeguards, offered no assistance. Despite the risks, more and more black swimmers came to the pool and endured the threats, assaults, and other "petty annoyances." When white swimmers found that violence no longer intimidated blacks from using the pool, many stopped coming. White attendance plummeted to one-tenth its normal level. The dislocated white swimmers redirected their threats and vitriol at city officials. They sent scores of "abusive" letters to the mayor and Recreation Commission promising widespread racial violence if the city did not bar blacks from entering the pool. City officials responded in the press that they could not officially segregate the pool. They could, however, close it, which is what they did. The official explanation was that attendance had sunk so low that the pool was no longer economical to operate. The fact that most of the swimmers were now black probably made the decision easier.[49]

The pool remained closed for three weeks. "Feeling that [the] immediate danger of racial disturbances had passed," the city reopened it on August 10 as an experiment to see if an integrated pool would be sufficiently patronized to cover the operating expense. Attendance rebounded to half the normal number as some whites returned. They came back, however, not because they accepted integration but to reclaim the pool as their public space. Once again, they assaulted and harassed black swimmers in an attempt to reestablish de facto exclusion. In a letter to the city council, Recreation Commission Secretary E. T. Noren reported that "every day at the pool some minor outbreaks occurred which might have developed into serious trouble."[50] Blacks and whites fought and quarreled in the water. Blacks were bombarded with tomatoes on their way to the pool. On one occasion, competing gangs of black and white youths threw rocks at one another near the pool entrance. The numerous police officers stationed at the pool, ostensibly to maintain order, did nothing to stop the rock fight. According to the local paper, they "kept watch" as the melee raged.[51]

Like the police officers, Elizabeth's recreation commissioners seemed ambivalent about the racial violence. They let the "minor outbreaks" continue for thirteen days before deciding to close the pool again—this time for the remainder of the summer. The racial conflict, however, seemed to play little role in their decision. As before, they closed the pool because it was losing money. The only concern the commissioners expressed about the violence was that it scared white swimmers away: "The decrease [in patronage] must be accounted for by the fact that the white users . . . refuse to use the pool if the colored patrons also use the pool, and because of the feeling on the part of parents of sending their children to the pool while the danger of potential race riots continue."[52]

City officials did not actively attempt to stop the racial violence, perhaps, because it served their interest. For eight years, the attacks on black swimmers had relieved them from having to resolve the thorny problem of mixed-race swimming at a gender-integrated pool. They avoided legal culpability by correctly claiming that the city did not bar blacks from using the pool and yet, at the same time, avoided backlash from whites by giving them free reign to assault prospective black swimmers. This arrangement was convenient for the city, but it had fallen apart during the summer of 1938. While the recreation commissioners claimed that the pool reopening in early August was an experiment to see if the city could operate Dowd Pool profitably on a truly integrated basis, it might also have been an experiment to see if a couple weeks of sustained violence might again intimidate blacks from using the pool.

When Dowd Pool opened for the 1939 swimming season, the social use had, apparently, returned to whites only. The evidence to support this conclusion is circumstantial yet compelling. Whereas the racial conflicts the previous summer were widely reported in the local newspaper and commented upon regularly in city council meetings, no mention of racial issues at the pool appeared in either of these sources. Perhaps most convincing, the attendance at Dowd Pool returned to the level of pre-1938 summers. During its first eight years of whites-only operation, attendance averaged around 70,000 swims per summer. During the brief periods of truly integrated swimming, it dropped to between one-quarter and one-half normal use. In 1939, however, total attendance rebounded to 63,612.[53] Either white people in Elizabeth suddenly overcame their racial prejudices, stopped abusing black swimmers, and willingly swam in the same pool with them, or, more likely, the city's black population decided that a swim in Dowd Pool was not worth the threat to their safety.

In some northern cities, especially large metropolises, public officials unofficially—but purposefully—segregated their municipal pools by locating one or two pools within black neighborhoods and the rest in white neighborhoods. This strategy succeeded, in large part, because the social geography of most large northern cities had become more rigidly divided along racial lines and because of increasing antagonism between blacks and working-class whites. Prior to the Great Black Migration, black settlement patterns were similar to those of ethnic whites. Immigrants and blacks typically lived in small clusters interspersed throughout the central city.[54] After 1916, however, black residents of northern cities increasingly became concentrated into one or two clearly defined neighborhoods.[55] In Cleveland, for example, historian Kenneth Kusmer found that by 1930 "at least 90 percent of the city's Afro-Americans lived within a region bounded by Euclid Avenue on the north, East 105th Street on the east, and Woodland Avenue to the south." Furthermore, the population within this area was predominately black.[56] The same concentration occurred elsewhere. Chicago's South Side, New York's

Harlem, and Detroit's Paradise Valley all emerged as distinct black "ghettos" during this period.[57]

This residential segregation helped cities separate black swimmers from white without officially segregating their pools. Recreation officials in Cincinnati, for example, purposefully located two of the city's eight pools "in districts where almost all the residents were colored," and the other six pools away from African American neighborhoods. This spatial arrangement made it inconvenient and potentially threatening for black residents to swim at any but the two pools designated for their use. In New York, Parks Commissioner Robert Moses similarly encouraged racially segregated use by locating most of the city's WPA pools within thoroughly white neighborhoods such as the Lower East Side, Greenpoint, and Red Hook. This ensured that if black New Yorkers attempted to swim in a pool intended for whites, they would have to trek through a white neighborhood to get to the pool and would be far outnumbered and more easily intimidated while in the water.[58]

Swimming pools in Harlem, however, required more finesse because blacks, Puerto Ricans, and whites lived in relatively close proximity to one another. African Americans and Puerto Ricans, whom Moses also considered "colored people," predominated, but many whites lived along Harlem's southern boundary. Moses encouraged segregation at the two pools in this area through strategic location and devious administration. He located one pool within the heart of black Harlem at Colonial Park (146th Street) and the other further south in Thomas Jefferson Park (between 111th and 114th Streets). He earmarked the first pool for blacks and Puerto Ricans and the second for whites. To deter the African Americans and Puerto Ricans who lived in lower Harlem from using Thomas Jefferson Pool, Moses employed only white attendants and lifeguards and, according to Moses biographer Robert Caro, kept the water in Thomas Jefferson pool unheated, assuming that cold water bothered "colored" swimmers more than whites. Whether true or not, pool use did divide along racial lines, but most likely due to the threat of violence from white swimmers. As Caro writes, "one could go to [Jefferson Park Pool] on the hottest summer days, when the slums of Negro and Spanish Harlem a few blocks away sweltered in the heat, and not see a single non-Caucasian Face. Negroes who lived only half a mile away, Puerto Ricans who lived *three blocks* away, would travel instead to Colonial Park, three miles away."[59]

De facto segregation, however, was inconsistent and unequal. Whites could and did swim at pools earmarked for blacks, but the reverse—as we have seen—frequently led to violence. In 1932, William Schultz, a superintendent

Colonial Park Pool, Harlem, New York, 1937. Through location and devious administration, New York public officials encouraged de facto segregation at its WPA swimming pools. New York City Parks Photo Archive, neg. M-14, 12482.

with the West Chicago Park Commissioners, reported to *American City* that "there are 15 swimming pools in the West Park system. Among these, two are used by both white and colored people. The others are used entirely by the white race. In the two pools first mentioned, the colored race predominates." Similarly, Detroit's commissioner of recreation, C. E. Brewer, noted in 1932 that "attendance is over 95 percent colored" at two pools located within the city's black belt, which meant that some of the swimmers were white. Mixed-race swimming clearly continued into the 1930s in some northern cities, but it occurred primarily at pools intended for African Americans or at pools that remained gender segregated.[60]

〰️ In the southern tier of northern cities, the story was much the same as in cities further north. Racial segregation and exclusion occurred at the same time for the same reasons. The only significant differences were

Thomas Jefferson Pool, Harlem, New York, 1936. Even though many African Americans and Puerto Ricans lived close to Thomas Jefferson Pool, it was used almost exclusively by "whites." New York City Parks Photo Archive, neg. M-47, 14774.

the means and consistency of separation. Whereas violence and pool location were the primary means used to separate black swimmers from white in Elizabeth, Pittsburgh, and New York, cities such as St. Louis, Washington, D.C., and Newton, Kansas, openly and officially segregated their pools along racial lines. In large cities, public officials relegated black swimmers to one or two Jim Crow pools. In smaller communities that operated only one pool, racial discrimination meant outright exclusion. One other difference between southern-tier and northern-tier cities was the response of black residents. Unlike in Elizabeth and Pittsburgh, blacks living in southern-tier cities generally did not aggressively protest racial segregation at municipal pools during the 1920s and 1930s. Instead, they demanded that the provision of pools for blacks and whites be equitable. In some cities it was, but in most it was not.

In the fall of 1925, Congressman Frederick Zihlman of Maryland introduced a bill authorizing the construction of two giant outdoor swimming pools in the District of Columbia. The federal government administered the district at the time, so Congress was responsible for funding recreation facilities. The Zihlman pool bill passed in the House but was held up in the Senate by Lee Overman of North Carolina because its wording did not indicate whether the pools would be racially segregated. Overman was adamant that blacks and whites not be permitted to swim and sunbathe together at pools that would be open to men and women. The bill's sponsor in the Senate, Royal Copeland of New York, assured him that district officials intended to operate the pools on a racially segregated basis, but Overman required more conclusive assurance. "I know the Senator from New York is all right; I have every confidence in him; but he will not have the authority to construct these pools and arrange for the bathing; that will be a matter which will be left to the Commissioners of the District of Columbia. There ought to be some language in the bill requiring that the pools be separate." Senator Copeland consented to make explicit what had been understood. He amended the bill by adding the line, "one for the white race and the other for the colored race." The amended bill passed the Senate and then returned to the House. When asked if he objected to the added phrase, the bill's sponsor, Representative Zihlman, replied, "I cannot conceive of any objection." The bill then passed the House and was signed by President Calvin Coolidge on May 5, 1926.[61] With this bill, the two political branches of the federal government did not merely sanction racial segregation at public swimming pools but actually mandated it.[62]

Several prominent black Washingtonians publicly protested the bill's amended language. Historian Carter G. Woodson stated that he "would rather bathe in Hell" than swim in a racially segregated pool. Nannie Burroughs, head of the National Wage Earners Association, quipped, "[w]hen I heard the bill was signed, I purchased a bath tub for my room so as to have no temptation to ever consider [using] the thing."[63] The leading African American newspaper in the city, the *Washington Tribune*, advised its readers to boycott the Jim Crow pool and swim instead at a supposedly integrated commercial pool that was scheduled to open that summer.[64] The paper went on to claim, as way of protest, that the swimming pool bill was the first time since the Civil War—when Congress authorized four black regiments—that a bill passed by the federal government explicitly segregated American citizens by race.[65]

To the *Tribune*'s chagrin, most black Washingtonians did not condemn the Jim Crow pool. Rather, they vied to have it located near their homes. According to the paper, individuals and neighborhood organizations began "a wild scramble to have the pool located here, there or elsewhere—preferably near 'our home district.'" The paper castigated local blacks for accepting segregation and implicitly blamed recent migrants from the South for not leaving their acquiescent habits of mind behind: "Had the Negro race the guts of the ordinary man, they would not care a whoop in h— where the insulting institution was located since a proper spirit of manhood and womanhood would forbid our noticing the existence of such excrescences of southern prejudice. The handkerchief clings tightly to most of our heads yet and apparently will stay there for some time to come."[66] Most black Washingtonians did not share the paper's acute sensitivity to segregation. They were more concerned with having convenient access to some public recreation facilities than with having equal access to all facilities.

White Washingtonians also voiced opinions as to where the blacks-only pool should be located. The district's Commission of Fine Arts, whose responsibility it was to choose the location, initially selected Anacostia Park, in the district's far eastern corner. Local white residents, who constituted a majority in Anacostia, "vigorously" opposed the choice, complaining that the pool would be "far removed from the center of population of those who might wish to use it." As the quote suggests, their concern related to the district's social geography. At the time, less than 10 percent of the district's total black population (11,838 out of 132,068) lived in Anacostia. By contrast, 36 percent of black Washingtonians (47,578) lived just north of downtown.[67] Several Anacostia citizen groups wondered why this area of more concentrated black settlement was not chosen as the site for the blacks-only pool. The Anacostia location, they complained, would set Washington's black population in motion, crisscrossing the District on their way to and from the enormous pool.[68]

In response to the public outcry, the Commission of Fine Arts reconceived the whole pool plan. Rather than build one giant pool for whites and another for blacks, the commission decided to build two medium-size pools for each, located in "closer proximity to the various centers of population." This "distributed system of bathing pools" would appease more of the people who wanted a pool near their homes and would encourage swimmers to stay within their own neighborhoods.[69]

The first pool for black swimmers opened in 1928 at 24th and N Streets, just across the Potomac Parkway from Georgetown on property adjoining Francis Junior High School.[70] It was a state-of-the-art outdoor facility containing two pools, broad concrete decks, and modern sanitation equipment.

The main tank measured 65 by 150 feet and ranged in depth from 3 1/2 to 11 feet.[71] According to James G. Tyson, one of the pool's first lifeguards and later its manager, it was one of the finest pools in the country "exclusively for black swimmers."[72] The same social integration that occurred generally at municipal pools during this period also occurred at Francis Pool. It was gender integrated, attracted a large number of adults, and was frequented by all levels of black society.[73] Scattered evidence also suggests that the culture and patterns of use at Francis Pool were the same as at the resort pools frequented by whites. In a brief history of the pool written in 1939, Tyson mentioned that the pool competed for patrons with "the beaches near Washington," which suggests that it served a similar function.[74] Attendance figures indicate that Frances Pool was also a popular place for people watching. In 1932, for example, "spectators" accounted for nearly 10 percent of the total admissions.[75] Like other swimming pools of the period, Francis Pool seems to have functioned as a leisure resort.

The district's second blacks-only pool—Banneker Pool—opened in 1934. It was located on Georgia Avenue near Howard University. Whereas the *Tribune* ignored the opening of Francis Pool out of protest, it reported positively on the opening of this pool, noting that "a grand and glorious time was had by all." Rather than advising readers to boycott Banneker Pool, it praised the facility in a front-page article as "one of the most elaborate [recreation] centers in the city." The paper also published photos of happy swimmers playing in the water.[76] The paper may have softened its stance on pool segregation by 1934 because the district's provision of pools for blacks and whites was relatively equal. Francis and Banneker pools were virtually identical to the two new outdoor pools opened for white residents. And, one of the district's three playground pools was earmarked for black children.[77] Given that blacks constituted 27 percent of the district's population in 1930, this provision may have seemed fair.[78]

Black Washingtonians did protest, however, when the provision of pools seemed unfair and inequitable. As the city's black population increased during the interwar years, black families moved into neighborhoods that had previously been inhabited mostly by whites. As these neighborhoods transitioned from being predominately white to predominately black, the new black majority often protested its exclusion from recreation facilities in the area. Such a dispute arose in 1940 at the Parkview playground and swimming pool. The surrounding neighborhood had become populated mostly by blacks, but the playground and pool remained earmarked for whites. Black children defied the whites-only policy by venturing onto the playground to use the slides and swings, but they did not enter the pool because attendants could better regulate access to it. During the midst of the grass-roots protest, district officials closed the pool until they could decide what to do. Eventually, they transferred use of the playground to black children but did not reopen the pool.[79] The decision to close the pool permanently rather than make it available to black swimmers foreshadowed the district's increasingly unequal provision of pools during the 1940s.

~~~~~ Unlike large cities, smaller communities could rarely afford to build separate pools for black residents. They either had to permit them to swim with whites, set aside separate days, or exclude them entirely. Most one-pool towns, especially those in the southern tier of northern states, chose exclusion, even though doing so clearly violated state civil rights laws and the Supreme Court's "separate but equal" interpretation of the Fourteenth Amendment. And yet, few African Americans filed suit challenging their exclusion from municipal pools during this period. The reasons, most likely, were the cost and potential consequences of such action for black plaintiffs. Lawsuits were expensive and time-consuming. Few small-town black communities, let alone individuals, had the financial resources necessary, especially during the Great Depression, to engage in a lengthy legal battle. Furthermore, blacks were in a vulnerable position in most small communities. They risked a range of reprisals—from losing already scarce jobs to physical intimidation—if they sued their city. Also, the national NAACP did not prioritize fighting discrimination at recreation facilities during this period. It devoted its limited resources to fight discrimination in education and employment as well as to lobby for a federal antilynching bill.[80] As a result, racial exclusion at municipal pools went almost unchallenged in the courts prior to the 1940s, except in Newton, Kansas.

During the 1930s, Newton was a small railroad town in the middle of the state that also served as a marketplace for surrounding wheat farms. The population was quite homogeneous. Eighty-seven percent of its 11,034 residents in 1930 were native-born whites; foreign-born whites and blacks each constituted about 5 percent of the population. Despite its small size, Newton's black community had a long history and maintained several civic and religious institutions. Blacks were among Newton's earliest settlers. Black "exodusters" from Mississippi, Louisiana, and Tennessee arrived during the late 1870s seeking the fruits of emancipation: security, freedom, and opportunity.[81] By the 1930s Newton's black community had realized some of these goals. It had established an NAACP chapter, a fraternal lodge, and at least three churches. A full 90 percent of black adults could read and write. Of the city's 518 black residents in 1930, 149 were adult males, 151 adult females, and 218 were children under twenty-one.[82] Although the black community was stable, educated, and family-oriented, race proved too significant a social division to permit blacks and whites to swim together.

Newton officials devised a strategy to circumvent Kansas's civil rights law before they began constructing the town's first pool. Shortly after town residents approved a $30,000 swimming pool bond in 1934, Samuel Ridley, president of the local NAACP chapter, asked Mayor McCulley Ashlock and City Commissioner Walter Trousdale to build two pools, one for whites and the other for blacks. Ridley explained that black residents were not "desirous of going into a swimming pool with other groups," just as he assumed whites did not want to swim with blacks. Ashlock and Trousdale no doubt concurred but replied that the town could not afford to build two pools. Trousdale also informed Ridley that the city intended to lease the pool to a private operator who would determine the admission policy. Wary of this arrangement, pastors from three local African American churches attended two city commissioner meetings to ascertain whether the city intended to guarantee black citizens equal access to the quasi-public pool. At both meetings, the commissioners refused to acknowledge the three men let alone address their concerns, blatant rebuffs that served as a harbinger of what would occur at the pool.[83]

After Athletic Park Pool was built, the city leased it to a local citizen named Harold Hunt, who opened it to the "public" on May 29, 1935. Many black residents sought admission that first summer, but in each case Hunt refused to let them enter. He bluntly told them that they could not swim in the pool because of their "racial identity."[84] Late in the summer, Ridley wrote to Ashlock and Trousdale protesting the racial exclusion and threatening legal action if the policy continued. He reiterated his earlier claim that blacks in Newton did not particularly want to swim with whites but stated that they would do so in order to secure their constitutional rights. Ridley received no response.[85] When Athletic Park Pool reopened the following summer, Ridley tested the admission policy by sending several black men to seek entry. Again, Hunt informed them that "colored people would not be permitted to swim under any conditions." As promised, Ridley quickly filed suit on behalf of one of the swimmers, D. E. Kern, in Kansas State Supreme Court through Topeka civil rights attorney Elisha Scott.[86]

In his pleadings and oral arguments, Scott presented a straightforward case of unlawful racial discrimination. He showed that black residents of

Newton helped pay for the pool through taxes, and then claimed that Hunt, with the blessing of city officials, denied all black persons use of it. Furthermore, the city failed to provide an alternative pool for their use. Scott emphasized that this case involved systematic racial exclusion, not segregation. He concluded that the actions of Hunt and Newton city officials clearly violated the state's civil rights law—which guaranteed citizens, regardless of race, equal access to public facilities—and the Fourteenth Amendment of the Constitution. Scott sought a court order "commanding defendants to admit plaintiff and other citizens of Newton of African descent and color to the privileges of the swimming pool."[87]

The defense's case was considerably more complicated. The city and Hunt conducted separate defenses, because city officials claimed that the lessee was solely responsible for the administration of the pool. If any discrimination occurred, they argued, Hunt was acting as a private citizen not as an agent of the city.[88] With the exception of this point, however, both defendants made the same subsequent arguments. Neither denied that black swimmers had been systematically denied access to the pool. In fact, Hunt's lawyer did his best to explain to the court why complete racial exclusion was necessary. Blacks could never be permitted to enter the water, he explained, because the Newton pool "is what is known as a circulatory type of pool," which meant "the water is only changed once during the swimming season." This was an important point because it explained why Hunt could not set aside separate hours or days for black swimmers. White patrons did not simply object to swimming with blacks; they feared coming into contact with water that had ever touched black skin. According to Hunt's lawyer, the only way white residents would swim in a pool after blacks was if the water was drained and the tank scrubbed. Since this happened only at the end of the summer, Hunt would lose white patrons for the whole swimming season if he ever allowed a black person to use the pool. "[I]f colored persons were permitted to swim in said pool," Hunt's attorney explained, "then the members of the white race would not."[89]

Rather than deny the charge of discrimination, lawyers for Hunt and the city attacked the plaintiff's case on technical grounds. They argued that Kern did not have the legal right to sue the city on behalf of anyone but himself. He could not, in other words, sue on behalf of the entire black community. The relevant question of fact therefore was not whether black people in general were excluded from swimming in the pool, but whether Kern in particular had been denied admission. Predictably, the defense claimed that Kern never presented himself for admission to the pool, which meant he had no basis for a complaint. Thus, while the defense admitted that Hunt denied all black people admission to the pool, it denied that he had violated D. E. Kern's constitutional or civil rights.[90]

After both sides presented oral arguments on April 5, 1937, lawyers for the city delayed the court's ruling through a series of deceptions and legal maneuvers. First, they asked the court to give the city time to settle the dispute with Kern before rendering its decision. The court agreed and stopped considering the case "until the matter [of settlement] had been considerably examined."[91] As would become clear later, the city had no intention of settling the matter; it simply wanted to delay the court's decision long enough for another summer of segregated swimming to pass. Next, the Newton City Commission authorized construction of a second swimming pool, "for colored people," and quickly forwarded the resolution to the court in hopes that it would bolster the city's defense. Whereas racial exclusion was clearly unlawful, the Kansas Supreme Court could easily countenance segregation based upon earlier U.S. Supreme Court rulings that upheld the doctrine of separate but equal. Back in Newton, the second-pool resolution seemed to give black residents what they wanted—a swimming pool for their own use. But Thurgood Marshall, whom Ridley had asked to consult on the case, quickly saw the catch.[92] The resolution mandated only that the new pool be built "as soon as funds are available." Marshall warned Ridley that "as soon as" would be a long time in coming.[93]

In response to the city's delays and deception, Ridley became more militant. "The Executive Committee of the Newton Branch is opposed to any kind of compromise in said case," he wrote to Marshall in 1937.[94] Black leaders no longer wanted a segregated swimming pool; they were determined to see the court open Athletic Park Pool to all swimmers. With this uncompromising position, black leaders in Newton, Kansas, legally challenged segregation head-on and, in doing so, leapt ahead of national protest strategies at the time, which focused on enforcing the "equal" mandate of the Supreme Court's 1896 *Plessy v. Ferguson* ruling.[95]

After Ridley put an end to the settlement talks canard, the city found yet another way to delay the court's decision. It filed a "motion to quash alternative writ" that asked the court to rule on a narrow point of law and then dismiss the case without considering the substantive issue of whether black citizens should have equal access to the pool. The point in question was the city's earlier argument that Kern did not possess the "legal capacity" as a private individual to sue on behalf of a community of people. In a ruling issued in January 1938, the court agreed with the city that Kern could only sue on his own behalf but refused to dismiss the case. "[W]e are not prepared to say that plaintiff can maintain this action on behalf of the group for which he pleads. But we think it clear that in the interests of justice and equity plaintiff is entitled to maintain the action in his own behalf."[96] This preliminary ruling dramatically circumscribed the scope of the case. As defense lawyers had originally hoped, the pertinent legal question became whether Kern himself had been denied admission to the pool, not whether Hunt barred black people in general.

The court finally ruled on the merits of the case on April 6, 1940, nearly five years after Ridley initiated the suit. The court found that the city could not escape responsibility for the lawful administration of the pool by leasing it to a private individual. Newton city officials were therefore liable for any violation of the law perpetrated by Hunt. Though meaningless for Kern and Ridley, this precedent became important in future swimming pool discrimination cases. Finally, the court ruled on the central question of whether Hunt and the city had violated state law or Kern's constitutional rights by refusing him admission to Athletic Park Pool. The court's answer was no. It ruled that Kern did not sufficiently prove that he had ever "presented himself at the pool and demanded to be admitted to it." Therefore, he had no basis for a complaint.[97]

This ruling effectively settled the case, but the court did not stop there. It went on to articulate a general legal basis for denying black Americans access to public pools. It ruled that pool operators and public officials had "wide discretion" to deny individuals access to municipal pools. This legal right to discriminate, the judges indicated, was particular to the administration of swimming pools because they were such intimate public spaces. "It is a peculiar situation [at a swimming pool] since more or less informality is the rule at such places. Mothers come there with small children and use the place as a playground. On this account there is a wide discretion vested in those in charge of such pools as to whether persons of a quarrelsome disposition or big boys known to be bullies or men or women known to be of immoral character generally should be admitted. This is true regardless of the color or race of the person excluded."[98] When coupled with the court's earlier finding that an individual could not sue on behalf of a group of people, this reasoning provided cities throughout the state the legal fencing necessary to bar all blacks from entering municipal pools. A person could only sue based upon his or her individual exclusion, yet city officials had considerable legal leeway to bar "undesirable" individuals from swimming pools. If a black person ever sued a city for denying him or her access, city officials could simply argue that this particular person was turned away for being quarrelsome or immoral. The fact that all other black people were similarly barred from the pool was, in the eyes of the court, immaterial.

Ridley was thoroughly disillusioned by the time the court issued its ruling. He wrote to Marshall in April 1940 asking whether the Newton branch should appeal the decision or send a well-known and undeniably respectable black resident to the pool, this time with ample witnesses, and then file another suit. The letter, however, revealed Ridley's deeply felt frustration. In a thinly veiled plea for help from the national office, he concluded the letter, "I have been fighting said case almost alone since 1936 with my personal funds. Will appreciate any advice you see fit to give us."[99] Whatever advice Marshall offered, Ridley neither appealed the Kern decision nor initiated a new lawsuit. His five-year odyssey had obviously shaken his confidence in the fairness of the courts. As a result, the only municipal pool in Newton remained for whites only.[100]

The Newton case highlights another primary cause of racial discrimination at swimming pools in the North. Many whites objected to swimming with blacks because they perceived them as unclean and likely to be infected with communicable diseases. According to his lawyers, Hunt had to exclude black swimmers from Athletic Park Pool because white patrons feared coming into contact with water that had touched black skin. This same concern pervaded the thinking of whites in other northern communities as well. A Marion, Indiana, woman explained that white residents of that city would not swim with "colored people," because they viewed them as "dirty" and "didn't want to be polluted by their 'blackness.'"[101] Similarly, the managers of Shady Grove Park, an amusement complex near Pittsburgh, permitted all classes of white patrons to swim in its pool during the early 1930s but excluded blacks, even though they had equal access to the park's other facilities. Black patrons could, however, swim in the pool "after the season for whites had closed" in early September. The manager explained that this arrangement gave the maintenance crew "sufficient time to properly cleanse and disinfect it after the Negroes have used it." White patrons would only swim in the pool after blacks if the water was drained and the entire basin scrubbed with a disinfectant. As there was not enough time to do this during the busy summer season, black swimmers had to wait until the fall.[102]

Cleanliness and health concerns based on social prejudices were not new in the 1920s and 1930s. Previously, however, such concerns were based on class prejudices. Middle-class Americans avoided swimming with the working classes—both black and white—because they viewed them en masse as dirty and likely to be infected by a communicable disease. By the 1920s and 1930s, however, these class-based prejudices had given way to more thoroughly race-based prejudices. Several factors contributed to this change. During the mid- to late 1910s, doctors and public health officials published several studies showing significantly higher rates of infectious diseases among blacks than whites. Some of these studies offered explicitly racial explanations to account for the difference. They concluded that blacks suffered disproportionately from tuberculosis and syphilis because of biological predisposition and "lower standards of morality." These widely reported studies began to uncouple the popular association of communicable diseases with social class and link it with race instead.[103] At the same time, a large black underclass appeared in northern cities. Most of the 1.5 million southern blacks who migrated to the North between 1915 and 1930 settled in overcrowded and unsanitary slums. The combination of their southern ways, low-level industrial occupations, and dilapidated homes stigmatized the migrants as "dirty, crude, and generally unpleasant," according to historian James Grossman.[104] The Chicago Commission on Race Relations found that even working-class whites, many of them immigrants, objected to the migrants because of their "soiled and ill-smelling clothes."[105] Because of the migration and the simultaneous drop in European immigration, black Americans quickly became the most conspicuous poor in northern cities, and race became perceived as the most meaningful social signifier of dirtiness. As a result, the sanitation and health concerns that divided Progressive Era swimmers along class lines now convinced all classes of northern whites that they should avoid swimming with blacks.

Intertwined with the racial violence and discrimination that occurred at municipal pools during the interwar years were acts of resistance. Black swimmers in Elizabeth, New Jersey, returned day after day to Dowd Pool during the summer of 1938 despite the threats and assaults. Black voters in Pittsburgh switched long-standing political allegiances to protest the city's sanctioning of discrimination and violence at Highland Park Pool. Samuel Ridley battled Newton, Kansas, in court for five years in an attempt to secure black citizens a place to swim. These examples testify to the social, political, and legal ways in which black Americans resisted the onset of racial segregation and exclusion at municipal swimming pools during the 1920s and 1930s.

Despite their courageous and sometimes perilous efforts, black Americans invariably lost these early civil rights struggles. By the end of the 1930s, communities throughout the North had successfully separated black swimmers from white at municipal pools. The protests over pool discrimination failed, in large part, because the government institutions responsible for protecting the civil and legal rights of citizens conspired to deprive black Americans of those rights. Social protests failed to integrate pools because police officers did not protect black swimmers or arrest the assailants. Rather, officers often encouraged the beatings and then arrested the victims. Political protests of the sort orchestrated by black leaders in Pittsburgh were ineffective because of black residents' numerical minority in northern cities and the pervasive racial prejudice among whites. As minority swing voters, blacks possessed limited political power. They might tip local elections to one candidate or another and thus sway municipal policy slightly. But, they did not have sufficient numbers to convince municipal officials to adopt policies offensive to the white majority. Neither Mayor Kline nor Mayor McNair would risk alienating white voters en masse by enforcing integrated use of Highland Park Pool. The courts proved no more responsive to legal arguments during this period than white swimmers and politicians did to social and political protests. The few judges faced with deciding pool discrimination cases during the 1920s and 1930s relied on legal technicalities and conjured tenuous legal logic in order to protect racial segregation and exclusion.

Despite early defeats in swimming pool cases, civil rights leaders in the North trusted that legal protest afforded black Americans the best chance to end racial discrimination at municipal pools. After 1945 more and more NAACP chapters sued their cities and towns over pool segregation and exclusion. Even before the United States Supreme Court effectively overturned the separate-but-equal doctrine in *Brown v. Board of Education* (1954), state and federal judges had already forced many cities to open their swimming pools to black citizens. Chapter 6 tells the story of this legal triumph and examines its paradoxical social consequences.

CHAPTER 6

"MORE SENSITIVE THAN SCHOOLS"
THE STRUGGLE TO DESEGREGATE
MUNICIPAL SWIMMING POOLS

Backed by Supreme Court decisions a powerful trend is breaking down segregation of the races. In this area, so far, the changes have been taken in stride without the racial trouble that many persons had feared. . . . But joint use of the city's major pool proposes a sudden jump all the way to one of the touchiest problems in race relations. —Editorial, **Kansas City Star** *(1952)*

On a hot summer day in 1952, seventeen-year-old Mamie Livingston and two younger sisters walked the ten blocks from their East Baltimore home to Clifton Park municipal swimming pool. The three had never plunged into the pool even though they grew up so very near to it. Mamie did not expect to enter that day either, but she hoped. A rather rude attendant turned the girls away "with scorn," according to Mamie, but added that the city would soon build a pool nearby that they could use. Mamie eagerly waited out the summer and her senior year at Carver High School but saw no evidence of a new pool. Finally, in late July 1953, she wrote to the *Afro-American*, Baltimore's leading black newspaper, asking if it knew what had happened to the pool for black swimmers. "As of yet," she lamented, "we have heard nothing more of this." At the end of her letter, Mamie linked the lack of an accessible municipal pool to the larger issue of civil rights: "If this country is ever going to have equal rights, why not start here?" For her, equal rights was not an abstract principle; it meant having a pool in which to swim just like her white neighbors.[1]

Baltimore operated seven outdoor pools at the time—six for whites and one for blacks. The whites-only pools were distributed throughout the city in Druid Hill, Patterson, Clifton, Gwynns Falls, Riverside, and Roosevelt Parks. Most were resort pools with large tanks, concrete decks, and sand beaches

"Outside Looking In"—Mamie Livingston, Baltimore, 1953.
Afro-American Newspapers Archives and Research Center, Baltimore.

or grassy lawns. In contrast, the city's only municipal pool for blacks, located in Druid Hill Park, was "quite small," according to the Department of Recreation, and provided virtually no leisure space. The tank was surrounded by a narrow concrete walkway enclosed by fencing. There was no sand beach, no pool deck, and no lounge chairs.[2] Furthermore, Druid Hill Park was located several miles northwest of downtown and not easily accessible from East Baltimore, where many black families lived. The park was four and a half miles, for example, from the Livingstons' home at 1027 North Washington Street. Mamie and her siblings could not reasonably walk the nine miles round trip to the pool, nor could Vonzella Livingston, their mother, afford to send them by car or bus. The Livingstons were not poor; they were just saving money to buy a house.[3]

Mamie's letter to the *Afro-American* prompted the paper to investigate the city's pool-building plans and publicize the unequal provision. It contacted recreation department officials and learned that the city did not plan to build a Jim Crow pool in East Baltimore. Shortly thereafter, three black boys drowned in two separate incidents while swimming in natural waters around the city. In one incident, Tommy Cummings and Bernard Hipkings were swimming with two white friends in the Patapsco River when Tommy slipped beneath the water and never came back up alive. The surviving trio later explained that they swam in the river because it was the only place in the city where they could all swim together.[4] In the wake of the deaths, the *Afro-American* and the Baltimore branch of the NAACP lobbied the city to end segregation at its swimming pools. The city's park board discussed the issue at a meeting in early September 1953 but "unanimously agreed not to change our policy at this time." Within days, Linwood Koger, a lawyer affiliated with the local NAACP, filed suit against the city in federal district court seeking an injunction "to restrain defendants from operating on a segregated basis any swimming pool established, operated, or maintained by the city of Baltimore."[5] What began with Mamie Livingston's ten-block walk to Clifton Park Pool had expanded into a legal assault on racial segregation at Baltimore's municipal pools.

While the case should have hinged on questions of constitutional rights and legal precedents, the real issue was interracial intimacy. During the hearing in June 1954, city solicitor Edwin Harlan argued that racial segregation must continue at swimming pools—despite the Supreme Court's recent ruling in *Brown v. Board of Education* that school segregation was unconstitutional—because swimming brought males and females into "physical" and "intimate" contact. "There must be segregation," Harlan exhorted, "in fields of intimate contact or else there may be trouble." Harlan predicted that whites would riot if black men were permitted to swim with white women. This reasoning convinced Judge Roszel Thomsen to uphold segregation at the city's pools. In reconciling his decision with *Brown*, Thomsen explained that swimming pools were "more sensitive than schools" because of the visual and physical intimacy that accompanied their use.[6] The NAACP quickly appealed the decision to the U.S. Court of Appeals for the Fourth Circuit, where a three-judge panel unanimously overturned the ruling and ordered the city to desegregate its pools. The justices concluded that "segregation cannot be justified as a means to preserve the public peace." The city appealed to the Supreme Court, but the nine justices effectively upheld the ruling by declining to review the case.[7]

City officials abided by the ruling and opened all seven outdoor pools to blacks and whites on June 23, 1956. Despite the dire predictions of race riots, desegregation occurred "without incident," according to the *Afro-American*. Local newspapers even portrayed the pools as harmonious racial melting pots. The *Baltimore Sun* printed a picture of two boys, one white and one black, clasping hands as they plunged into the water from a high dive.[8] The *Afro-American* ran a picture of two male sunbathers laying side by side with the caption: "This scene showing colored and white swimmers basking in the sun together in a relaxed manner shows how amicably the changeover was effected."[9] Attendance statistics, however, indicate that these snapshots of racial harmony were misleading.

Desegregation did not really integrate the city's municipal pools. Rather, it transferred use of some pools to black residents. The three pools located in overwhelmingly white sections of the city—Riverside, Roosevelt, and Patterson—continued to attract only white swimmers. The pools located near black or racially mixed neighborhoods attracted almost exclusively black swimmers. That first summer of "integrated" use, the total number of swims citywide by whites dropped 62 percent from the previous year. Even more revealing, the number of whites swimming at pools now frequented by blacks plummeted more than 95 percent. In 1955, the summer before desegregation, the whites-only pool in Druid Hill Park attracted 23,320 swimmers during the season's first thirty days. The next year, only 870 whites entered the pool during the same month-long period, but 700 of them came on opening day. Once local whites realized that blacks were using the pool, an average of only six whites swam in it each day. The previous year, before desegregation, daily attendance averaged 775. "The white people in Druid Hill Park and Clifton Park areas have deserted [these pools]," noted Director of Parks and Recreation R. Brooke Maxwell, "because of the integration policy."[10]

The racially divided use of Baltimore's municipal pools continued for many years. In 1963 Floyd Stevens, director of the Clyburn Home for Orphans, brought a group of parentless children to swim at Riverside Pool. As the group approached the water, swimmers began to shout, "Nigger, get out of here." Two of the children—a ten-year-old boy and thirteen-year-old girl—were black. Stevens let the white orphans enter the pool but took the unnamed black boy and girl back to the orphanage. As a newspaper account of the incident explained, "municipal pools in Baltimore have been declared integrated, but the one visited by the orphans has been used only by whites."[11] In response to racial desegregation, many white swimmers simply retreated to pools that were difficult and threatening for black Americans to access.

The desegregation of Baltimore's municipal pools occurred a few years later than in most northern cities, but the process and social effects were the same. Between 1945 and 1955, progressive-minded Americans, both black and white, challenged racial discrimination at municipal pools throughout the northern United States. The protests were local in orientation but national in scope. They were frequently organized by branch chapters of organizations such as the NAACP, the Young Progressives, and the American Youth for Democracy, but many protests were spontaneous and individual, like Mamie Livingston seeking entry to a whites-only pool on a hot summer day. These efforts to integrate municipal pools were opposed by determined and often violent resistance. Groups for and against segregation threw rocks and tomatoes at one another, swung bats and fists, and even stabbed and shot at each other. And so, the process of desegregating municipal pools was just as contested as the process of segregating them had been back in the 1920s and 1930s. When social protest proved ineffective, local NAACP chapters sought court orders forcing city officials to open pools to black swimmers. Unlike the earlier period, they usually triumphed. By the mid-1950s—the period when most accounts say the civil rights movement began—local protesters and plaintiffs had successfully desegregated municipal pools throughout the northern United States.

Several factors account for their success. The experience of fighting tyranny in Europe and the Pacific during World War II emboldened black Americans to fight racial discrimination at home. After the war, many steadfastly refused to accept exclusion from municipal pools or their inequitable distribution. Also, black swimmers received institutional support in their efforts to desegregate pools. After Mamie wrote her letter, the *Afro-American* and the local NAACP both joined the fight, eventually carrying it to federal court. World War II also brought about an important shift in the attitude of many northern whites. The horror of seeing deterministic views of race carried to extreme ends by Nazi Germany caused many Americans to question their own racial assumptions. Furthermore, the impassioned and heartfelt assertions that the nation was fighting the war to defend freedom and democracy forced many white northerners to grapple with the contradiction between American ideals and the nation's treatment of black citizens.[12] After the war, some progressive-minded whites joined blacks in their fight to desegregate swimming pools. Many more northern whites simply concluded that blatant forms of public discrimination were wrong. Finally, state and federal judges became much more sympathetic to charges of racial discrimination than they had been before the war. Rather than conjure tenuous legal logic to sustain discrimination, the courts, in many cases, forthrightly upheld the law.[13] Federal courts in particular played a critical role in desegregating municipal pools during this period.

Although many northern whites no longer condoned public forms of discrimination after World War II, most still refused to swim with blacks. When black Americans began using a pool that had been desegregated, whites generally abandoned it. In large cities, desegregation transferred use of some pools from white swimmers to black but rarely led to meaningful interracial swimming. In smaller communities, desegregation was more consequential. Public officials in many one-pool cities, especially those in the southern tier of northern states, closed their pools rather than permit interracial swimming. When one-pool communities kept their desegregated pools open, many whites retreated to private pools or simply stopped swimming. One consequence of desegregation was that white attendance at municipal pools plummeted in many northern cities.

~~~~~~ Americans began protesting pool segregation in the North as soon as World War II ended.[14] Two of the most significant early desegregation struggles occurred in Warren, Ohio, and Montgomery, West Virginia. In both cities, public officials had leased their municipal pool to a private organization in order to circumvent state civil rights laws that prohibited racial discrimination at public facilities. When the private operators refused to admit black swimmers, local branches of the NAACP sued. Unlike the Newton, Kansas, case ten years earlier, the black plaintiffs triumphed in court and established legal precedents that tipped the scales of justice in the favor of black swimmers throughout the North. The social outcomes of the Warren and Montgomery cases, however, show that racial prejudice persisted long after the public discrimination ended.

The struggle to desegregate Warren's Packard Park Pool began early in the summer of 1945. Representatives from the Warren NAACP chapter and leaders of the Warren Inter-Racial Committee asked Mayor Robert Roberts to ensure black citizens equal access to the city's one municipal pool. Roberts refused but did offer black residents exclusive use of it one day a week. The biracial group rejected the offer, claiming that any form of segregation violated black citizens' civil rights. The group's uncompromising position put Mayor Roberts in a difficult spot. He recognized that the city could no longer openly violate Ohio's civil rights law, but he did not want blacks and whites to swim and sunbathe together. Perplexed by the dilemma, he decided to close the pool to all swimmers that summer.[15]

The swimming pool was a much-debated topic during the municipal elections that fall. Roberts held to his position of segregation or closure, while challenger Henry Wagner promised to reopen the pool and admit "all citizens regardless of race or color." Wagner won the election. As promised, the new mayor opened Packard Park Pool to all citizens during the 1946 swimming season. Some local whites willingly swam with fellow black residents, but most would not. Overall attendance plummeted that summer. As a result, the city lost $3,500 operating the pool, whereas in past years the deficit had never exceeded $1,000.[16]

Wagner was committed to ending public forms of discrimination, but not so much that he would let it bankrupt the city. As the deficit mounted that summer, he approached the Inter-Racial Committee, the local NAACP, and the Warren Urban League asking if they would accept segregated use. He explained that the pool was losing so much money that the city would have to close it "unless separate days could be designated for Negroes and Caucasians." Again, the civil rights groups refused, explaining that they would not sacrifice the legal rights of black residents for a few thousand dollars of savings. When the segregation talks failed, the Warren City Council pursued an alternative solution. Late in the summer, it passed Emergency Ordinance 3518 authorizing the city to lease the pool to a private swim club. By doing so, the city sought to relieve itself of the financial burden of operating the pool as well as the headache of regulating its use.[17]

In January 1947 the newly formed Veterans Swim Club leased the pool from the city. City officials required no up-front compensation for use of the $100,000 facility, only 10 percent of any profits. The club implemented an elaborate process for screening applicants. All members had to be veterans or related to one, be recommended for membership, and pass a two-thirds secret ballot vote by the executive board. Despite the stringent requirements, the club quickly enrolled 4,600 members. Not one was identifiably black. Many black veterans and their families applied for membership, but all were rejected. The Warren branch of the NAACP complained to Mayor Wagner that this was obviously racial discrimination, but he had washed his hands of the pool "problem." Local black leaders finally decided that the courts were their best recourse.[18]

James Culver, president of the local NAACP, hired Youngstown attorney William M. Howard to sue the city and the Veterans Swim Club. Howard quickly wrote to Thurgood Marshall, head of the NAACP Legal Defense Fund, asking for advice on the matter. The response by Marshall's associate, Marian Wynn Perry, never made it to Howard, which caused a bit of a rift between them.[19] Without advice from the more experienced civil rights attorneys in New York, Howard proceeded on his own, filing suit in the Trumbull County Court of Common Pleas. The case involved two principal questions. Did the city lease the pool to the swim club with the intent to deprive black residents use of it? If so, the lease was clearly illegal. Second, did the swim club exclude applicants based solely on their racial identity? If so, was that illegal?

Howard focused his case on the validity of the lease, an approach that at first seemed ill-fated. He argued that the real purpose behind the lease was to exclude black residents from the pool, which, under Ohio law, made it illegal. Howard called several witnesses to substantiate this point, but they gave rather weak testimony. William Burd, a member of the Warren Inter-Racial Committee, testified that city officials had approached the group, prior to authorizing the lease, asking it to support segregated use or risk having the pool closed entirely. Other witnesses gave similar testimony. Howard concluded that the either-or proposition—accept segregation or closure—showed that, from the start, the city was searching for a way to separate black swimmers from white.[20] On cross-examination, however, each of the witnesses admitted that city officials had always presented the pool issue as an economic problem, not a social one. City Solicitor Donald Del Bene used these admissions to bolster the city's argument that it had leased the pool not with the intent to exclude blacks, but because the pool was "economically unsound and a financial loss to the City." As such, Del Bene asserted, the lease was perfectly legal. Del Bene next claimed that the Veteran's Swim Club was solely responsible for the administration of the pool, and the city was therefore not legally liable for its membership decisions. In its defense, the Veteran's Swim Club denied excluding applicants based on their racial identity, but went on to claim that, as a private organization, its board could admit or exclude applicants based upon any criteria it chose.[21]

In his decision, Judge J. Graham focused on the discrete legal issues of the case and refused to speculate on the motives of city officials. First, he ruled that the swim club could indeed admit and exclude prospective applicants at its own discretion: "If the Veteran's Swim Club holds a valid lease, that club, being a private club, can determine who its members are to be and can refuse use of the pool to nonmembers." The pertinent legal question therefore was whether the city leased the pool with the intent to deny black swimmers access or to avoid financial loss. Judge Graham accepted the word of city officials and ruled that their decision to lease the pool was based solely on financial considerations. "The court," he explained, "cannot delve into the recesses of the minds of the councilmen for the purpose of discovering any [malicious] motive." The lease therefore was legal, and Graham dismissed the case.[22]

Howard was eager to appeal and again wrote Thurgood Marshall asking for advice. After attorneys in the national office scrutinized the case "backward and forward," Marshall advised Howard not to appeal. The national NAACP was dedicated to fighting discrimination, even at swimming pools, but it did not want to argue weak cases that might add another precedent to the bulwark of case law that sanctioned racial segregation. Marshall did not doubt that the city leased the pool in order to exclude black residents, but city officials had been careful not to leave any evidence that proved this was their intent.[23] Even though the prospects for reversal seemed slim, Howard appealed the ruling anyway and soon benefited from a federal court decision on a similar case that originated in Montgomery, West Virginia.

Montgomery, a small community located in the southwest corner of the state, constructed its municipal pool in 1942 but did not open it until 1946. The delay had nothing to do with the war, however. During construction, local black leaders met with city officials on several occasions to ascertain whether black residents would be guaranteed equal access. On one occasion, the city attorney replied that he "would resign rather than advise the city to permit [interracial] use." Members of the city council held similar views but realized that officially excluding black citizens would clearly violate West Virginia's civil rights law. Unwilling to permit interracial swimming or brazenly defy the law, they decided not to open the pool. The summers of 1942, 1943, 1944, and 1945 all passed without anyone using it.[24]

Early in 1946, a less scrupulous city administration took office. Mayor R. M. Holstine devised a strategy for excluding black swimmers without, at least on the surface, violating state law. That summer, he leased the pool to the Montgomery Park Association for one dollar. Like the Veteran's Swim Club in Warren, the park association was a private corporation formed solely for the purpose of administering the pool. The pool finally opened in June 1946, four years after it had been built. The racial discrimination that occurred at the Montgomery pool was much more blatant than in Warren. Prospective swimmers simply came to the pool and paid $7.50 for a season pass. Every white person who paid the "membership fee" was admitted, while every identifiably black person was turned away. Shortly after the pool opened, Paul Lawrence, Dr. R. A. Mead, Colbert Coleman, and Willard Divers, all members of the local NAACP chapter, walked into the pool office and handed thirty dollars to the pool manager for four season passes. The manager slid the money back to the men, explaining that he "didn't have any orders to sell tickets to colored people." Rather than argue with the manager, the group complained to F. B. Eberhart, president of the Montgomery Park Association. Eberhart responded that the association "hadn't made arrangements to sell colored people tickets." While both carefully avoided associating themselves personally with the policy, the pool manager and Eberhart freely admitted that the association was excluding black residents because of their racial identity.[25]

The following summer, the same four men returned to the pool and attempted to purchase season passes. Again, the manager refused to accept them as members. This time Lawrence, Mead, Coleman, and Divers called on Mayor Holstine and threatened to sue the city if it did not open the pool to black residents. Holstine responded, rather colloquially, "That won't do for you to use the pool." Shortly thereafter, Dr. Meade—who was a longtime dentist in town—hired Charleston attorney T. Gillis Nutter to file suit against the city on behalf of Paul Lawrence in particular and all black residents of Montgomery in general. Nutter was an experienced civil rights attorney who had been fighting racial discrimination in West Virginia since 1928, when he successfully desegregated Charleston's public library.[26]

Nutter recognized that the choice of venue was critical both to the outcome of the case and the significance of the decision. He filed suit in U.S. District Court in part because he believed that black plaintiffs could not get a fair hearing in local court, especially involving a dispute with public officials. "We have been absolutely unable to gain a single victory in Fayette County," Nutter wrote Thurgood Marshall, "although we have had two killing scrapes by officers and other matters but we have lost every effort we have made to protect Negroes in their rights."[27] Nutter also filed suit in federal court because he hoped that victory in the Montgomery case would strike a blow for black swimmers across the nation. "I had in mind," he wrote Marshall on another occasion, "that the present use of swimming pools had become almost a nation wide question and I thought possibly that we might be able through the Montgomery suit to establish the right of Negroes to use swimming pools without discrimination or segregation, throughout the country." Only a federal court ruling, Nutter believed, would have such a far-reaching effect.[28] But, the potential reward was offset by considerable risk. Defeat in federal court would hinder other pool discrimination cases as much as victory would help.

In his complaint, Nutter repeated the facts of the case—describing the multiple times Lawrence had been denied access to the pool—and focused on two arguments. First, he claimed that the city could not escape lawful administration of the pool by leasing it to a private group. Second, he argued that Lawrence had the right to sue on behalf of all 600 black residents of Montgomery. Both arguments harkened back to issues raised in the *Kern v. Newton* case from the late 1930s, which Nutter had studied in preparation for the Montgomery case.[29] Although Kern had lost the earlier case, Nutter hoped to take advantage of the Kansas Supreme Court's ruling that cities could not lease away their legal obligation to ensure black citizens equal access to public pools. He also filed suit on behalf of the whole black community in an attempt to preempt the legal sophistry the Kansas court used to dismiss the *Kern* case. Nutter concluded the complaint by asking the court to permanently enjoin the city and/or park association "from denying plaintiff, and all other citizens of Montgomery, West Virginia, equal access to and enjoyment of the aforesaid recreation facilities."[30]

Both the city and the park association did their best to ignore or complicate the central issue of racial exclusion. As in the Warren case, the city argued that it had leased the pool because it did not have sufficient funds to operate it, not as a means to exclude black residents. Next, the city claimed that it bore no responsibility for the park association's administration of the pool. In its defense, the Montgomery Park Association argued that it did not "unlawfully discriminate" against black Americans, which was not to claim that it did not discriminate, but that the discrimination was lawful because the association was "a private corporation and in no sense a [public entity]." The association further argued that no "actual controversy" existed between it and the plaintiff because the pool lease had expired on September 30, and it no longer operated the pool. The combined arguments of the city and park association suggested that there was no one for Paul Lawrence to sue. The city was not liable because it did not operate the pool when the discrimination occurred, and the association could not be sued because it did not operate the pool when the suit came to trial.[31]

Unlike previous judges faced with swimming pool discrimination cases, Federal District Judge Ben Moore focused more on the larger issues of justice and equality than discrete questions of law. Whereas Judge Graham in the Warren case was not willing to "delve into the recesses of the minds" of public officials to divine their motive, Judge Moore was. "Justice would indeed be blind if she failed to detect the real purpose in this effort of the City of Montgomery to clothe a public function with the mantle of private responsibility. 'The voice is Jacob's voice,' even though 'the hands are the hands of Esau.' It is clearly but another in the long series of stratagems which governing bodies of many white communities have employed in attempting to deprive the Negro of his constitutional birthright; the equal protection of the law." In an opinion issued February 11, 1948, Moore instructed Nutter to prepare an order in the form of a declaratory judgment stating that the park association's refusal to admit Lawrence "was an exercise of governmental power by the city of Montgomery" in violation of the Fourteenth Amendment. Conforming his ruling to the Supreme Court's 1896 *Plessy v. Ferguson* decision, Moore ruled that the order should include an injunction restraining the city "from again denying plaintiff the right to use the swimming pool at any time when the pool is open for public use, unless there be provided by the City other and equal swimming facilities available to persons of the Negro race."[32] *Lawrence v. Hancock* therefore did not necessarily desegregate the pool, but it did ensure that black residents would have a pool in which to swim if the city provided a pool for whites.

Montgomery city officials were amenable to neither option. They would not permit interracial use but could not afford to build a second pool. So, they closed the pool and kept it closed until 1961. For fourteen years, the unused pool stood as a conspicuous reminder of the city's racial divide.[33]

Despite its bittersweet outcome for local blacks, the Montgomery decision set a historic precedent. It was the first substantial legal victory for black Americans fighting swimming pool discrimination in the courts. One hopes that Samuel Ridley, who brought the *Kern v. Newton* case to the Kansas Supreme Court, learned of the Montgomery legal triumph and realized that his earlier odyssey provided Nutter a map for navigating the tricky waters of swimming pool discrimination cases.

As Nutter intended, the *Lawrence v. Hancock* decision immediately benefited black plaintiffs in other cases—particularly William Howard's fight to end discrimination at Packard Park Pool in Warren. Nutter immediately sent Moore's ruling to Thurgood Marshall, who quickly forwarded it to Howard.[34] In this way, the New York office not only provided legal advice to civil rights attorneys across the country but also served as a clearinghouse of the latest legal opinions, which proved invaluable. When Howard received the correspondence, the Warren case was before Ohio's Eleventh District Court of Appeals. Howard introduced the Montgomery decision to the court, and it immediately tipped the scales of justice in his favor. In its eventual ruling, the court liberally paraphrased from the Montgomery decision and even quoted Moore's reference to Jacob and Esau verbatim. "Many cases have been cited as authority for the proposition herein discussed. The case most nearly analogous is the case of *Lawrence v. Hancock*. Except that the names of the parties are different and the locale is different, the opinion of the court in that case could well be the opinion in this case." The court determined that the city and swim club "quite obviously conspired to prevent the use [of the pool] by plaintiffs and other colored persons," and then ordered the city to admit black swimmers to Packard Park Pool on an equal basis with all other citizens.[35]

By the time the court of appeals issued its ruling, Warren mayor Harold Smith had already decided to desegregate Packard Park Pool. He declined to renew the Veteran Swim Club's lease and announced in early June 1948 that the pool would be open to all citizens. It was probably no coincidence that the change in policy occurred immediately after Howard gave a copy of the Montgomery decision to city attorneys. The local Warren newspaper covered the June 15 pool opening and published a front-page picture showing a dozen kids waiting to enter. The last two children in line were clearly black and the caption read, "Last one in the water is a monkey."[36] Attendance at the pool plummeted as a result of desegregation. Although it did not provide exact numbers, the *Warren Tribune Chronicle* reported that "records indicate that no where near as many persons are using the pool this year as last."[37] The attitudes and prejudices that led to racial exclusion at the pool were much more difficult to eradicate than the discrimination itself.

~~~~~ The Montgomery and Warren cases were important precedents, but they were not as widely applicable as Nutter had hoped. Both dealt specifically with the question of racial exclusion—cases where whites had access to a municipal pool, but blacks did not. The judges ruled that racial exclusion was unconstitutional but explicitly affirmed each city's right to segregate black swimmers at separate-but-equal pools. Desegregation became an issue only because neither city could afford to build a second pool. Discrimination cases in larger cities, which did provide separate pools for black residents, would be more difficult to prove. They would hinge on the more subjective question of whether the Jim Crow pools were in fact equal to the pools open only to whites. The first such case originated in St. Louis in 1950 and dealt with access to Fairgrounds Park Pool, the earliest segregated pool in the northern United States. The story of its desegregation, however, begins several years earlier, when black swimmers directly challenged segregation by repeatedly seeking admission.

At the end of the World War II, the provision of municipal pools in St. Louis was decidedly unequal for black residents. They had access to two indoor "bathhouse" pools, whereas whites could choose to swim at any of six pools, including two gigantic resort pools in Fairgrounds and Marquette Parks.[38] The wartime experience predisposed black residents to question public forms of discrimination, but it was the city's changing demography that prompted the swimming pool protest. The black population of St. Louis increased 42 percent during the 1940s as migrants flooded into the midwestern metropolis from the South and the surrounding hinterland.[39] Traditional black neighborhoods could not absorb all the migrants, so black families gradually pushed the boundary of residential segregation both north and west from the city's Central Corridor. As they moved into new areas, local blacks demanded access to neighborhood recreation facilities. In 1946, for example, black residents living in south central St. Louis informed Commissioner of Parks and Recreation Palmer B. Baumus that they intended to use the Buder Recreation Center with or without the blessing of the city. The Buder facility, which contained a playground, athletic facilities, and an indoor swimming pool, was "designated" for white use because the surrounding neighborhood had been overwhelmingly white when the recreation center opened back in 1930. The area was now inhabited predominately by black Americans. Commissioner Baumes acquiesced to black residents' demand, desegregating the playground and athletic fields but not the pool. He could accept black and white children playing on swings and slides together but not swimming together. While Buder playground was now ostensibly integrated, the reality was that its use passed almost completely to blacks. When black children stepped onto the grounds, whites walked away in protest and did not return. Angry parents sent petitions to the mayor, and a few locals even burned a cross on the contested playground but to no avail. City officials would not resegregate the facility, and the flaming cross did not scare black children away. The city did, however, quickly construct a new whites-only playground nearby. Eventually, the city opened Buder pool to black children as well.[40]

Black St. Louisians next sought to integrate Fairgrounds Park Pool. The park was, as one black resident recalled, "right on the cutting edge of [residential] segregation" during the late 1940s.[41] As more and more black families moved into this area northwest of downtown, they periodically sought admission to the pool. Whereas pool segregation had been official city policy during the 1920s and 1930s, it had become more a matter of custom in the postwar period. Sometimes pool attendants told prospective black swimmers outright that they could not enter, whereas at other times the attendants strongly discouraged them but added, "If you really want to swim, you can get in line." If the swimmers did not yield to the implicit threat and actually got in line, they were explicitly denied admission once they reached the gate. Commissioner Baumes considered each of these episodes to be of such importance that he instructed pool officials to notify him "immedi-ately" whenever a black swimmer sought admission to the pool.[42] Although no black swimmers entered Fairgrounds Pool as a result, this social protest was nonetheless effective because it forced the city to enforce its segregation policy. Segregation was strongest and most viable when it was an accepted and uncontested habit of community life. Black residents upset this habit in St. Louis by repeatedly seeking entry to Fairgrounds Pool and eventually forced the city to rethink its policy.

The rethinking occurred in 1949, when a new city administration under the direction of Mayor Joseph Darst took over the offices at city hall. A real-estate man who had been involved in Missouri politics for twenty-five years, Darst was a close friend of President Harry Truman and shared a likeness to him as well. Darst was bald on top with a ring of gray hair around the sides and back of his head. He had a warm, round face, accentuated by round steel-rimmed glasses. Darst's election ended eight years of Republican control in St. Louis.[43] The new mayor brought in his own staff and department heads, but retained many high level civil servants. He appointed his campaign man-ager, John J. O'Toole, to direct the Department of Public Welfare, which over-saw the Division of Parks and Recreation, but retained Palmer Baumes as the Commissioner of Parks and Recreation.

Early in the spring of 1949, Baumes asked O'Toole what the new adminis-tration's policy would be regarding black citizens seeking admission to Fair-grounds and Marquette Pools. O'Toole responded, "Why do you ask this ques-tion? What is the problem?" Baumes informed him that black citizens were causing "trouble" by challenging the traditional practice of racial segregation. "It's a question," he told O'Toole, "that comes up every year that is difficult to handle and we ought to decide on a policy." For several months leading up to the pool openings, O'Toole avoided deciding. He later recalled: "Frankly, I did not know what to do. I couldn't see where there was any basis for ex-cluding Negroes under the law. I kept postponing giving an answer. I really thought that the man who had been the commissioner of parks for a long time should know what to do." O'Toole never consulted with Mayor Darst, which suggests he did not recognize the sensitivity of the issue. Finally, four days before the pools were set to open on June 21, Baumes sought a definite answer from O'Toole. "I told him I could see no basis for keeping Negroes out of the pools," O'Toole recalled. "They are citizens like everybody else and have every legal right to enter any public facility."[44]

The day before the pools opened, a reporter from the *Post-Dispatch* found out about O'Toole's decision. He and a reporter from the *Globe-Democrat* asked the director for a statement. O'Toole denied integrating the city's pools but added that blacks would not be denied admission. Unsure of the distinction, the reporters asked him to clarify. O'Toole explained that the city was not inviting blacks to swim in the outdoor pools, but, if they sought admission, attendants would let them enter. Mayor Darst finally became involved when the same reporters asked him to comment on the new policy. Caught by surprise, Darst declined, saying he needed to consult with his advisers. Later that day, Darst contacted the papers to confirm O'Toole's directive but asked them to give the story "only factual and routine coverage." He no doubt realized this was an explosive issue but, as subsequent events would show, did not realize just how explosive.[45]

The next morning, June 21, the *Globe-Democrat* plastered across its front page the headline, "Pools and Playgrounds Opened to Both Races." The opening line of the article read: "Negroes and whites hereafter may swim together in all of the city's nine pools . . . , Director of Public Welfare John J. O'Toole announced yesterday."[46] More in line with what the mayor had hoped, the *Post-Dispatch* buried the story on an inside page with the less arousing title, "Negroes Will Not Be Denied a Swim in Any City Pool."[47] If Darst or O'Toole wondered how the new policy was being received by the public, they merely had to ask local insurance executive John O'Toole. Mistaking him for the director of public welfare, scores of angry citizens made threatening phone calls to his home. Concerned that the callers would soon be ringing his bell, the businessman quickly asked for police protection. Fortunately for the welfare director, his phone number and street address were listed in the city directory under his nickname, Jack O'Toole.[48]

That afternoon, 30 black swimmers and about 200 white swimmers waited outside the male entrance to Fairgrounds Pool. A much smaller number of girls, all of them white, waited outside their entrance. When the gates finally opened, the young swimmers entered the facility without incident but did break into separate racial groups in the water. Black swimmers tended to gather in one area of the enormous pool and whites in another. This was the first time in the pool's thirty-six year history that the city permitted identifiably black swimmers to enter its expansive waters. The lifeguards considered quitting in protest but decided to stay on.[49]

〰〰 As the boys and girls tentatively played in the pool, a large crowd gathered in the park. About 200 teenagers and young men peered in from outside the fence and began shouting threats. More menacing than their words, however, were the bats, clubs, bricks, and knives they carried in their

Black Swimmers at Fairgrounds Park Pool, St. Louis, June 21, 1949. These were the first identifiably black swimmers to enter Fairgrounds Park Pool, pictured here before they were assaulted by a mob of angry white residents. From the St. Louis Globe-Democrat Archives of the St. Louis Mercantile Library at the University of Missouri—St. Louis.

hands. Neither Darst nor O'Toole had informed the police about the pool-integration order, so no officers were on hand to quell the angry crowd. The pool custodian eventually called the police to get them to escort the black swimmers out of the park. Seven officers arrived but did little to protect the boys. As the swimmers walked through a human gauntlet, white youths would, according to an eyewitness, "dart in and strike the Negro children from time to time . . . and this was not prevented by police action." Nor did the police disarm the protesters, except for one young man who brandished a large hunting knife.[50]

Over the next couple of hours, the police and the mob chased after small groups of blacks that approached the park. The officers sought to turn them away so as to avoid violence, while the protesters sought to pummel them. The mob eventually tired and dispersed, perhaps going home for dinner. By 6:45, twenty more black youths had lined-up outside the pool waiting to enter. White swimmers also waiting in line warned, or perhaps threatened, "You'd better get out of here if you don't want trouble." The boys heeded the warning and left the park. Shortly thereafter, the mob reconstituted itself outside the pool fence, and, again, the police did not disperse it. When a small group of black youths approached, someone shouted, "there's some niggers," and the rioters chased after them. The mob surrounded the boys, shouted a few epithets, and then beat them, according to the *St. Louis Star-Times*, with "clubs, bats, bricks, sticks, and their fists." One of the victims, Arthur Goodin, pulled out a knife to protect himself and stabbed Rolland Erbar, a twenty-year-old white cement finisher. The mob shouted—"He's got a knife." "He cut him."—and then intensified its assault. The onslaught ended only when the mob took off after two other black children approaching on bicycles. The young bicyclists escaped, but an unsuspecting man exiting a streetcar was attacked and beaten.[51]

Up to this point, the mob consisted of several hundred teenagers and a few older men, who incited the passions of the younger rioters with inflammatory rhetoric. "You want to know how to take care of them niggers," a burly man of about thirty asked rhetorically. "Get bricks and smash their heads." One of the teens expressed concern that the police would arrest him for smashing a black child's head with a brick. "No, they won't," the man responded. "Kill a nigger and you will make a name for yourself." As night approached, the crowd grew considerably, reaching an estimated 5,000 by eight o'clock. It now included many women, children, and adult men.[52]

The mob chased every black person who approached the park. A local newspaper described one of these episodes: "At 7:50 pm a Negro was seen on the east side of Spring Street, and another chase was underway. He ran, stumbled, and fell about 100 feet west of Grand Ave. Members of the crowd pounced on the Negro, beating him severely. Plainclothes police rushed to the spot and formed a protective cordon around the man. A detective sergeant tried to learn the man's name, but he was so severely beaten he could not speak." Then, someone hollered that another black man had been spotted on the other side of the park. The crowd and the police raced toward him. A smaller group of rioters had cornered the man on the front porch of a home adjacent to the park. Before the police could rescue him, the mob beat him with clubs and sticks, then kicked him as he lay motionless on the ground. As the police carried the limp but still breathing body away, one of

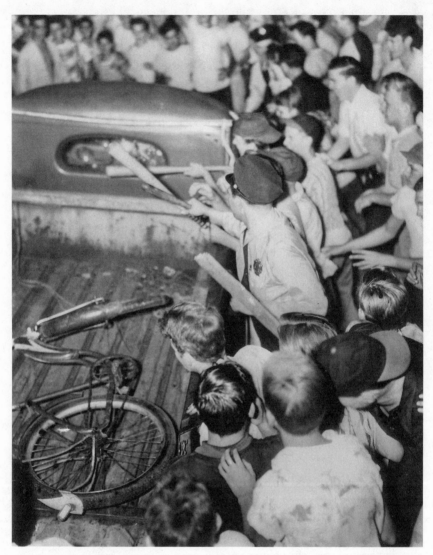

Rioters outside Fairgrounds Park, St. Louis, June 21, 1949. Young white men brandishing bats and clubs attack a truck driven by a black man during the Fairgrounds Park Riot. The role of the police officer in the melee is unclear. From the St. Louis Globe-Democrat Archives of the St. Louis Mercantile Library at the University of Missouri—St. Louis.

the attackers could not believe the man survived. "Why I kicked him twice in the head myself," remarked the sixteen-year-old boy.[53]

Some black bystanders were brave beyond reason. One young man driving past the park stopped, got out of the car, and challenged some of the rioters to

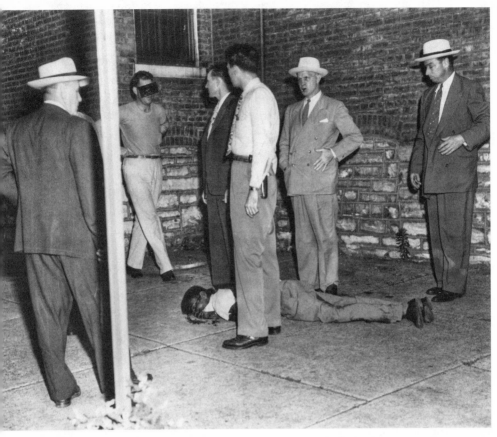

Victim of Fairgrounds Park Riot, St. Louis, June 21, 1949. From the St. Louis Globe-Democrat Archives of the St. Louis Mercantile Library at the University of Missouri—St. Louis.

a fight after they yelled obscenities at him and his wife. Police Chief Jeremiah O'Connell, who was now on the scene with about 150 officers, rushed to the enraged man and persuaded him to drive away. The police eventually blocked all roads leading to the park and created a cordon around the area to warn black residents away. The violence soon ended, but the crowd stayed in the park until late that night. Twelve people—ten blacks and two whites—suffered injuries that required hospitalization. The black victims were treated at segregated Homer G. Phillips Hospital for a variety of injuries, including stab wounds, fractured jaws, skull fractures, scalp lacerations, and countless cuts and bruises. The two white men were treated at City Hospital, one for a stab wound and the other for facial abrasions.[54]

For all the violence and lawlessness, the police arrested only eight people—five of whom were black. Goodwin, who stabbed the white cement finisher, was charged with inciting to riot and assault with intent to kill. Three other young black men were charged with disturbing the peace and inciting to riot. James Wallace, a thirty-seven-year-old black man who claimed to be on his way to the St. Louis Cardinals–New York Giants baseball game at nearby Sportsman Park when the mob attacked and stabbed him in the chest, was, according to the charge, suspected of affray. The white man who was stabbed, Roland Erbar, was charged with disturbing the peace and inciting to riot, while Aaron O'Neal, a thirty-eight-year-old white welder, was also suspected of affray. All seven of these men were arrested at their respective hospitals while receiving treatment for their various wounds. Only one person was taken into custody at the scene, as the riot raged. The police arrested eighteen-year-old Clyde Monroe and charged him with interfering with police business. Officers found the youth letting the air out of their police car tires. The charges were eventually dropped on all except one, Clyde Monroe. He pled guilty and paid a five-dollar fine.[55]

In response to the violence, Mayor Darst closed Fairgrounds and Marquette Pools and announced that the city would return—at least in the short term—to the "time-honored policy" of segregation at the pools. The mayor acknowledged that O'Toole was legally correct in opening the pools to black residents but rescinded the integration order anyway, "in the general public interest."[56] Darst did promise to build an outdoor pool for black residents sometime in the near future.[57] He also formed a fifteen member Council on Human Relations, composed of twelve whites and three blacks. The members were community leaders, labor-union representatives, and business people. Darst assigned the council two broad tasks: counteract racial prejudices among the people of St. Louis and seek a way to end "discriminatory practices" in the city. To achieve these ambitious ends, he allocated the group $5,000 and an office in city hall.[58]

The local media blamed the riot on "hooligans" and "young rowdies," thereby absolving the larger white community of complicity. The *Post-Dispatch* reported that "the disturbances in large part were created by irresponsible teenagers" who were being directed by a few older agitators.[59] Rumors also circulated through the city that communists or fascists or perhaps both groups were responsible for the violence.[60] The black press was especially eager to point the finger of guilt at extremist groups. The *St. Louis Argus* blamed the violence on followers of Gerald L. K. Smith: "The Fascists and the crowds who are still fighting President Truman's Civil Rights program will be found among the 'inciters to riot.' Included in those, of course, is the Gerald L. K. Smith–Ku Klux Klan, race baiting conglomerations. They claim to have a bait for all suckers who thrive on slime and ignorance."[61] By blaming irresponsible youths and extremist groups, the St. Louis press suggested that the mob did not reflect the views of most whites. When local religious leaders issued a public statement condemning the violence and supporting pool desegregation, the *Post-Dispatch* editorialized that "[t]hese—and not the Fairground Park hoodlums—represent the real sentiment of the community."[62] And yet, one local paper questioned these judgments. The *Globe-Democrat* agreed that most reasonable whites regretted the violence and the black eye it caused the city but doubted that most whites wanted the pools integrated: "The violences [*sic*] at the Fairgrounds Park pool were precipitated by whites. That they were rash and thoughtless youths, with a content of plain hoodlumism, does not mean that within the city generally cannot be found numbers of more sober whites who seriously object to indiscriminate bathing by whites and Negroes."[63] Subsequent events would validate the paper's assertion.

The mayor's Council on Human Relations hired George Schermer, director of Detroit's Interracial Committee, to investigate the causes of the riot and recommend ways to improve race relations in the city. Schermer interviewed police officers, city officials, victims of the violence, witnesses, and pool employees. His final report offered a very different interpretation of the riot than appeared in local papers. Schermer determined that the riot resulted solely from the introduction of mixed-race swimming and did not reflect blind racial hatred or underlying social or economic tensions in the city. He acknowledged that the racial contest over the pool stemmed from increasing black settlement in the area, but he did not find overt racial antipathy among local whites. He pointed out that three days after the riot, blacks and whites were back at Fairgrounds Park playing baseball with one another. He further concluded that the riot was really a protest that turned violent but never lost its protest character. People in the mob "discussed" the pool integration order and condemned O'Toole for issuing it, even during the height of violence. This in part explains why the riot did not radiate out from the park and engulf the surrounding neighborhood. Schermer concluded that the mob did not raze black homes and businesses, as was the case in so many other twentieth-century race riots, because the protesters were motivated by a specific goal rather than general racial hatred. They intended to reestablish the traditional boundaries of racial interaction in the park. They accepted interracial baseball but not interracial swimming. Despite obvious resistance to the policy, Schermer concluded that the city had no option but to reopen the pools on an integrated basis. To avoid another riot, he advised the city to begin a public relations campaign designed to counteract fears about mixed-race swimming and station enough police officers at the pools to protect black swimmers.[64]

The Council on Human Relations agreed with Schermer in principle, but a slim majority decided that the risk of further violence was too high to immediately open the outdoor pools to black swimmers. The council concluded that "the transition from a policy of segregation in the operation of swimming pools . . . to one of non-segregation must be made with careful planning and preparation."[65] By an eight-to-seven vote, the council advised Mayor Darst to continue racial segregation for the time being. Darst agreed. "Public safety," he wrote to the council, "demands the approach you have outlined."[66] Local and national civic groups, including the Urban League, League of Women Voters, and the Interracial Ministerial Alliance, objected to the decision but could not sway the mayor.[67]

When Fairgrounds Pool opened for the 1950 season on June 19, three black residents—attorney George Draper and two women affiliated with the local NAACP chapter, Katie McCullough and Rose Taylor—sought admission to the pool but were denied. An attendant claimed that they had to have a "permit" issued at city hall to enter the pool. Draper asked whether all swimmers needed this permit, to which the attendant replied, no, "only Negroes."[68] Three days later, the St. Louis chapter of the NAACP filed suit against Darst, O'Toole, Baumes, and the City of St. Louis in U.S. District Court on behalf of Draper and Taylor seeking a court order forcing the city to desegregate all of its municipal pools.[69]

The case was assigned to Judge Rubey M. Hulen. Hulen was a pensive-looking fifty-five year old man with dark hair and a long, stern face. He was a lifelong Missourian. Born in tiny Hallsville, Hulen attended night classes at Kansas City Law School, served as Boone County prosecutor, and was a Democratic Party leader in the state. His ascension to the federal judiciary resulted from political favoritism, not distinction as a jurist. President Franklin Roosevelt appointed him to the federal bench in 1944 as a favor to Missouri Senator Bennett Champ Clark, who Hulen helped get elected six years earlier.[70] If either party to the pool suit assumed that Hulen's small-town upbringing and membership in the state's political establishment meant that he was partial to the traditional practice of racial segregation, they were wrong.

In court, the city mounted a vigorous defense of its segregation policy. The city's attorney, who was appropriately named James Crowe, offered two principal arguments. First, he claimed that the city was in the process of constructing a relatively large outdoor pool at the Vashon Community Center that would be open to blacks. The city would therefore, Crowe argued, soon meet the constitutional standard of separate but equal established by the Supreme Court's 1896 *Plessy v. Ferguson* decision. He then claimed that the city was committed to integrating all of its swimming pools "as expeditiously as public feeling will permit," but asked the judge to permit them to move slowly so as to avoid additional violence.[71]

The plaintiff's attorney, S. R. Redmond, dismantled the city's defense through a series of strategic cross-examinations. First, he argued the city's superintendent of recreation John Turner into admitting that the soon-to-be-completed Vashon Pool was not in fact equal to Fairgrounds or Marquette Pools. It was much smaller and lacked a sandy beach. Turner also admitted that the indoor pools currently open to black citizens were "undoubtedly" less desirable than the outdoor pools. Redmond next cornered St. Louis chief of police Jeremiah O'Connell into admitting that the police could in fact maintain order at the outdoor pools if they were thrown open to blacks and whites. He asked O'Connell a clever question: "Would you say that the trouble at Fairgrounds on June 21, 1949 was due to incompetence in the police department?" Recognizing the trap, O'Connell stuttered and hedged, trying to think of a way out. Associate City Counselor John McCammon objected to the question, but Judge Hulen overruled. The police chief had to answer. Unwilling to take the blame for last year's debacle, O'Connell stated that the police could have maintained order if only he had been informed about the integration order ahead of time. Redmond then asked him if the police could maintain order if the pools were integrated this summer. "Yes," the chief replied. Redmond had effectively dismantled the city's principal arguments but that did not ensure victory. Black plaintiffs had learned through decades of less-than-color-blind justice to expect the worst.[72]

In his decision, Judge Hulen granted Draper and Taylor the injunction they sought, ordering the city to open Fairgrounds and Marquette Pools to black swimmers on July 19, 1950. Hulen first addressed the question of whether the city could legally exclude black citizens from the most desirable municipal pools if it promised to desegregate them at some later date, when racial prejudices had weakened. He mocked this argument as "a new and novel theory" of law. "Defendants would delay the granting of equal rights to plaintiffs, as guaranteed by the Constitution to some unannounced date to be determined by the Council of Human Relations. The law permits no such delay in protection of plaintiffs' constitutional rights."[73] Hulen next addressed the issue of the soon-to-be-completed Vashon Pool. He warned the city that even when it was completed and open to black residents, Vashon Pool would not make continued segregation at Fairgrounds and Marquette Pools constitutional. The Vashon Pool was, Hulen concluded, "in a setting far less attractive than the present outdoor pools." Citing the U.S. Supreme Court's recent *McLaurin v. Oklahoma State Regents for Higher Education* decision, Hulen stressed that separate facilities must be equal in fact.[74]

The judge, however, did not stop there. He tentatively waded into unchartered legal waters by suggesting that racial exclusion from any municipal pool, even if another truly equal pool were provided, might still violate the Constitution. A comparable pool "may mitigate discrimination," Hulen concluded, "but it will not validate it as to other sections of the city." Hulen seemed to be saying that a black swimmer who had to walk past a whites-only pool to get to a truly equal Jim Crow pool would not be receiving equal treatment under the law, as mandated by the Fourteenth Amendment. Convenience was a component of equality.[75]

James Crowe was startled by the implication of Hulen's ruling and asked him to stay the integration order until a higher court could review it. During a tense verbal exchange, Crowe pointed out that the decision conflicted with social tradition and legal precedent: "We feel that this cause presents a most serious question and most important decision. We feel that the condition that has existed—the status quo, if you will,—that has existed for this and many decades in this country, the decisions of the courts which have been in being, they have recognized as Constitutional rights equal facilities provided between the races." Unmoved, Hulen responded that neither social nor legal custom would make him disregard his oath to uphold the Constitution. "Does the viewpoint of the community set aside the Constitution?" Hulen asked Crowe. "Is the Constitution to be shelved for an hour, or set aside, because one part of the community happens to have an antipathy towards it? . . . I have no intention of putting my ear to the ground, to see what the people are thinking. I think any judge that would do that would be a dishonor to the bench."[76]

When Thurgood Marshall read a transcript of this exchange several weeks later, he forwarded it to two other NAACP attorneys with a note attached proclaiming, "This is really good." The future Supreme Court justice no doubt recognized in the sentiments of Judge Hulen—his rigid definition of equal and his unwillingness to be swayed by popular sentiment—a shift in the legal tide that would lead inevitably to the *Brown v. Board of Education* decision that he would argue before the U.S. Supreme Court four years later.[77]

Back in St. Louis, Judge Hulen's decision caused not one, but two social changes at Fairgrounds and Marquette Pools. Mayor Darst announced that the city would abide by the ruling, but added that beginning July 19 — the same day Hulen set for racial desegregation — the pools would become segregated along gender lines. Men and women would have to swim separately, Darst decided, if blacks and whites swam together.[78] The mayor had essentially turned the clocks back thirty-seven years to 1913, when an earlier city administration had simultaneously gender-integrated and racially segregated Fairgrounds Pool. Darst no doubt sensed that most whites still harbored the same sex-based racial prejudices that led the city to racially segregate the pools in the first place.

As it turned out, most white St. Louisians were not willing to accept any form of interracial swimming. They virtually stopped using the city's municipal pools after desegregation. On July 19 the police and white protesters outnumbered swimmers at Fairgrounds Pool almost forty to one: 170 police officers and about 200 white protesters watched as 10 swimmers (3 blacks and 7 whites) plunged into the enormous pool. Only three women entered Marquette Pool on its first day of interracial swimming — all of them were black.[79] The number of black swimmers gradually increased that first summer, as they felt secure about their safety, but the number of whites did not. A month after "integration," the *Post-Dispatch* reported that Fairgrounds and Marquette Pools "have been almost completely boycotted by residents in the vicinity who ordinarily use the facilities."[80] The boycotts were not short-lived. Before desegregation, the outdoor pools attracted hundreds of thousands of white swimmers each summer. Fairgrounds Pool recorded 313,000 swims during the summer of 1948. The pool was closed throughout 1949 because of the riot. The first summer of interracial swimming, 1950, the pool reported only 60,000 swims, 80 percent less than the last summer of "whites only" swimming. Even this number was artificially high because the pool was still segregated during the first month of summer, before Hulen's ruling took effect. The attendance statistics for subsequent summers reveal the full effect of desegregation: 10,000 swims in 1951, 20,000 in 1952, 20,000 in 1953, and 25,000 in 1954. The attendance at Marquette Pool was equally depressed, plummeting from an average of nearly 300,000 swims per summer to an average of 24,000. And, almost all the swimmers at both pools were now black.[81] In its 1954 *Annual Report*, the parks and recreation division blamed desegregation for the dwindling number of swimmers: "[I]t appears likely that the failure of the large outdoor pools to draw the huge number of swimmers that were attracted in the past may be a reflection of passive resistance to inter-racial swimming."[82]

〰〰〰 In 1956 St. Louis closed Fairgrounds Pool.[83] Just as the pool's opening back in 1913 foreshadowed a new era in the history of swimming pools, its closing symbolized the end of that era. Beginning in the mid-1950s, northern cities generally stopped building large resort pools and let the ones already constructed fall into disrepair. They became decrepit monuments of a bygone age when tens of millions of white Americans spent their summers swimming and suntanning at municipal pools. Although many whites abandoned desegregated municipal pools, most did not stop swimming. Instead, they built private pools, both club and residential, and swam in them instead. Racial integration was not the only cause of the dramatic proliferation of private swimming pools after the early 1950s, but it was a direct and immediate cause. As one disgruntled St. Louis citizen asked rhetorically in a letter to the *Post-Dispatch*, "What is going to happen to the whites who do not want to mix?" "They will go to a pool where they have to pay a fee," he answered.[84] And so they did.

CHAPTER 7

"ALONE IN THE BACKYARD"
SWIMMING POOLS IN RECENT
AMERICA

*I suppose like many people I really didn't believe when the issue had to be
faced that intelligent, well-educated, financially secure suburban middle-class
people would effectively exclude a neighbor from a community [swimming
pool] solely on the basis of race.—Frank Kratovil,* Washington Star *(1968)*

In 1961 New York City mayor Robert Wagner announced that the
city intended to construct a swimming pool in the northernmost section of
Central Park, just below 110th Street. Much like the Central Park pool John
Mitchel proposed back in 1910, Wagner intended it to provide recreation for
the disadvantaged "young people" who lived nearby.[1] Unlike Mitchel's proposal, the public responded favorably to Wagner's announcement. "Usually
a 'dissenter' when encroachments are attempted in Central Park," Irene
Roth Gould wrote the *New York Times*, "I am all for the building of the pool."
Gould's support rested on her assumption that the pool would combat juvenile delinquency in the city: "[It] can serve many of the underprivileged, who
may skate in winter, swim in summer, leaving little energy for miscreancy."[2]
Gould's justification of the pool reflected a fundamentally different view of
municipal pools than was common a generation earlier. In her mind, the
pool would serve as an asylum for poor inner-city youths, not as a community resort.

The proposed Central Park pool exemplified yet another redefinition of
municipal swimming pools, a redefinition that harkened back to the Progressive Era. During the 1960s, large cities once again built pools within or
near poor residential areas and intended them to combat crime and juvenile
delinquency by giving idle youths something constructive to do during the
summer. By the time Central Park's Lasker Pool opened in 1966, the ap-

parent need for inner-city pools had become particularly acute. Black Americans were rioting in cities across the country—burning, looting, and even killing. Local and national politicians believed that swimming pools would help alleviate the social tensions that precipitated the violence and quite literally cool down angry and frustrated urban blacks. With the help of federal "anti-poverty" funds, cities throughout the country built hundreds and hundreds of municipal pools, most within black "ghettos." It was a building spree reminiscent of the Great Depression. And yet, unlike the New Deal resort pools, the prototypical municipal pool of the late 1960s was small, shallow, offered no leisure space, and attracted only children. They were comparatively inexpensive and quick to construct but failed to provide viable recreation for America's urban poor.

The building spree was short-lived. Municipal-pool building slowed dramatically in the 1970s, when a prolonged fiscal crisis hit urban America. Rising budget deficits combined with diminishing tax bases precluded many cities from building new pools or even repairing and maintaining existing ones. As a result, municipal pools crumbled into disrepair. Pool closures became commonplace at the end of the century. Some cities closed a majority of their pools. The decline of municipal pools was evidenced in other ways as well. Attendance dropped steadily between 1970 and 2000, which contributed to the closures. Widely reported incidents of gang shootings, drug dealing, and sexual assaults at municipal pools stigmatized them as centers of urban crime and juvenile delinquency. As a result, many Americans came to see municipal pools not as antidotes to urban blight but as emblems of the urban crisis.[3]

The history of private swimming pools during the second half of the twentieth century is a very different story. Prior to 1950, only the richest Americans owned residential pools, and relatively few private club pools existed in the United States.[4] After 1950, however, the number of private swimming pools skyrocketed. Most private-pool building occurred in the suburbs. When Americans moved into postwar suburbs, they invariably chose to organize private-club pools rather than fund public pools. The "swim club" quickly became a ubiquitous suburban institution. The proliferation of residential pools was even more dramatic. By 1999, 4 million American families owned in-ground pools as compared to only 2,500 in 1950.[5]

Several factors enabled this dramatic growth. General economic prosperity, less expensive pool construction techniques, and mass suburbanization all created the material conditions necessary for millions of Americans to join private clubs or install backyard pools. The underlying cause of the private-pool boom, however, was middle-class Americans' desire to recreate within more socially selective communities. Private pools enabled Americans to exercise much greater control over whom they swam with than was possible at public pools. Joining a club pool ensured that other swimmers would be of the same social class and race. Installing an at-home pool ensured that other swimmers would be limited to family and friends.

The privatization of swimming pools during the second half of the twentieth century degraded the quality of community life in America. From the 1920s until the early 1950s, tens of millions of Americans frequented municipal pools each year. Hundreds and even thousands of people at a time interacted and socialized at these public spaces. Americans also determined cultural standards and the social boundaries of their communities at municipal pools. In short, community life was fostered, monitored, and disputed. After racial desegregation, millions of Americans consciously chose to stop swimming at municipal pools and chose instead to organize and join private swim clubs. Collectively, these choices represented a mass abandonment of public space and effectively resegregated swimming along class lines, which meant that the frequent and sustained interactions that occurred between middle-class and working-class Americans at municipal pools dwindled. As Robert Putnam points out in *Bowling Alone*, the lack of "repeated interactions with fellow citizens" has significant social costs. It breeds mistrust, intolerance, and a lack of empathy.[6] The proliferation of residential swimming pools represented not simply an abandonment of public space but a profound retreat from public life. At-home swimmers isolated themselves from their communities, even the white, middle-class crowds that congregated at club pools. They fenced themselves into their own backyards and almost everyone else out. As a result, public discourse diminished and the social life in American communities became further atomized.

Poor and working-class Americans suffered most directly from the privatizing of swimming pools. When middle-class Americans abandoned municipal pools in favor of private pools, cities downgraded the public importance of swimming pools. They built relatively few new pools, neglected maintenance on existing pools, and eventually closed dilapidated pools rather than pay for costly repairs. As a result, those Americans who could not afford to join a swim club or install a backyard pool had less access to swimming and recreation facilities than did previous generations. By the end of the twentieth century, many poor and working-class neighborhoods in American cities lacked appealing public spaces where residents could gather to socialize, exercise, relax, play, and forge community bonds. Middle-class abandonment of municipal pools also caused public officials to reconceive the design of pools. The municipal pools constructed during the second half of the twentieth century were almost never large resorts. Instead, cities built small, austere facilities that offered few of the amenities that made municipal pools so popular during the 1920s and 1930s. The assumption seemed to be that the urban poor required recreation asylums, not leisure resorts.

Municipal-pool building stalled during the fifteen years following the end of World War II. Whereas cities opened thousands of pools during the interwar years, they built relatively few between 1945 and 1960. Washington, D.C., and New York City combined opened nineteen pools during the 1930s but none during the fifteen years after World War II.[7] Kansas City likewise built no new pools between 1945 and 1960, even though it operated only three at the time.[8] St. Louis did open one new pool in 1959, but it was a replacement for the old Fairgrounds Park Pool, which closed in 1956. The new pool, however, was nothing like the original. It was rectangular, measured only 82 by 115 feet, and lacked a sandy beach.[9]

There were several reasons for the lack of new construction during the postwar period. In some communities, additional pools were not needed. Pool building during the interwar years had been so comprehensive that existing pools continued to meet local demand. At the same time, overall demand for public swimming facilities declined as many white swimmers abandoned municipal pools after racial desegregation. This was particularly true in the southern tier of northern states. Overall white attendance at public pools in St. Louis, Washington, D.C., and Kansas City dropped 60 to 80 percent. White attendance at some pools dropped by more than 90 percent.[10] Declining attendance made it difficult for public officials to justify costly new facilities. The fact that many municipal-pool swimmers were now poor and nonwhite also deterred new construction. Providing public recreation for the urban poor, especially black Americans, was not a priority during the postwar period.[11]

In addition to not building new pools, many cities closed existing ones—especially those serving minority swimmers—and underfunded maintenance and upkeep.[12] In Washington, D.C., for example, federal officials let McKinley Pool fall into disrepair after it was desegregated in 1950 and its use changed from exclusively white to "predominately" black. By 1960 the "pipes were corroded," the drainage system backed up, and the filtration system did not work properly. According to city engineers, the pool had become "a health hazard." Rather than repair it, which is what local residents wanted, the federal government decided to close it.[13] Public officials in Kansas City closed one of its pools in 1957 for similar reasons. After Grove Pool was desegregated in 1954, attendance plummeted and city officials began to view it as a financial burden, not a civic asset. Rather than pay the yearly operating deficit of $6,000, the city closed the facility even though it operated only two other swimming pools.[14] During the same period, Philadelphia closed its municipal pool located at Memphis and Albert streets and replaced it with a parking lot.[15] Swimming pools were clearly no longer the high public priority that they had been during the interwar years.

Public officials suddenly reconsidered the value of municipal pools during the mid-1960s however, when cities across the nation erupted into violence. According to one count, 329 separate "black riots" occurred in 257 American cities between 1964 and 1968.[16] Most of these riots occurred during the hottest days and nights of summer. The high heat and humidity made the already oppressive inner-city environment intolerable and heightened the frustrations of its inhabitants. In an effort to dampen the anger and frustration that inflamed the rioters, cities scrambled to build swimming pools as quickly as possible in their poorest neighborhoods, especially those populated by black Americans. One riot in particular highlighted the lack of municipal pools in poor, black neighborhoods and spurred a nationwide effort to redress the past neglect.

On a hot, mid-July afternoon in 1966, several teenagers opened a fire hydrant near the corner of Roosevelt Road and Loomis Street on Chicago's West Side. As was common, they crowded in front of the wide-mouth spout and let the cool water gush over their bodies. Before long, patrolmen Melvin Clark and Arthur Secor arrived in their police cruiser and shut off the hydrant. Opening hydrants was prohibited in Chicago although, according to the Chicago *Defender*, the city only seemed to enforce the ordinance in black neighborhoods. A local community leader, Chester Robinson, implored the officers to leave the hydrant open, explaining that it was the children's only source of relief from the heat. Clark and Secor refused. As the officers were leaving, Donald Henry emerged from the crowd that had gathered and reopened the hydrant. Miffed by this act of defiance, Clark and Secor moved to arrest him. "You're not going to let these policemen arrest me," Henry reportedly shouted to the crowd. "Why don't you do something about it?" The onlookers began throwing rocks at the two officers, who quickly retreated to their squad car and radioed for backup. Within minutes, fifteen more police cars had rushed to the scene. The crowd greeted them with a barrage of rocks, bottles, and bricks.[17]

The hydrant dispute sparked three days of intense rioting on Chicago's West Side. That first night, several hundred black men roamed the area smashing windows, burning buildings, and looting stores. The mob fought off the police with bricks, Molotov cocktails, and even gunfire. Two of the stores looted that night sold liquor, but the rioters were more intoxicated with anger than alcohol. "The police ain't gonna mess with me tonight," proclaimed one man. "I am not about to take nothin'. My jive is ready, man, and if a cop comes at me I'll give him some of what he dishes out."[18] The rioting escalated the next night as a larger mob roamed the area, burning and looting. When firemen arrived to douse the flames, rioters pelted them with rocks. When policemen attempted to arrest the looters and restore order, snipers hiding atop the high-rise public housing in the area shot at the officers. When the violence continued into a third day, Illinois Governor Otto Kerner dispatched 1,500 National Guardsmen, who patrolled the riot zone on foot and in jeeps mounted with .30 caliber machine guns. The guardsmen were given orders to shoot back if fired upon. Their overwhelming force eventually quelled the riot. In the end, three people were killed, countless were injured, and 300 were arrested. Six police officers were shot and many more were injured from the rocks and bricks. The amount of property damage was not immediately known.[19]

The fire-hydrant confrontation did not just precipitate the riot—it revealed an underlying cause of it as well. Black Chicagoans seethed with anger in part because they lacked summertime recreation opportunities, especially swimming pools. "Hell, it's so God Damn hot," explained one man. "I'll cool my ass anywhere I want to. They ought to take some of that poverty money and put a swimmin' pool over here." The *Chicago Defender* agreed, noting that "[a] swimming pool may be the most immediate need the community faces."[20] There were three municipal pools within a mile of the riot flashpoint, but they were inaccessible to black residents. The pools were located within white neighborhoods, where, according to one West Side resident, blacks "can't go without being beaten." Chester Robinson added, a bit hyperbolically, that a black swimmer would "need a Gatlin gun" to enter one of the nearby pools.[21] Even city officials acknowledged that the pools were not "readily available to Negroes because of hostility in the white communities." A few years earlier, for example, 750 whites attacked a group of black swimmers with bricks and stones as they left the South Side's Bessemer Park Pool.[22]

The conspicuous lack of municipal pools in Chicago's black neighborhoods dated back to the Progressive Era, when reform-minded public officials built ten pools in poor, immigrant neighborhoods near the stockyards and steel mills, but none within the emerging "black belt." During the interwar years, white swimmers and local residents effectively segregated the city's pools by assaulting and intimidating black swimmers.[23] Not much had changed by the 1960s. Ironically, black swimmers in Chicago, New York, and Detroit were worse off than those in Washington, Baltimore, and St. Louis. In these southern-tier cities, black residents gained access to most municipal pools after official segregation ended because blacks constituted a relatively large percentage of the population and were not as concentrated in just one or two neighborhoods. Desegregation rarely led to meaningful mixed-race swimming in these cities, but it did transfer use of many municipal pools to black swimmers. In more northern cities, especially large metropolises, no such transfer of use occurred during the 1950s. Black residents generally remained confined to neighborhoods with few municipal pools and still faced violent reprisal for attempting to swim in pools traditionally used by whites. The old means of de facto segregation still functioned.[24]

The fire-hydrant riot prompted Chicago officials to redress the historically inadequate provision of pools in the city's black neighborhoods. During the third day of violence, Martin Luther King Jr. met with Chicago mayor Richard Daley and advised him that swimming pools would help alleviate some of the tensions that caused the riot. Three days later, the city purchased ten small, pre-fabricated pools and quickly set them up in the "troubled neighborhoods." Daley also announced a long-range plan to build more than 100 "neighborhood pools" in the city.[25] The very first neighborhood pool opened a year after the riot and was located less than a block and a half from the disputed fire hydrant. Over the next two years, the city opened thirty-two new pools. Twelve were located within or next to public housing projects inhabited predominately by black Americans.[26]

The Chicago riot spurred a nationwide pool-building spree as well. Four days after the riot ended, President Lyndon Johnson announced that federal "anti-poverty" grants would be used to fund swimming pools for "disadvantaged youth" in cities across the country. Within a month, the federal government had disbursed pool money to forty metropolitan areas, including Chicago, New York, Philadelphia, Washington, and Atlanta.[27] New York City built thirty new pools over the next two years and eighty-four in total between 1966 and 1971. As in Chicago, the city targeted black neighborhoods in particular. The first two pools were located in Harlem's Morris Park and the Brownsville section of Brooklyn.[28] New York parks commissioner Thomas Hoving expressed the general sense of urgency for inner-city pools at the time: "Some projects that have waited five years to get built are going to have to wait another five years. Pools, school playgrounds, and street carnivals which reach the people in the ghetto have to come first."[29] Providing summer recreation for urban blacks had suddenly become a national priority.

Public officials intended the inner-city pools to cool off angry young men and make the summer months bearable for the poor and unemployed. The *New York Times* explained that the federal pool-building program was "designed in part to relieve the strong social pressures that build up in poor urban areas during the summer."[30] The *Chicago News* noted more colloquially that the pools were intended to "cool hot tempers" and "head off racial trouble."[31] City officials also intended the pools to show aggrieved black residents that local government was not ignoring their needs as had so often been the case in the past. They were a gesture toward improving the intolerable conditions that existed in inner cities at the time, especially during the long hot days and humid nights of summer.[32]

Most of the municipal pools opened during the late 1960s, however, did not provide viable recreation for teens and young adults. Seventy of the eighty-four pools opened in New York and all but one of the thirty-two pools opened in Chicago were "mini-pools." They were rectangular and measured only twenty by forty feet. They were a uniform three feet deep and could accommodate about forty children at a time. The pools were usually too crowded for actual swimming, so youngsters stood in the water talking and splashing. Nor did the mini-pools provide any leisure space. The tanks were surrounded by a narrow concrete perimeter and enclosed by a chain-link fence. Most did not even have dressing rooms, so swimmers traveled to the pools in their suits. Children in one New York neighborhood dubbed them "giant-sized urinals." And yet, hundreds of children frequently waited an hour or two in the hot sun for a chance to splash with friends.[33] Municipal pools were clearly needed, but mini-pools did not meet most people's needs.

Mini-pools were the prototypical municipal pool of the late 1960s, but some cities did build larger pools as well. The most noteworthy was Bedford-Stuyvesant's People's Pool. The residents of this poor, predominately black area of Brooklyn had been clamoring for a municipal pool for years. City officials finally agreed in 1966. At a cost of $4 million, the pool complex opened in 1971. It contained three tanks—a main pool 100 by 230 feet, a diving pool, and a shallow wading pool for young children. The facility also contained a playground and community amphitheater. It resembled the resort pools of the 1920s and 1930s in size but not appearance. The entire structure was vandal-proof concrete: concrete walls, concrete pool deck, decora-

Morris Park Pool, Harlem, New York, 1967. A typical mini-pool. Daniel McPartlin / New York City Parks Photo Archive, neg. M-58, 329913.

tive concrete blocks, and concrete walkways connecting the pools with the playground and amphitheater. The facility was utterly unnatural. There were no trees, no grass, and no sandy beach, just colorful graffiti-like art. Without the graffiti art, the People's Pool might have passed for a prison recreation facility.[34]

The municipal pool renaissance was short-lived. Whereas public pools were a national priority during the tumultuous late 1960s, pool building stalled during the 1970s. The primary reasons were economic. The 1970s were a period of "fiscal crisis in older central cities," according to urban historian Jon Teaford. New York City went bankrupt in 1975, and other large northern cities faced ballooning deficits and shrinking tax bases.[35] In an attempt to cut costs without eliminating existing services, cities abandoned plans for future pools and put off costly maintenance and repairs on existing

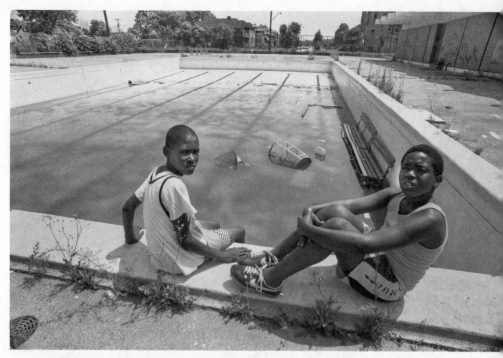

McCabe Pool, Detroit, 1989. Many northern cities neglected maintenance and repairs on municipal pools during the 1970s and 1980s, resulting in dilapidated and often unusable facilities. Detroit News Photo Archive.

pools. As a result, municipal pools deteriorated and came to reflect the poverty of urban America. "Boards have replaced broken windows. The water fountain is broken. Walls are smeared with graffiti. The ground is littered and a burned car sits in the parking lot."[36] Although a bit extreme, this description of a Detroit swimming pool captures the general state of municipal pools during the 1970s and 1980s, especially in large cities.

The fate of municipal pools in Youngstown, Ohio, exemplifies the general decline of public pools in the urban North. Between the end of World War II and the late 1960s, Youngstown operated six municipal pools. Yearly attendance at the pools averaged about 200,000.[37] The city opened two more pools during the 1970s for a total of eight. Thereafter, however, the city struggled to keep the pools open due to declining attendance and budget shortfalls. In 1981 the city's recreation commission planned to close two underused pools—Bailey and Chase—but decided instead to shorten the season at all eight pools. The pools closed that year on August 9, saving the city $50,000.[38] Pool attendance continued to decline after 1981. In 1984, the eight pools recorded a combined 42,835 swims—80 percent lower than pool attendance had been during the 1950s and 1960s. Attendance at four of the pools was particularly woeful. Mill Creek Pool averaged sixty-one swimmers a day, Lincoln fifty-seven, Johnson forty-four, and Chase Pool attracted an average of only thirty-three swimmers a day.[39] The following year, the city began closing its most underused facilities. Between 1985 and 1987, Youngstown closed Chase, Mill Creek, and Lincoln pools. "Financially, we can't afford to keep these places up," explained Parks and Recreation Commissioner Angelo Pignatelli. The city next closed Pemberton pool after the 1988 season, leaving residents with four pools—one for each region of the city.[40]

Violence, rowdiness, drug dealing, and vandalism also plagued Youngstown's municipal pools during this period. On one occasion, a group of swimmers maliciously threw a pool manager into the water and held him under until he nearly drowned. The manager quit that evening. Another altercation occurred between a college-age lifeguard and a misbehaving swimmer. As the lifeguard futilely sought to enforce the pool rules, the swimmer confronted the guard, stepped on his foot, and then cocked his elbow back threatening to pummel him with a closed fist.[41] In 1988 an all-out gang war occurred at North Side Pool. Rival youth gangs had battled for control of the pool throughout the summer. On a 100-degree August afternoon, the usual taunts and threats boiled over into a brawl involving 200 people. The lone security guard at the pool was no match for the young hooligans. They beat him, they beat bystanders, and they beat one another.[42] After the riot, hundreds of nearby residents petitioned the city to close the pool. They claimed that it turned their North Side neighborhood into a "crime zone" each summer. They cited fighting, drug use, vandalism, "undesirables hanging around," and even break-ins as a result of the pool. "I grew up near the pool, and I loved it," recalled Deborah Duffy, who still lived across the street. "But it's not a neighborhood pool anymore. The fights and the drugs have scared everybody away. I won't let my daughter go there, and nobody in the neighborhood will go there."[43]

Although Duffy did not mention race explicitly, it was a primary source of concern for local residents. Youngstown's North Side was racially diverse, but the pool was located within a white enclave. The city had officially desegregated its municipal pools back in the early 1950s, but racially divided use persisted into the 1980s.[44] This in large part explains why pool attendance remained relatively high during the 1960s and 1970s. The city's North Side had two pools during this period. Blacks predominated at Chase Pool and whites at North Side Pool. Duffy's mention of North Side Pool as a "neighborhood" institution recalled the days when it was used almost exclusively by whites. The racial composition of swimmers changed, however, when the city closed Chase Pool in 1986, and black swimmers migrated to North Side Pool. Two years later, the *Youngstown Vindicator* reported that "the vast majority of swimmers [at North Side Pool] are black." As Duffy indicated, local residents, most of whom were white, had stopped using it.[45]

In response to local efforts to close the pool, black community leaders lobbied the city to keep it open. City councilwoman Darlene Rogers pointed out that closing the pool would deprive area youths of one of the few recreation spaces accessible to them. "My concern is that it is the only pool left on the North Side. If we close the pool, there won't be any place for those kids to swim. And we don't have many other recreational activities for them."[46] The comments of Duffy and Rogers reveal the divergent views of municipal pools that had developed by the 1980s. Rogers viewed them as antidotes to inner-city living, whereas Duffy viewed them as sources of crime and delinquency.

The city decided not to close North Side Pool, but it could not justify operating all four pools given the minuscule attendance. In 1989 the city recorded 20,500 total swims at its remaining four pools and then 15,075 the following summer. Attendance now totaled roughly 8 percent of what it had been back in the 1950s and 1960s. The city closed two pools in 1991, leaving only Borts and North Side pools still open. Between 1985 and 1991, Youngstown closed 75 percent of its municipal pools.[47] As of 2004, the city still operated only two pools and attendance had dropped even further, to about 10,000 a year.[48]

The story in other northern cities was much the same. Because of neglect during the 1970s, the physical condition of New York City's pools was dreadful by the early 1980s. "There is decay in these old structures," wrote the *New York Times* in 1981. "Maintenance is minimal. Obviously vandalism is ever present throughout the system."[49] The comptroller's office offered a similarly scathing assessment four years later. Only three of the city's thirty-six full-sized outdoor pools were in an acceptable condition. In total, inspectors found 136 problems severe enough to be termed "hazardous."[50] Because of the deterioration and the high cost of operation, the city closed some of its large outdoor pools and most of its mini-pools. Of the seventy small pools opened between 1966 and 1971, only twenty-three remained in 1994.[51] The destruction of municipal pools in Pittsburgh came later than in New York but was far more severe. Between 1996 and 2004, the city permanently closed twenty of its thirty-two pools in an effort to reduce its ballooning budget deficit. Some members of the city council complained that pools should be one of the last city services suspended, but most did not agree. As a result of the closings, Pittsburgh offered residents fewer municipal pools in 2005 than it had in 1925.[52]

In 1991 a *New Yorker* article commented on the pool closings in New York City. The author claimed that closing municipal pools significantly degraded the quality of community life in the city. The neighborhood pools, he observed, brought people together and provided a public space—amid the high-rise apartments, passing cars, and hurrying pedestrians—where neighbors actually communicated with one another. Closing the pools, he implied, would make local residents more anonymous to one another and erode the local sense of community that they fostered. The author also related the pool closings to what he saw as the increasing privatization of life in the city. New Yorkers, he noted, spent untold billions on Hampton summer homes, artwork and furnishings, and entertainment. And yet, amid such plenty, the city could not afford to operate its municipal pools. "We are not poor as a people, yet somehow we have become bankrupt as a society. We are—to use an old-fashioned word—*ruined*. . . . We seem to have accepted two separate economies: one of abundance, ruling the way that many of us eat and sleep and entertain ourselves, and one of absolute hand-to-mouth impoverishment, ruling our civic life."[53] The closing of municipal pools only added to the civic poverty.

≈≈≈ In 1959 the *Washington Star* surveyed the capital's public pools and noted the conspicuous absence of white swimmers. As in other cities, white Washingtonians had largely abandoned public pools after they were racially desegregated. The paper wondered where all the white swimmers had gone. Had they stopped swimming? T. Sutton Jett, a local recreation official, provided the answer. Whites had not stopped swimming, Jett told the *Star*; rather, they had switched to swimming in private pools. Jett estimated that 125 club pools had opened in the Washington, D.C., area since 1953, and dozens more were under construction. Private pools appealed to white swimmers, Jett surmised, because access could be restricted to "members and their guests."[54] In this way, the abandonment of public pools and the proliferation of private pools were inextricably linked. White, middle-class Americans organized and joined club pools precisely because they did not want to swim in socially unrestricted waters, and the availability of private pools surely made the decision to stop using public pools easier.

Private club pools were mostly a suburban phenomenon. As millions of mostly white American families moved into suburbs following World War II, they found an inadequate supply of swimming pools.[55] A small number of country club pools existed in established suburbs, but new subdivisions obviously lacked existing pools.[56] Some postwar suburbs, most famously Levittown, included swimming pools in the community plan, but most did not.[57] So suburbanites took it upon themselves to build their own. Beginning in the early 1950s, neighbors joined together to form swimming pool associations. Three hundred to four hundred families pooled their resources in order to build a swim club. Depending on the size of the pool and the number of members, each family usually contributed between $150 and $200 for an ownership share, which covered the initial construction cost, and then paid yearly dues for upkeep and operating expenses. In 1958, 125 of these club pools were operating in the Washington, D.C., area with a combined membership of about 40,000 families.[58] That same year, the *Philadelphia Evening Bulletin* reported that "swim-club pools have sprung up in every direction."[59]·

Swimming pools served a vital social function in the nation's burgeoning suburbs. These new communities lacked the social bonds that knit older communities together. Neighbors did not know one another, nor did they necessarily share the same ethnic or religious heritage. Furthermore, single-family homes in sprawling suburbs best navigated in a car tended to isolate families from their neighbors. This spatial arrangement afforded residents desired privacy, but that privacy could turn into isolation. Swimming pools brought suburban families together. They were one of the few civic spaces where suburbanites could socialize and integrate themselves into the community. The *Philadelphia Evening Bulletin* commented in 1958 that joining a swim club served as "a means of becoming acquainted with neighbors, forming friendships among children and uniting a community in a common purpose. The community swim pool is an investment not only in money but in neighborhood co-operation, enjoyment and friendliness."[60] Club pools were vital social centers in America's postwar suburbs.

Suburban communities could have chosen to fund public pools—which would have served the same social function at less cost and effort per family—but most did not. In July 1954 Donald Hunt, chairman of the Montgomery County Council in Maryland, noted that there was "no interest" in public pools, even though a dozen groups were organizing private swim clubs in the county at the time. Montgomery County did not open its first public pool until 1968.[61] As late as 1974, Montgomery County and neighboring Prince George's County operated a total of two public pools. By contrast, there were well over 100 club pools scattered throughout the two counties.[62] The same was true in suburban Philadelphia. The *Philadelphia Inquirer* reported in

1964 that "private swim clubs are flourishing in all areas of suburban Philadelphia" but counted only one public pool in Delaware County.[63]

Suburbanites organized private club pools rather than fund public pools because club pools enabled them to control the class and racial composition of swimmers, whereas public pools did not. As one critic commented in 1955, club pools were built "not for all persons regardless of race or creed, but for a group of affluent citizens."[64] Class exclusion was achieved through residency requirements and membership fees. Many pool associations mandated that most or all members had to live within a certain distance of the club or within a particular subdivision.[65] This limited the social makeup of the membership to the social makeup of the community. The typical $200 membership fee and $30 annual dues reinforced the residency requirement by restricting membership to families earning a middle-class income. Finally, as one writer made clear, the tasks necessary to organize a private swim club were definitely white-collar work: "If you can, include [among the founding members] an engineer, a lawyer, a contractor, and architect and/or an accountant. The architect and engineer can work on site selection and planning. A lawyer can untangle zoning codes and create the non-profit body corporate. An accountant can keep the records."[66] As a result of their social exclusivity, club pools redivided swimmers along class lines. Americans from different social classes once again swam and socialized at different pools.

The primary appeal of club pools, however, was the assurance of not having to swim with black Americans. Civil rights laws applied only to "public accommodations," so private pools could legally continue to exclude black swimmers even after the courts had forced cities to desegregate municipal pools. Many swim clubs, especially those located in suburbs accessible to black Americans, explicitly barred black families from joining. For example, swim clubs in Chevy Chase, Bethesda, and other suburbs close to Washington, D.C., passed bylaws when they first organized in the 1950s that limited membership to white persons.[67] Other swim clubs relied on the racial exclusivity of their surrounding neighborhood to prevent black families from joining. One club in suburban Maryland passed a residency requirement in 1958 mandating that members live within three-fourths of a mile of the pool. So few blacks lived in the area that the club did not receive a membership application from a black family until 1968. When the first black family applied, the club rejected its application, and the membership quickly voted not to allow any black members. Since the club could no longer rely on residential segregation to protect the racial composition of its membership, it now needed an explicit policy.[68] Noting the pervasive discrimination against black

Americans at club pools, a Washington, D.C., judge lamented, "I suppose like many people I really didn't believe when the issue had to be faced that intelligent, well-educated, financially secure suburban middle-class people would effectively exclude a neighbor from a community [swimming pool] solely on the basis of race."[69] In this case, he clearly misunderstood the suburban middle class.

It is also clear that racial desegregation deterred suburban communities from building public pools during the 1950s and 1960s. Again, Montgomery County offers a particularly revealing example. In May 1955 the county council authorized construction of two public swimming pools. Its rationale was that moderate-income residents could not necessarily afford membership at a private club.[70] The council suddenly scrapped the two pools one month later, however, just days after a federal court ordered that public recreation facilities throughout Maryland be racially desegregated.[71] A year earlier, a local citizen had asked rhetorically, "Is [approving club pools] to be the easy way for the County Council, other municipal bodies and civic associations to avoid the issue of public pools?"[72] In many suburban communities, the answer was yes.

Racial exclusion at private pools came under attack during the mid-1960s, as black families moved into suburbs served by whites-only club pools. After breaking the residential color-barrier, black suburbanites sought to break the pool color-barrier as well. An early challenge occurred in 1965, after Paul Sullivan rented a house in a Fairfax County, Virginia, suburb to a black couple, Theodore and Laura Freeman. Freeman was an economist at the U.S. Department of Agriculture. Sullivan included a membership at the nearby Little Hunting Park Swim Club with the rental. After the Freemans registered at the pool, however, the club's board of directors revoked their membership. Sullivan, who was also a member, protested, claiming that the board's decision was based solely on racial prejudice. He circulated a petition among the club's membership, made phone calls to the board members accusing them of bigotry, and wrote letters to local religious leaders—including the board president's pastor—claiming that the club had perpetrated a "real moral evil." Eventually, the board agreed to let the entire club vote whether to admit the Freemans. On July 29, hundreds of members crowded into a local elementary school gymnasium to decide the matter. The Freemans attended the meeting to show everyone that they were a likable, middle-class family. Even so, a majority of the club's membership refused to admit them. Most members did not want to swim with blacks no matter their class status and personal disposition.[73]

Three years later, a similar dispute arose at another Washington-area pool. Dr. Harry Press, chief radiologist at Howard University, his wife Francella, and their two daughters had purchased a home in Wheaton, Maryland, a suburban community north of the capital. In the spring of 1968, the Presses applied for membership at the Wheaton-Haven Recreation Association, a swim club located a few blocks from their home. The board of directors summarily rejected their application.[74] Later that summer, a white couple who belonged to the same pool, Murray and Rosalind Tillman, brought Grace Rosner as their guest. Rosner's appearance created quite a stir. "It was such a terribly big scene," she later recalled. "There was this man shouting and carrying on. I was so mortified and so . . . angry. He was a member of the association board. He was obnoxious, but he never said 'nigger' or anything. He never even said anything to me directly, but he kept saying things like, 'she ain't coming in here.'" Eventually, the pool manager let Rosner into the pool, but the board of directors held an emergency meeting the next day to pass a more restrictive guest policy. Only relatives of members would henceforth be admitted as guests.[75] Since no blacks were members, the new policy ensured they would not enter as guests either.

The Tillmans, the Presses, and Grace Rosner joined together and filed suit in federal court, claiming that the club violated both the 1866 Civil Rights Act and the more recent Civil Rights Act of 1964 by denying membership and guest privileges on the basis of race. The critical legal question was whether the Wheaton-Haven Recreation Association was, in the eyes of the court, a private club. Both civil rights laws applied only to public accommodations. The club claimed that it was a private organization, and therefore its board of directors could refuse to admit anyone it pleased. The plaintiffs countered that the pool operated as a public facility—except when it came to admitting black members—and therefore should be legally treated as one. In siding with the swim club, the U.S. District Court for Maryland and the U.S. Court of Appeals for the Fourth Circuit both concluded that the association was a private club and dismissed the case. The courts justified the decision by pointing to the apparent fact that at least one white family had been denied membership. This was a critical point because it seemed to indicate that the pool was not simply a "public accommodation masquerading as a club" in order to "exclude persons of other races." The judges also emphasized the association's inherent class exclusivity to support their conclusion that the organization was private. "Some considerations of social and financial standing are implicit in the size of the fees and dues," which meant that there were "selective elements other than race alone."[76]

The Tillmans, the Presses, and Rosner appealed the ruling to the U.S. Supreme Court, where they were joined in their fight by some powerful allies. The U.S. Department of Justice, the Maryland Commission on Human Relations, and Montgomery County all filed *amici curiae* (friend of the court) briefs urging the justices to apply civil rights laws to club pools. The participation of the federal, state, and local governments on behalf of the plaintiffs indicated how much the political tide had shifted by the late 1960s. Whereas public institutions had lined-up against black swimmers to prevent interracial swimming in the 1930s and 1940s, they now fought to ensure equal access. In its unanimous ruling, the Supreme Court concluded that the pool was, as far as the law was concerned, a public accommodation and therefore subject to the Civil Rights Act of 1964. Membership was "open to every white resident" who lived within three-quarters mile of the pool, wrote Justice Blackmun, "there being no selective element other than race." The one white family denied membership, it was discovered, lived more than three-quarters of a mile from the club and was not admitted for that reason. In essence, the justices concluded that the primary reason this suburban community organized a private swim club rather than a public pool was so its residents could avoid swimming with black Americans.[77]

Even though the Presses triumphed in court, they never joined the club. By the time the Supreme Court issued its ruling in 1973, they had installed a pool in their backyard. The family made a special event of "integrating" the residential pool by throwing the Tillmans' daughter into it fully clothed. The Presses, Tillmans, and Grace Rosner had all become friends during their collective fight against racial discrimination. When a local paper asked Rosner if she intended to swim at the Wheaton-Haven pool, she replied with a wry smile, "Sure, you bet I do."[78]

〜〜〜〜 The Presses were just one of several million American families that installed a swimming pool at their home during the second half of the twentieth century. Much as with club pools, residential pool-building was enabled by mass suburbanization and expanding economic prosperity. Large backyards provided the space necessary for a residential pool and rising salaries made them affordable to the middle class. These material developments, however, do not explain why having a pool in one's backyard appealed to so many Americans. Residential pools became so popular after the mid-1950s because they satisfied several desires common among the suburban middle class. For one, they advertised material success and upward mobility. Installing a backyard pool was a conspicuous way for status-conscious Americans to show who was getting ahead.[79] Residential pools also enhanced domestic family life by keeping mom, dad, and the kids at home to recreate. Finally, backyard pools enabled Americans to retreat from public life. They provided the privacy, security, and social exclusivity that so many suburbanites desired during the tumultuous postwar decades.

In 1950 *Beach and Pool* magazine counted only 2,500 residential swimming pools in the United States.[80] At the time, Americans rightly associated them with Hollywood stars and Long Island estates. Over the next twenty years, however, the number of residential pools in the United States increased rapidly, and pool ownership was democratized. This building spree began in 1952. Americans built about 7,000 residential pools that year and about the same number each of the next three years. By the end of 1955, the number of residential pools nationwide topped 26,000.[81] Despite the tenfold increase since 1950, backyard pools were still beyond the means of middle-class Americans. In 1954 a real-estate developer offered pools as an add-on feature to homes he was building in a Long Island subdivision. The homes stood on two-acre plots and cost more than $40,000. The pool was an additional $4,500. This was not Levittown.[82] Two years later, the *St. Louis Post-Dispatch* noted that "while [backyard] pools are becoming more popularly afforded every year, they're still not cheap."[83]

Residential-pool building exploded after 1956 precisely because backyard pools became affordable to the middle class. Americans built 30,500 such pools in 1957; 37,400 the following year; and 46,200 in 1959. Families with an annual income between $7,000 and $12,000 purchased half of all the at-home pools installed in 1957. As one observer noted, this was "a far cry from a few year ago, when most pools were sold to families with incomes above $25,000—and, in many cases, $100,000."[84] One of the definitive symbols of the leisure class had suddenly become accessible to the middle class.

Several factors contributed to the affordability of residential pools during the late 1950s. The unprecedented economic prosperity of the period meant that many more American families could afford to install backyard pools. Per capita income grew by 35 percent between 1945 and 1960, and the country's gross domestic product rose nearly 250 percent. Real wages among American workers increased more during the 1950s than in the previous half-century. This prosperity swelled the ranks and bank accounts of the middle class. The number of salaried employees increased 61 percent between 1947 and 1957, and, by the mid 1950s, 60 percent of American households earned a "middle-class income" as compared to 31 percent during the 1920s.[85] These tens of millions of middle-class Americans had money to spend on cars, televisions, and even swimming pools. They also bought homes in record numbers. More Americans purchased single-family homes between 1946 and 1956 than in the previous 150 years. Sixty-two percent of American families owned their own homes in 1960 as compared to 43 percent in 1940. Furthermore, 85 percent of the new housing starts during this period were in the suburbs.[86] These suburban homes provided Americans the physical space necessary to build backyard pools.

At the same time, the cost of residential pools dropped due to an improved construction technique. The "Gunite method" enabled builders to spray a concrete mixture of dry sand, cement, and water through an air-pressurized hose into a steel-meshed cage formed into the shape of the pool. At $3,000 to $4,000, many middle-class Americans could afford a Gunite pool.[87] Financing also helped make residential pools more affordable. Prior to the 1950s, banks generally refused to loan money for at-home pools. The lack of financing meant that only those people who could pay the full cost of the pool upfront could afford to buy one. During the 1950s, however, banks reclassified pools as home improvements and began loaning money for their construction. By 1958 more than two-thirds of all residential pools built in the United States were financed through banks or mortgage and loan companies.[88]

Financing, large backyards, and disposable income explain how middle-class Americans were able to own their own swimming pools, but they do not explain why residential pools became so popular. Americans chose to add swimming pools onto their homes during the 1950s for the same reasons they moved out to the suburbs in the first place. For one, residential pools promised to strengthen family relationships by providing an at-home space for the whole family to recreate. According to historian Stephanie Coontz, "[t]he 1950s was a pro-family period if there ever was one. . . . the family was everywhere hailed as the most basic institution in society."[89] Residential pools appealed to suburbanites because they reinforced this domestic culture. Pool owners often cited keeping the family at home as a primary reason for purchasing backyard pools. A suburban Philadelphia family, for example, installed a backyard pool in 1955 after the arrival of their fourth child. "It's wonderful to know where they are," explained Mrs. Allan Johnson. "Even more wonderful to know this will continue to be true in the years ahead." When asked in 1957 why he thought so many families were buying residential pools, a pool builder responded, "[I]t's a good way to keep the children at home."[90]

Residential swimming pools also appealed to America's burgeoning middle class because they were emblems of success and upward mobility.

"Of all the symbols of wealth you can imagine," the *Washington Star* wrote in 1957, "having a private swimming pool for your own family probably would rank among the highest."[91] Backyard pools were status symbols that accorded owners social prestige. The *New York Times* noted in 1957 that "the man with his own pool is likely to be a middle-class commuter or small city professional, who may or may not be able to swim, but is certainly in a position to impress his neighbors."[92] As the quote suggested, pool ownership at this time signaled individual success. The family with a pool in its backyard was keeping ahead of the Joneses.

Finally, backyard pools enabled owners to control their social environment. Whereas joining a private club ensured that members would swim with people of the same class and race, installing a residential pool ensured that owners would swim only with friends and family. One Long Island resident explained in 1956 that he installed a backyard pool because membership policies at private clubs had become too liberal: "Almost anyone can join a beach club. They've had to take in members to make up the deficit. It's the man with the pool in his yard who gets ahead these days."[93] Private pool owners also sought to escape the crowds that congested club pools and beaches. "Our [local] pool is so crowded on a hot day," complained one suburbanite, "that you can't dive in without getting tangled up in a pair of flippers or impaled on a snorkel. The nearest beach is fifteen miles away and the traffic is awful. With three kids we were stuck." What was the family's solution? "We built a pool for $3,500 and are finally living the kind of life we moved out here to find."[94] Residential pools facilitated the private, domestic, and comfortable life that suburbanites desired during the postwar period.

The trend toward swimming at home accelerated during the 1960s. By 1965 Americans owned 575,000 residential pools. Five years later, the total reached almost 800,000. "Just about any wage earner, it seems, can afford to own a pool," observed the *Philadelphia Evening Bulletin* in 1965.[95] This was an overstatement, but a new construction method using vinyl rather than cement did further reduce the cost of an in-ground pool. Pool builders dug a hole in the ground, lined the sides and bottom with concrete blocks, wood, or cheap metal, and then draped thick-gauge vinyl over it to prevent leaks. Dubbed "blue-collar pools" by some in the industry, the vinyl pools cost under $3,000 as compared to the nearly $5,000 that a concrete Gunite pool cost at the time.[96] One-third of all residential pools installed in 1965 were vinyl-lined. Concrete pools were still the most popular with a 57 percent market share. Comparatively expensive aluminum pools were a distant third in sales.[97]

The further democratization of pool ownership during the 1960s subtly eroded the popular perception of residential pools as symbols of upward mobility and high social status. In 1967 the *Philadelphia Evening Bulletin* encapsulated how commonplace they had become: "We seemed to have moved from the fabulous idea of a chicken in every pot to a swimming pool in every backyard."[98] As the quotation suggests, residential pools were no longer symbols of individual success but rather reflected a general standard of living in middle-class America. Owning a backyard pool now meant keeping up with the Joneses but not necessarily surpassing them.

After the 1960s, residential pool building fluctuated with the ups and downs of the American economy. During periods of prosperity and optimism, pool sales boomed. When the economy lagged, pool sales typically followed. During the 1970s, "stagflation," rising unemployment, and general economic uncertainty caused the number of in-ground pool starts to drop from 83,500 in 1972 to 66,000 in 1975.[99] The economic malaise of the period also spurred the market for less expensive alternatives to the traditional in-ground pool. Americans purchased 300,000 aboveground pools in 1974, which was six times the number of in-ground pools installed that year. Aboveground pools were typically round, with an eighteen-foot diameter and a depth of between three and a half and five feet. They cost between $500 and $1,000, as compared to between $5,000 and $8,000 for an in-ground pool. Despite their popularity during the 1970s, aboveground pools had an image problem. "They are not exactly pretty," observed the *Washington Post* in 1975. "While the inviting pool's cool, blue water may make you forget the high-rise framework in the summer, you might think about what you're going to do with it in the winter. Is that really the view you want out your back window?"[100] Eventually, their conspicuous appearance and popularity among working-class and lower-middle-class families led some critics to stigmatize aboveground pools as tacky symbols of social pretension.

The economic recovery of the mid-1980s—at least for the middle and upper classes—reignited the residential pool building boom. Americans installed 113,400 pools in 1984, 120,500 in 1986, and 149,000 in 1989. Concerns about water pollution and beach closings along the Atlantic also spurred sales. With beaches from New England to the Mid-Atlantic littered with medical and industrial waste, chicken bones, and broken bottles, a chlorinated backyard pool seemed much more sanitary than the Atlantic Ocean. In 1990 the total number of in-ground residential pools in the United States approached 3 million. California and Florida had the most, followed by northeastern states such as New York, Pennsylvania, New Jersey, and Connecticut.[101] Residential-pool building continued to boom during the prosperous 1990s. In 1998 Americans installed 172,184 pools, more than in any previous year. At the end of the century, the total number of in-ground residential pools in the United States topped 4 million.[102]

Many of the residential pools installed around the turn of the century were monuments to the astounding personal wealth many Americans had accumulated. In 2000 retired Wall Street CEO Matthew Cody commissioned a pool "worthy of boom times," according to the *New York Times*. He hired a small army of construction and landscape specialists to build an elaborate pool at his Belle Terre home. The pool was shaped like a half moon with a raised spa in the middle. A bridge connected the spa with the backyard, which was outfitted with fountains, a cabana, a pavilion, and a barbeque area. All of this sat atop a 110-foot bluff overlooking Long Island Sound. The total cost was between $1.5 and $1.7 million. Cody built his backyard retreat in order to escape from Long Island society. "There is nothing like walking out your backdoor and into your own little world," he told the *New York Times*. "Going to the Hamptons and doing all that is nice, but no matter when you go it's almost always traffic now. Sitting in traffic is not my idea of enjoying oneself. That's why we are building this."[103] That same year, Laurie and Scott Booth installed a designer pool behind their South Barrington, Illinois, home. The pool resembled a natural lagoon, with rock formations, a waterfall, and lush vegetation. The pool also featured very modern design elements, including a deck with sharp geometric lines, a raised platform in the middle of the water, and a bridge arching out to the island. The Booths' commissioned such an elaborate pool because they did not want their private oasis to resemble a typical pool. "We didn't want some stark white, rectangular pool like you see at the park district," they explained.[104] As had been the trend since the 1950s, the Codys and the Booths used their wealth to separate and distinguish themselves from the general public.

While privacy was a primary appeal of residential pools, some families concluded that swimming in their own backyard was just plain lonely. "This swimming pool isn't that neat all of a sudden," concluded Buckie Padgett. Padgett explained that after installing a pool at their Long Island home, her family began to feel isolated from their friends and the larger community. So the Padgetts joined a local beach club and mostly stopped swimming at home.[105] The family's decision was surprisingly common. In 1976 the *Philadelphia Evening Bulletin* reported on the paradoxical trend of residential-

Residential Pool, South Barrington, Illinois, 2000. At the end of the twentieth century, many wealthy Americans installed elaborate residential pools that provided domestic oases for their families. Courtesy of Mariani Landscape, Lake Bluff, Illinois.

pool owners joining community swim clubs. The reason, according to the paper, was that "they get bored swimming with their own families and want a change of scenery."[106] In 1999 more families in Massachusetts filled-in existing pools than built new ones. Susan Marandett, who spent thousands of dollars to decommission her family's backyard pool, explained, "if we kept the pool, it would be hard to justify our joining a swimming complex, which is far more fun for my kids than to be alone in the backyard."[107]

〜〜〜〜 The privatizing of swimming pools corroborates Robert Putnam's claim in *Bowling Alone* that the quality of community life in America has deteriorated due to a widespread retreat from public life. The choices of millions of Americans to join private club pools and install residential pools exemplify what Putnam calls "civic disengagement." And yet, the timing and causes of pool privatization complicate Putnam's interpretation. He claims that community life flourished during the 1950s and 1960s and then began to decline during the 1970s. He explains the timing of the flourishing and then the decline primarily as generational turnover. Americans who came of age during the Great Depression and World War II, he claims, were exceptionally active in the civic life of their communities. By the 1970s and 1980s, this generation was beginning to pass away. Subsequent generations, according to Putnam, have been much less civically active. Furthermore, Putnam explicitly downplays racial prejudice and racial desegregation as causes of Americans' retreat from public life. "[My] evidence is not conclusive," Putnam concludes, "but it does shift the burden of proof onto those who believe that racism is a primary explanation for growing civic disengagement."[108]

The history of swimming pools locates the beginning of civic disengagement in the 1950s and 1960s—the period when Putnam claims community life flourished—and links it quite clearly with racial prejudice and racial desegregation. Between 1950 and 1970, millions of Americans chose to stop swimming at municipal pools. This represented a mass abandonment of public space and was caused most directly by racial desegregation. When municipal pools were desegregated, white swimmers generally fled. Those who could afford the expense organized or joined private club pools. The primary appeal of club pools was that members could avoid interacting with people who were socially different from themselves. Club pools contributed to a vibrant community life, but access to these communities was restricted along class and racial lines. Although difficult to prove empirically, the absence of meaningful interaction between socially diverse people and the lack of an immediate common interest—such as a shared swimming pool—surely hardened social divisions, limited understanding of and empathy for people who were socially different, and segmented community life.

The proliferation of residential pools, which also began during the postwar period, represented a much more profound civic disengagement. Between 1950 and 1970, nearly 800,000 American families spent considerable sums of money in order to recreate at home rather than in public. They installed backyard pools precisely because they wanted to turn inward and privilege family over community. As Alexis de Tocqueville observed back in the nineteenth century, "each person, withdrawn into himself, behaves as though he is a stranger to the destiny of all the others. His children and his good friends constitute for him the whole of the human species. . . . And if on these terms there remains in his mind a sense of family, there no longer remains a sense of society."[109] This retreat from public life accelerated after 1970, when 3 million more American families installed at-home pools. But, it originated during the postwar period among the generation that came of age during the Great Depression and World War II.

〰〰 In 1988 a local dispute in East Hampton, Long Island, received national attention. A couple was threatening to sue the town for refusing a permit to build a second swimming pool at the couple's oceanfront home. The second pool was necessary in part, Joseph Papandrea claimed, because a neighbor was building a two-story house that would overlook the existing pool and take away the couple's privacy. "We won't be able to go nude sunbathing anymore," he explained. While the dispute hinged on issues of zoning restrictions and environmental protection, the story was widely reported due to its almost comical justification of Thorstein Veblen's 1899 critique of the "leisure class." While one backyard pool was an emblem of comfort and affluence, two pools at an oceanfront home exemplified conspicuous consumption run amuck.[110]

At the same time, a different sort of swimming pool controversy was raging in Greenpoint, New York. Residents of this Brooklyn neighborhood bitterly disagreed about what should be done with the crumbling remains of McCarren Pool, one of the giant New Deal pools opened back in 1936. Larger than a football field, it could accommodate 6,800 swimmers at a time and, according to the *New York Times*, had served as "the hub of the working-class neighborhood's summertime social life." Over the years, however, the pool had been "devastated by neglect, vandals and drug addicts." The city eventually closed it in 1983. Some in the community, especially Latino and black residents, wanted the pool restored to its former splendor. Other area residents, mostly whites, wanted the pool closed permanently or rebuilt on a much smaller scale. They feared that such a large public pool would become a locus for urban crime and social disorder. "Put 6,000 people in one pool and you can imagine the chaos that will follow," explained one critic.[111]

These two episodes reveal the diverse and often discordant social and cultural meanings Americans attached to swimming pools at the end of the twentieth century. Private pools came to symbolize, sometimes in an extreme way, the "good life"—a life of material comfort and leisure—and yet also domestic isolation. Public pools evoked very different images. For some, they exemplified urban decay, while others saw in them the possibility of a rejuvenated and vibrant community life. The Greenpoint controversy shows that public debate at and about municipal pools was not silenced by the privatization of swimming pools after 1950. However, too many controversies in contemporary America resemble the East Hampton dispute: people fighting to get away from their community rather than fighting to be part of it.

THE PROMISE AND REALITY
OF SWIMMING POOLS AS PUBLIC
SPACES

While conducting the research for this project, I frequently visited the swimming pools I was studying, if they still existed. On one occasion, I spent an evening at Athletic Park Pool in Newton, Kansas—the same pool that Samuel Ridley attempted to desegregate back in the 1930s. In some ways, the scene in 2000 was much as it might have been during the swimming pool age. Hundreds were congregated at the pool. Children played in the water and waited in line for the diving board. Teens gathered around the concession stand and chased one another on the lawn. Some fathers played in the pool with their children, but most adults sat along the pool deck chatting with friends and neighbors. The pool was the town's social center that warm summer evening. In other ways, however, the scene in 2000 was markedly different than it would have been back in the 1930s. Most notably, blacks, Hispanics, and whites all mingled together, content to be a part of the same community. I seemed to be the only one who noticed or cared that the crowd was racially diverse. And yet, as an outsider, I could not tell anyone's social position. Some swimmers may have been affluent; others may have been poor and unemployed. Whatever inequalities and social divisions existed in Newton, they were not apparent at the pool. Once people left their cars and changed into their swimsuits, signs of social status were difficult to detect.

After spending the day at Newton's public library reading about how Athletic Park Pool divided residents back in the 1930s, my swim that evening reminded me of the promise of municipal pools as public spaces. Swimming pools and public space generally have the potential to foster a vibrant community life by counteracting many of the segmenting and alienating aspects of modern life. They offer an informal social space—a meeting ground—where people separated by social differences, large yards and high fences, busy lives, and electronic entertainment can interact and communicate face to face. Municipal pools can humanize relationships between people. They enable the sustained and unhurried interaction necessary for members of a community to meet, forge bonds of friendship, and develop a sense of shared interest and identity. This is what a reporter for the *Wilmington Evening Journal* observed at Price Run Pool back in 1925. He wrote that "everyone seemed imbued with the community spirit." Residents became "acquainted with each other" at the pool and "cement[ed] bonds of community friendship."[1] The same was true at Newton's Athletic Park Pool when I visited it in 2000.

The scene at Athletic Park Pool also reminded me that municipal swimming pools and other public spaces can level social differences. For one, they diminish social distinctions by bringing diverse people together at the same place doing the same things. This was certainly the case in Palmerton, Pennsylvania, during the 1930s. Eighty-something-year-old Joseph Plechavy reminisced to me about his childhood days at the town's swimming pool, where this son of an immigrant laborer "yakked" and played with children who lived on the other side of town. "It didn't matter who you were," Plechavy recalled, "you swam at the pool."[2] Municipal pools can also diminish the significance of economic inequality by affording all social classes access to some trappings of the good life. The resort pools of the interwar years, for example, democratized the life-style of the leisure class. The poor and working classes could lie out on a sandy beach, refresh themselves in cool water, and visually consume attractive bodies just as though they were on vacation at a shore resort. Finally, pools force swimmers to cast off most material accoutrements of life. Swimmers leave behind their homes, cars, clothing, and other outward signs of status that define people's identity in a consumer society. Swimmers return to something resembling nature, in a more natural state themselves. As an Allegheny County public official insisted in 1939, "let's build bigger, better, and finer pools, that's real democracy. Take away the sham and hypocrisy of clothes, don a swim suit, and we're all the same."[3] In all these ways, the stark inequalities of life could become less apparent and less meaningful at municipal pools.

While not immediately visible at the Newton pool, municipal swimming pools highlight another virtue of public space. They allow ordinary and even marginalized members of society to participate in the production of public culture. The way ordinary swimmers appeared and what they did at municipal pools shaped American culture in profound ways. Working-class swimmers helped popularize and legitimate pleasure-centered recreation during the late nineteenth century by defying the expectations of Victorian public officials. All levels of society participated in the redefinition of pools as leisure resorts and sexualized spaces during the interwar years. Without public spaces such as swimming pools, the production of public culture would be less democratic. Cultural elites—such as marketers, movie producers, television programmers, writers, and editors—would exercise greater control over defining social and cultural norms. This is precisely what Lewis Mumford feared back in 1961, when it appeared to him that suburbanites were becoming too susceptible to the messages they received through their individual encounters with mass culture: "With direct contact and face-to-face association inhibited as far as possible, all knowledge and direction can be monopolized by central agents and conveyed through guarded channels. . . . Each member of suburbia becomes imprisoned by the very separation he has prized: he is fed through a narrow opening: a telephone line, a radio band, a television circuit."[4] Swimming pools and other democratic public spaces limit the cultural power of mass media precisely because they encourage "direct contact and face-to-face association."

Despite their considerable potential to foster community life, level social differences, and empower ordinary Americans, municipal pools rarely realized their full promise as public spaces. Since their origin in the mid-nineteenth century, Americans mostly used municipal pools in ways that divided communities and reinforced social distinctions. Social segregation is the most persistent theme in the history of swimming pools. At first, use divided along class, gender, and generational lines, which reflected the prevailing public social divisions in industrial America. When these divisions mostly evaporated during the interwar years, racial separation took their place. In the northern United States at least, the 1920s and 1930s were years of unprecedented racial separation and antagonism. When courts forced northern communities to desegregate their municipal pools after World War II, most whites chose to maintain this racial boundary through violence or retreat. In some cases, as in Chicago, working-class whites violently resisted attempts by black swimmers to use traditionally whites-only pools, even into the 1960s. As Thomas Sugrue found when studying housing disputes in Detroit during the postwar period, the poorest class of urban whites resisted black "intrusions" most fiercely because they could least afford to move out, or, in the case of swimming, join a private club.[5] Middle-class whites, on the other hand, who were already moving out to the suburbs in droves, simply organized and joined swim clubs so they would not have to swim with black

Americans or working-class whites. Since the late nineteenth century, simply looking at the composition of municipal-pool swimmers clearly reveals the social fault lines in American communities.

Americans used segregation at municipal pools to reinforce social differences in two opposite ways. During the Progressive Era and much of the second half of the twentieth century, municipal pools isolated socially marginalized groups from mainstream society. Public officials used municipal pools as asylums, to concentrate the urban poor at particular public spaces so that they would not wreak havoc elsewhere. This is why New York City parks commissioner Charles Stover and the *New York Times* proposed in 1910 to locate the city's municipal pools underneath bridges rather than in Central Park. The same was true in the 1960s, when cities throughout the country rushed to build pools that would essentially quarantine angry black citizens. During both periods, swimming at a municipal pool marked you as socially marginal. During the interwar years, however, swimming at a municipal pool meant just the opposite. All those permitted access to the giant resort pools—white Americans—were accepted as members of mainstream society, whereas those excluded—black Americans—were defined as social others. In both cases, Americans used municipal pools to determine the social boundaries of their communities, one in the negative and the other in the positive.

Municipal pools reinforced social distinctions in more subtle ways as well. During most periods, public officials and reformers intended municipal pools to solve problems that they associated with a particular social group. The earliest pools were intended to provide baths for the urban working classes, because they were dirty and posed a threat to public health. Progressive Era pools were intended to offer asylum to working-class youths, because they were potentially delinquent and posed a threat to the social order. The municipal pools of the late 1960s were intended to cool down angry black Americans and stop them from rioting. In each case, the expenditure of money for municipal pools required a justification explaining how the larger community would benefit. The only period of significant pool building in which reformers and officials did not emphasize the public good to justify municipal-pool construction was during the interwar years, when pools were intended to serve middle-class Americans as well. The designs of municipal pools reflect this same class distinction in the provision of public recreation. When communities built pools intended for middle-class residents, they adorned them with sandy beaches, grassy lawns, and sundecks. When poor and working-class Americans were the intended users, cities generally

Sterling Playground Pool, Brooklyn, New York, 1967. Many municipal pools constructed during the late 1960s were small, austere facilities, located in out-of-the-way places that essentially quarantined minority youths. Daniel McPartlin / New York City Parks Photo Archive, neg. B-356, 32992.7.

built austere facilities that offered minimal leisure space. Throughout the twentieth century, public officials shared an assumption that middle-class Americans deserved publicly funded leisure that enhanced their individual lives, whereas poor and working-class Americans required publicly funded recreation that mitigated social problems.

All too often, the interaction and close contact that occurred at municipal pools did not foster mutual understanding and friendship across social lines, but rather enabled individuals and groups to act out social antagonisms. Racial violence is the most obvious example. From the 1920s to the 1950s, northern whites took advantage of the physical intimacy at swimming pools to dunk, punch, kick, and club black Americans. Pools have also been the scene of gender violence. During the mid-1990s, an epidemic of sexual assaults occurred at New York City's municipal pools. In dozens of separate "whirlpooling" incidents, groups of teenage boys surrounded a girl in the water, tore off her swimsuit top and then grabbed her breasts. In some cases, the assault went further. One seventeen-year-old boy inserted his finger into a girl's vagina, and a twenty-six-year-old man attempted to rape and sodomize a girl. In each case, the pools were filled with hundreds of other swimmers. The crowded environment and close physical interaction enabled the boys and young men to publicly act on their contemptuous lust for females.[6] In these instances, contact at municipal pools between Americans with different social identities did not lead to greater trust, empathy, and understanding but rather just the opposite.

In response to the first few whirlpooling incidents, New York City parks commissioner Betsy Gotbaum quipped that, "this has been going on [for] time immemorial."[7] It was an impolitic comment, but it correctly placed sexuality at the heart of the history of swimming pools. Since their origin in the nineteenth century, sexuality and concerns about sexuality have profoundly shaped the use and regulation of municipal pools. During the Gilded Age and Progressive Era, cities gender-segregated pools in order to protect women's modesty and protect them from advances by anonymous men. Gender separation also served as a means of social control. It limited the opportunities unrelated males and females had to meet and interact in public, thereby maintaining traditional family authority over mixed-gender socializing and courtship. This all changed during the 1920s and 1930s. Gender integration was *the* watershed in the history of municipal swimming pools. It marked a historic social and cultural reconstruction of public space. Concerns about sexuality remained, but they were redirected at a particular social group— black Americans. For the rest of the community, sexuality became the magnet that drew hundreds and even thousands of males and females together at swimming pools. *Fortune* was not wrong when it claimed in 1934 that swimming pools became so popular after gender integration because they sparked "the full voltage of cosmic urge."[8] As this quotation suggests, gender integration also transformed pool culture. Shrinking swimsuits, bathing beauty contests, exhibitionism, and voyeurism all reflected the explicit sexuality that pervaded mixed-gender pools. The consequences of the sexualization of pool culture have been profound, especially for women. It heightened the importance of physical appearance as a source of identity and contributed to women's anxiety about the size and shape of their bodies. It also cast women into the public role of visual objects. It became culturally normal for males to visually consume females at swimming pools. Given this subject-object relationship, it is perhaps not surprising that some male swimmers sexually assaulted females at pools. As a fourteen-year-old girl who witnessed one of the whirlpooling incidents remarked to the *New York Times*, "when guys see a girl in a bathing suit, they just see her as being naked."[9] So, perhaps Gotbaum was only half right. Sexuality at swimming pools does have a long history, but to claim that it goes back "time immemorial" misses the point that it is really a product of history and not a natural state.

~~~~~ Municipal swimming pools are becoming endangered in the United States. At the same time that cities such as Pittsburgh and Youngstown are closing most of their pools, suburban communities are generally choosing to build "water theme parks" rather than traditional pools.[10] Given their tumultuous history, some may welcome the extinction of municipal swimming pools. Not me. Growing up in Seattle, I spent most summer days swimming and playing with friends at Olympic View Swimming Pool. So many memories are still vividly etched on my mind—being thrown up in the air and into the water by my father, "showing off" in an attempt to impress two particular girls, beating all comers at pickleball, and trading baseball cards on the pool deck. By contrast, my memories of watching television, playing soccer, attending church, and being at school are much less vivid. There was something special about the pool. It would be a shame if future generations did not have the same opportunity to create their own vivid childhood memories. Perhaps our children will be more successful at realizing swimming pools' full promise as public spaces. I hope so.

NOTES

INTRODUCTION

1. Boston City Council, *Report of the Proceedings* (1898), 619; Philadelphia, *Annual Report* (1897), 150.
2. Watkins, *Dancing with Strangers*, 127–29.
3. By "northern United States" I mean the northeast quadrant of the country, roughly bounded by Washington, D.C., St. Louis, Milwaukee, and Boston.
4. Nasaw, *Going Out*, 2; Kasson, *Amusing the Million*, 4. See also Peiss, *Cheap Amusements*.
5. McGreevy, *Parish Boundaries*, 4.
6. Matthew Pratt Guterl identifies a corresponding intellectual and cultural shift in the urban North. Building on the work of Matthew Jacobson, he argues that northerners reconstructed their notions of race along rigid black-white lines during the 1920s and 1930s. Early in the twentieth century, most northern whites perceived black Americans to be one among many different "races." After World War I, however, they began to reconceive race along a biracial, black-white, race-as-skin-color division. See Guterl, *Color of Race in America*.
7. John Higham makes a similar argument about the cultural agency of the working classes in his seminal essay "The Reorientation of American Culture in the 1890s," esp. 86–87.
8. National Recreation Association, *Leisure Hours of 5,000 People*, 9.
9. Fox and Lears, *Culture of Consumption*, x; Leach, *Land of Desire*, xv. See also Cross, *An All-Consuming Century*.

CHAPTER ONE

1. "Almost a Riot: An Attack by Roughs on the Down-town Free Bath-House," *Philadelphia Evening Bulletin*, June 25, 1884, 6.
2. For an institutional history of public baths in nineteenth-century America, see M. Williams, *Washing "The Great Unwashed."*
3. Boston, *By-Laws and Town-Orders*, 74–75, in Altherr, *Sports in North America*, 21.
4. New York, *Laws and Ordinances*, 4, in Altherr, *Sports in North America*, 34.
5. *Boston Columbian Sentinel*, September 6, 1820, in Altherr, *Sports in North America*, 60–61.
6. Daniels, *Puritans at Play*, 174.
7. "Justis Runnin' Wilde," *Milwaukee Sentinel*, September 3, 1878, 8.
8. *Milwaukee Sentinel*, July 9, 1878, 2.

9. "Cherry Hill Swimmers: What Spring Means to Pier-Haunting East Side Boys," *New York Times*, May 27, 1900, 8.

10. *Milwaukee Sentinel*, July 7, 1860, 1.

11. On the lax enforcement of municipal ordinances during the nineteenth century, see Hantzmon, "Forestalling."

12. "Bathing within the City Limits," *Milwaukee Sentinel*, June 25, 1858, 1.

13. Ibid.

14. On Victorian culture, see Howe, "American Victorianism as a Culture," 507–32. Years after this first public debate about the swimming and bathing ordinance, an unnamed citizen wrote to the *Sentinel* a sardonic critique of the Victorian sensibilities that made such a law necessary. "The ordinance is made and enforced for the express accommodation of a parcel of weak, unwomanly, pinched-waisted abortions of what might have been women, but who are nothing but walking dummies to exhibit dry goods upon; who never have children themselves, and do all they can to check health, happiness, and life in others. These are the namby-pamby, wishy-washy, poor excuses of poodle-dog fondling feminines, who are neither fish, flesh, nor good red herrings, but who float along in the scum of upper-tendom. Some of these, who pretend to be wives, but are not, complain to their male partners, who ought to be men and fathers but are not, that the sight of naked boys in the water, or on the beach, half a mile off, offends their sense of decency; and an ordinance prohibiting bathing is the consequence." Implicit in this caricature of the men and women who favored the ban as being feminine, sterile, and morose was a serious critique of the Victorian moral order. The author praised the masculine, irreverent, and pleasure-centered behavior of the swimmers and denigrated the restrained culture of the middle class. In essence, he flipped the prevailing moral order on its head. See "Wash and Be Clean," *Milwaukee Sentinel*, June 27, 1874, 3.

15. *Milwaukee Sentinel*, June 29, 1858, 1.

16. *Milwaukee Sentinel*, July 3, 1860, 1.

17. "Where Shall the Boys Swim?," *Milwaukee Sentinel*, July 3, 1860, 1.

18. *Milwaukee Sentinel*, July 7, 1860, 1.

19. "Where Shall We Expose Ourselves?," *Milwaukee Sentinel*, July 7, 1860, 1.

20. See Howe, *Victorian America*; Stevenson, *Victorian Homefront*.

21. "Where Shall We Expose Ourselves?," 1.

22. *Milwaukee Sentinel*, June 25, 1858, 1.

23. Ryan, *Women in Public*, 58–94.

24. There were a few famous exceptions, most notably Benjamin Franklin and John Quincy Addams, but they were unusual among their contemporaries. The vast majority of early Americans did not know how to swim and rarely, if ever, entered the lakes and rivers that dotted the landscape. There were several mineral-water spas popular with colonial and early American elites, but visitors

plunged into the water and quickly got out to improve their health, not for recreation or amusement. See Bridenbaugh, "Baths and Watering Places."

25. "Swimming," *New England Magazine*, June 1832, 508.

26. Muths, "Bathing and Swimming," 339–59, in Altherr, *Sports in North America*, 27.

27. *Boston Columbian Sentinel*, September 6, 1820, in Altherr, *Sports in North America*, 60–61.

28. Aron, *Working at Play*, 34–40.

29. Higginson, "Saints and Their Bodies," 583. See also Aron, *Working at Play*, 42.

30. Higginson, "Saints and Their Bodies," 583–84.

31. Aron, *Working at Play*, 45–68, 72–79.

32. "Swimming," *Godey's Lady's Book*, August 1858, 123–25.

33. Higginson, "Gymnastics," 284.

34. Higginson, "Saints and Their Bodies," 588. For a more complete account of the midcentury fitness movement, see Green, *Fit for America*, 85–121.

35. Higginson, "Saints and Their Bodies," 592.

36. Referenced and quoted in Kirkbride, "Private Initiative," 280.

37. "Chicago Natatorium and Institute for Physical Culture," *Art Exhibit of Fashion* 3 (1878).

38. Chudacoff and Smith, *Evolution of American Urban Society*, 60.

39. Ibid., 115–33; Handlin, *Boston's Immigrants*, 88–123; Boyer, *Urban Masses and Moral Order*, 67; Barth, *City People*, 28–57. See also Anbinder, *Five Points*.

40. Boyer, *Urban Masses and Moral Order*, 67–84; Jackson, *Crabgrass Frontier*, 69–72.

41. Griscom, *Sanitary Condition*, 7–8.

42. Ibid., 15, 3.

43. Boston, for example, established its board of health in 1849, founded its first municipal almshouse in 1852, and passed ordinances to build a city hospital in 1857. See "Index to City Documents," Government Documents Reading Room, Boston Public Library.

44. See Lubove, "New York Association for Improving the Condition," 307–27; New York Association for Improving the Condition of the Poor, *Eighteenth Annual Report*, 65–69.

45. Boston Joint Special Committee on Public Bathing Houses, *Report* (1860), 7.

46. Reprinted in *Water-Cure Journal* 7 (February 1849): 46.

47. Boston Committee on Public Bathing Houses, *Report* (1860), 3–4.

48. Lubove, "New York Association for Improving the Condition," 307–27.

49. New York Association for Improving the Condition of the Poor, *Tenth Annual Report*, 26–27, 30–31; M. Williams, *Washing "The Great Unwashed,"* 16.

50. Boston Joint Special Committee on Public Bathing Houses, *Report* (1860), 8.

51. Ibid., 4.

52. Boston Joint Special Committee on Free Bathing Facilities, *Report* (1866), 4–5.

53. Tomes, *Gospel of Germs*, 27.

54. Boston Joint Special Committee on Free Bathing Facilities, *Report* (1866), 4.

55. Ibid., 6–7, 9, 16.

56. In 1866 "women" and "girls" accounted for 51,836 out of 433,690 total baths, 101,228 out of 807,201 in 1867, and 104,513 out of 842,617 in 1868. See Boston Committee on Bathing, *Report* (1868), 8.

57. Boston Joint Standing Committee on Bathing, *Report* (1867), 9. Boston's poor were the most common bathers at the public houses. The men's Dover Street Bridge Bath, located among the "throngs of the foreign population" in East Boston, attracted more bathers than any other facility. During the summer of 1867, the men and boys of the area visited it 137,000 times. The entire population of East Boston at the time was only about 20,000, which meant that each bather must have come often. The second most popular bath was attached to Warren Bridge, which was used by the "North End working population." It attracted more than 127,000 bathers in 1867. By comparison, only 59,000 baths were taken at the more socially exclusive L Street Bath. See Boston Joint Standing Committee on Bathing, *Report* (1867), 17–19.

58. Boston Joint Special Committee on Free Bathing Facilities, *Report* (1866), 6 (emphasis added).

59. Ibid.

60. *Roxbury Gazette and South End Advertiser*, July 30, 1868, 2. See Peiss, *Cheap Amusements*, 11–33; Powers, *Faces along the Bar*, 26–47.

61. Boston Committee on Bathing, *Report* (1868), 6–7; "The Public Baths for Roxbury," *Roxbury Gazette and South End Advertiser*, June 25, 1868, 2.

62. Boston Committee on Bathing, *Report* (1868), 6.

63. Boston Committee on Bathing, *Report* (1869), 10–11.

64. Boston Committee on Bathing, *Report* (1870), 8–9.

65. Boston Committee on Bathing, *Report* (1869), 10–11.

66. Some cities did provide public parks during the mid-nineteenth century, but they were not intended to provide amusement for the working classes. As Rosenzweig and Blackmar show in *The Park and the People*, 211–306, New York's Central Park initially served the city's upper classes. Furthermore, to the extent that park designers and municipal officials intended public parks to serve the working classes during the nineteenth century, they intended them to promote their conception of the public good by instilling the working classes with middle-class values and sensibilities. They did not intend parks to promote individual pleasure or amusement. See Kasson, *Amusing the Million*, 11–17. Frederick Law Olmsted, one of Central Park's designers, conveyed this point in 1870, when he wrote: "No one who has closely observed the conduct of the people who visit the Park can doubt that it exercises a distinctly harmonizing and refining influence upon the most unfortunate and most lawless classes of the city—an influence

favorable towards courtesy, self-control, and temperance." (Quoted in Kasson, *Amusing the Million*, 15.)

67. Boston Committee on Bathing, *Report* (1876), 1.
68. Philadelphia, *Annual Report* (1883), 1057.
69. Philadelphia, *Annual Report* (1884), XLIX.
70. *Philadelphia Evening Bulletin*, June 4, 1883, 4.
71. "Another Free Bath Opened," *Philadelphia Evening Bulletin*, June 21, 1884, 7.
72. Philadelphia, *Annual Report* (1884), 1371.
73. 1880 U.S. Census, Philadelphia County, Pennsylvania (Philadelphia, Ward 26), Enumeration District No. 551, National Archive Microfilm T9-1185, vol. 75, p. 518A, National Archives and Records Administration.
74. 1880 U.S. Census, Philadelphia County, Pennsylvania (Philadelphia, Ward 27), Enumeration District No. 551, National Archives Microfilm T9-1186, Vol. 76, p. 6D, National Archives and Records Administration.
75. Boston City Council, *Report on the Proceedings* (1898), 619.
76. Ibid., 619; Philadelphia, *Annual Report* (1897), 150.
77. Philadelphia, *Annual Report* (1884), 1371.
78. Philadelphia, *Annual Report* (1888), 503; (1889), 518.
79. Philadelphia, *Annual Report* (1891), 675. Some evidence suggests that the attendance figures for the Philadelphia swimming baths were inflated. This seems likely in that for the 1891 attendance figures to be correct, each pool would have had to average 2,855 bathers every day for ninety days. In all likelihood, however, the accurate figures would show a similar ratio of swims taken by boys as compared to men, women, and girls, if not a more lopsided ratio. If the city was going to fabricate numbers, it would have wanted to overstate the proportional use made by adults, because that is who the public was most willing to spend money to clean.
80. "Almost a Riot: An Attack by Roughs on the Down-town Free Bath-House," 6.
81. "Free Bath Houses," *Philadelphia Evening Bulletin*, June 18, 1888, 6. It is hard to believe that all these boys would express such enthusiasm for the opportunity to clean themselves. Children, especially boys, have never been quick to embrace bathing and other habits of civility, according to sociologist Norbert Elias. Instead, they take them on reluctantly as they enter adulthood. See Elias, *Civilizing Process*, 166–67, 188.
82. Kirkbride, "Private Initiative," 281.
83. Natatorium was a term used at the time mainly to refer to an indoor pool.
84. "The Natatorium Finished: A Party of Aldermen Inspect It but Do Not Take a Plunge," *Milwaukee Sentinel*, August 15, 1889, 3.
85. Veblen, *Theory of the Leisure Class*, 167–87.
86. "Use for Fat Men, Come Handy for Natatorium Use," *Milwaukee Sentinel*, February 26, 1890, 5.

87. The custom at the time was for men and boys to "bathe" naked at indoor pools and wear suits at outdoor pools.
88. "Use for Fat Men," 5.
89. Ibid.
90. Ibid.
91. Considine and Jarvis, *First Hundred Years*, 27, 47.
92. Hopkins, *History of the Y.M.C.A.*, 154.
93. Worman, *History of the Brooklyn and Queens*, 63.
94. Young Men's Era, *Book of Young Men's Christian Association Buildings*, 30.
95. Worman, *History of the Brooklyn and Queens*, 65.

CHAPTER TWO

1. West Chicago Park Commissioners, *Proceedings of the Board*, 1398.
2. Ibid.
3. "Improvements for West Side Parks," *Chicago Times-Herald*, August 23, 1896, 27.
4. *Turner* societies were exercise clubs popular in central and eastern Europe that immigrants established in America. Bicycling was a middle-class activity during the 1890s as the bikes were quite expensive. Contemporaries would have been hard pressed to find a more definitively middle-class organization than a bicycle club. See Green, *Fit for America*, 98–99, 228–33.
5. "Douglas Park Natatorium Is Open," *Chicago Tribune*, August 23, 1896, 6.
6. "West Side Free Baths," *Chicago Times-Herald*, August 23, 1896, 30; "Free Baths at Last," *Chicago Record*, August 24, 1896, 4; "An Excellent Park Feature," *Chicago Journal*, August 24, 1896.
7. "Small Boy's Paradise," *Chicago Record*, August 24, 1896, 7.
8. "Where All May Dip," *Chicago Record*, August 22, 1896, 7.
9. West Chicago Park Commissioners, *Annual Report* (1900), 14–16.
10. "Small Boy's Paradise," 7.
11. Tomes, *Gospel of Germs*, 27–28, 92–96, 109.
12. Boston City Council, *Report of the Proceedings* (1896), 419.
13. Boston Department of Baths, "Free Municipal Baths in Boston," 36, 45.
14. M. Williams, *Washing "The Great Unwashed,"* 44–49, 57.
15. U.S. Department of Commerce and Labor, "Public Baths in the United States," 1254–57.
16. Higham, "Reorientation of American Culture," 80. See also Smith, *Social History of the Bicycle*.
17. Green, *Fit for America*, 233–50.
18. Rozenzweig, *Eight Hours for What We Will*, 140–41.
19. See Green, *Fit for America*, 219–25; Mrozek, "Sport in American Life," 18–23.
20. Brookline, *Report* (1884), 129–30.

21. Brookline, *Report* (1885), 113; (1887), 87.

22. Brookline, *Report* (1890), 327–28.

23. "Annual Town Meeting," *Brookline Chronicle*, April 19, 1890, 122.

24. Brookline, *Report* (1894), 171. For accounts of the rising popularity of athletics and fitness during this period, see Green, *Fit for America*; Mrozek, "Sport in American Life," 18–48; Higham, "Reorientation of American Culture," 73–102.

25. *Brookline Chronicle*, October 26, 1895, 338.

26. Walter Channing, "Municipal Bath-houses," *Brookline Chronicle*, August 7, 1897, 3.

27. Brookline Building Committee, "Brookline Public Bath," 8.

28. "Model Establishment: Tappan-Street Bath-House an Institution to be Proud Of," *Brookline Chronicle*, January 2, 1897, 6.

29. *Brookline Chronicle*, March 6, 1897, 6; May 29, 1897, 1; June 5, 1897, 1.

30. "Art of Swimming," *Brookline Chronicle*, May 29, 1897, 1.

31. "In Running Order: The Tappan-Street Bath-House Now a Town Institution," *Brookline Chronicle*, January 9, 1897, 1.

32. Brookline Building Committee, "Brookline Public Bath," 18.

33. Channing, "Municipal Bath-houses," 3.

34. Brookline, *Report* (1897), 297; Channing, "Municipal Bath-houses," 3.

35. Channing, "Municipal Bath-houses," 3.

36. Brookline Building Committee, "Brookline Public Bath," 19–20.

37. Denehy, *History of the Town of Brookline*, 206, 142, 223, 230–31.

38. Howe, "Victorian Culture in America," 18–21.

39. Stevenson, *Victorian Homefront*, xx.

40. Brookline, *Report* (1900), 238–39; Channing, "Municipal Bath-houses," 3.

41. Brookline, *Report* (1898), 297; Channing, "Municipal Bath-houses," 3.

42. "Swimming and Bathing," *Brookline Chronicle*, March 6, 1897, 6.

43. Brookline Building Committee, "Brookline Public Bath," 9.

44. Channing, "Municipal Bath-houses," 3.

45. Brookline Building Committee, "Brookline Public Bath," 17–18.

46. Channing, "Municipal Bath-houses," 3.

47. Massachusetts Bureau of Statistics of Labor, *Twenty-Eighth Annual Report*, 22–23.

48. Brookline, *Report* (1898), 293–94.

49. A total of 41,853 swims was taken in the pool, and the receipts were $6,151.50. Brookline Committee on Care and Management, "Report," 3–4.

50. Brookline, *Report* (1897), 298.

51. Brookline Committee on Care and Management, "Report," 6–8.

52. Brookline, *Report* (1898), 293; Brookline Committee on Care and Management, "Report," 3.

53. Brookline Committee on Care and Management, "Report," 6.

54. Brookline, *Report* (1904), 193–94.

55. As to the behavior and activities of urban working-class children at the time, see Nasaw, *Children of the City*, 17–38. Peter C. Holloran explores the public response to "wayward" children in Boston in his book, *Boston's Wayward Children*.

CHAPTER THREE

1. "Report to the Chief of Bureau of City Property," December 18, 1912, Department of City Property, Papers, 1892–1947, Philadelphia City Archives.
2. Ibid.
3. Blodgett, *Gentle Reformers*, 131.
4. Blodgett, "Josiah Quincy, Brahmin Democrat," 437.
5. Quincy, "Development of American Cities," 536.
6. Boston City Council, *Report of the Proceedings* (1898), 387–88. Although Quincy never stated so, he probably did not see the Frog Pond pool as a public health hazard because it originated as a natural body of water.
7. Ibid., 450.
8. Ibid., 414.
9. Ibid., 388.
10. Ibid., 450.
11. Ibid., 414.
12. Ibid., 422, 449.
13. Ibid., 505–6.
14. Ibid.
15. Boston Department of Baths, "Free Municipal Baths in Boston," 23.
16. Boston City Council, *Report of the Proceedings* (1898), 371.
17. "The Cabot Street Bath House," *Roxbury Gazette and South End Advertiser*, August 27, 1898, 1.
18. Boston Department of Baths, *Annual Report* (1898), 49.
19. "The Cabot Street Bath House," 1.
20. Boston Department of Baths, "Free Municipal Baths in Boston," 24.
21. *Roxbury Gazette and South End Advertiser*, August 20, 1898, 4.
22. *Boston Daily Globe*, September 1, 1898, 4.
23. Ibid.
24. Quincy, "Development of American Cities," 536.
25. As to nineteenth-century municipal functions, see Novak, *People's Welfare*.
26. Hardy, *How Boston Played*, 87, 97.
27. Cavallo, *Muscles and Morals*, 17.
28. Boston City Council, *Report of the Proceedings* (1898), 616.
29. Ibid., 618, 623.
30. Ibid., 620, 624, 637.
31. "To Keep Baths Open," *Boston Daily Globe*, September 5, 1898, 3.
32. "To Bathe or Not to Bathe," *Boston Evening Transcript*, September 2, 1898, 4.

33. *Roxbury Gazette and South End Advertiser*, August 20, 1898, 4.

34. Boston City Council, *Report of the Proceedings* (1902), 113–14, 332, 311.

35. Quoted in Blodgett, "Josiah Quincy, Brahmin Democrat," 451.

36. Boston Park and Recreation Department, *Annual Report* (1917–18), 80.

37. Four different park boards administered the parks, playgrounds, and recreation centers in Chicago until they were eventually unified in 1934. The South Park District extended south from the South Branch of the Chicago River. The West Park District covered the western part of the city, while the Lincoln Park District extended north from the North Branch of the Chicago River. The Special Park Commission administered the playgrounds and beaches in the immediate downtown area.

38. See Philpott, *The Slum and the Ghetto*.

39. Breen, *Historical Register*, 362–63, 320–22.

40. Philpott, *The Slum and the Ghetto*, 27.

41. Breen, *Historical Register*, 379.

42. Duis, *Challenging Chicago*, 99–103.

43. Pacyga and Skerrett, *Chicago*, 409–16.

44. Philpott, *The Slum and the Ghetto*, 41.

45. Cavallo, *Muscles and Morals*, 31.

46. Playground Association of Philadelphia, "Advance of the National Playground Movement," 4.

47. J. Frank Foster, "An Article for Small Parks Read before the Chicago Society for School Extension" (1903), 15–16, Special Collections, Chicago Historical Society.

48. Carbaugh, *Human Welfare Work*, 94; South Park Commissioners, *Annual Report* (1909), 50.

49. See Boyer, *Urban Masses and Moral Order*, 146–50.

50. New York Association for Improving the Condition of the Poor, *Ninth Annual Report*, 18–21. The AICP did not provide aid for "incorrigible mendicants, the willfully improvident, the indolent who will not work, and the intemperate." Nor did it provide support for those who had "become so pauperized in spirit by long continued vagrancy, or other causes, that there is no hope of inciting them to self-support, and to aid whom would foster a great social evil."

51. On the prevalence of environmental social theories among Progressive reformers, see Moore, "Directions of Thought," 38–41.

52. Taylor, "Recreation Developments," 317.

53. Addams, "Public Recreation and Social Morality," 494.

54. Taylor, "Recreation Developments," 317.

55. Quoted in ibid., 316–17.

56. Ibid., 316–18; Playground Association of Philadelphia, "Play as Citizen Maker."

57. Addams, "Recreation as a Public Function," 617.

58. Cary Goodman argues this point most forcefully in *Choosing Sides*. Like Good-

man, Roy Rosenzweig contends that the play movement represented a "frontal assault on the dominant characteristics of [the working class's] defensive culture." Unlike Goodman, Rosenzweig claims that play reform did not succeed in socializing working-class children. "The limited available evidence suggests that instead of being reshaped by playgrounds, workers and their children actually reshaped the playground . . . according to their own needs." See Rosenzweig, *Eight Hours for What We Will*, 148, 149.

59. Foster, "An Article for Small Parks," 12.

60. Some Progressive play reformers, especially those based in New York, disagreed with Foster. They argued that only through "directed" play could children be properly socialized. Baseball and basketball, they claimed, taught players to follow the rules, work as a team, and respect authority. These activities also necessitated quick thinking and decisive responses to changing circumstances. Uncontrolled play, on the other hand, would unleash self-abandon and promote moral delinquency, they contended. On play reformers' assumptions about directed play, see Cavallo, *Muscles and Morals*, 73–106.

61. South Park Commissioners, *Annual Report* (1909). The photographs are interspersed throughout the report on unnumbered pages.

62. Ibid.

63. Osborn, "The Development of Recreation in the South Park System of Chicago," 49.

64. Playground Association of Philadelphia, "Play as a Citizen Maker," 5.

65. See Chicago Commission on Race Relations, *The Negro in Chicago*, foldout leaf between pages 110 and 111. Although residential segregation in Chicago was not as rigid at this time as it would become after 1920, identifiable neighborhoods where most of the residents were black existed on both the South and West Sides. See Spear, *Black Chicago*, 11–27.

66. Beginning in 1913, blacks on the South Side swam at the Wabash Avenue branch of the YMCA, one of many racially segregated Y facilities opened early in the twentieth century in cities throughout the country. The building was paid for by the Pullman Railroad Car Company, the national YMCA, individual black Chicagoans, and local white philanthropists. See "Race Gives Small Amount," *Chicago Defender*, June 28, 1913, 1; "YMCA Building Dedicated with Imposing Ceremonies," *Chicago Defender*, June 21, 1913, 1; "The Y.M.C.A.," *Chicago Defender*, September 13, 1913, 6.

67. Chicago Commission on Race Relations, *The Negro in Chicago*, 279.

68. Ibid., 287.

69. Ibid., 278, 294–95.

70. Ibid., 276, 278, 282.

71. M. Williams, *Washing "The Great Unwashed,"* 62; Todd, "Municipal Baths of Manhattan," 901.

72. "New Public Bath Opened," *New York Times*, June 29, 1906, 9.

73. Todd, "Municipal Baths of Manhattan," 901; M. Williams, *Washing "The Great Unwashed,"* 61.

74. M. Williams, *Washing "The Great Unwashed,"* 62; Todd, "Municipal Baths of Manhattan," 900.

75. "Public Bathing Establishments," *Brickbuilder*, January 1915, 16; Todd, "Four New City Baths and Gymnasiums," 683.

76. "City's Swimming Schools," *New York Times*, September 23, 1900, 22.

77. Kisseloff, *You Must Remember This*, 127.

78. Ibid., 566.

79. Ibid., 350.

80. "Nine Persons Drowned, One Missing, after Sultry Day," *New York Herald*, July 4, 1910, 3.

81. Kisseloff, *You Must Remember This*, 567.

82. "Divergent Views of Seaside Park," *New York Times*, December 3, 1909, 7.

83. Lewinson, *John Purroy Mitchel*, 11, 41–44, 55–58, 62.

84. Ibid., 43.

85. See Stewart, "Boston's Experience with Municipal Baths," 419.

86. New York City Board of Estimate and Apportionment, *Minutes, Financial, and Franchise Matters*, 3487–89; "Plans a Playground for Central Park," *New York Times*, May 20, 1910, 6; "Plans Drawn for Great Park Changes," *New York Times*, July 1, 1910, 1.

87. "Plans a Playground for Central Park," 6; "Central Park," *New York Times*, July 3, 1910, 6.

88. New York City Board of Estimate and Apportionment, *Minutes, Financial, and Franchise Matters*, 3487–89.

89. The committee was loosely composed of the following individuals: Gibson, former New York mayor and Columbia University president Seth Low, real-estate magnate and philanthropist William Rhinelander Stewart, College of the City of New York president John H. Finley, banker and capitalist Jacob Henry Schiff, financier George Walbridge Perkins, sculptor and painter Gutzon Borglum, U.S. Steel Corporation general counsel Francis Lynde Stetson, lawyer Eugene Ambrose Philbin, and industrialist Henry Phibbs.

90. *National Cyclopaedia of American Biography*, 13:533.

91. Ibid., 6:348; 12:236; 13:503, 533; 14:50, 503; 15:33; 22:22; 43:191.

92. "Can't Change Park without Parsons," *New York Times*, July 3, 1910, II-3.

93. *New York Times*, July 3, 1910, 6.

94. "McAneny for Park Pool," *New York Evening Post*, July 6, 1910, 2.

95. "Mitchel Backs Park Plan," *New York Evening Post*, July 7, 1910, 9.

96. *New York Times*, July 6, 1910, 6.

97. "Plans a Committee to Save the Park," *New York Times*, July 5, 1910, 5.

98. A study of New York housing conducted in 1900 by Lawrence Veiller found that nearly 400,000 poor and working-class people lived north of 86th Street on Manhattan's East Side. See Veiller, "A Statistical Study of New York's Tenement Houses," 195, 203.

99. "Can't Change Park without Parsons," II-3.

100. *New York Times*, May 22, 1910, 10.

101. Rosenzweig and Blackmar, *The Park and the People*, 412–13.

102. "Can't Change Park without Parsons," II-3.

103. "Stover Wants No Park Wading Pools," *New York Times*, July 4, 1910, 3.

104. Ibid., 3. Stover was certainly aware of the two pools housed within the East 23rd Street and West 60th Street bathhouses; but, as his statement suggests, he did not consider them swimming pools. They were bathing pools, which, in his mind, were distinct from swimming pools.

105. "Says Building in Park Is Necessity," *New York Herald*, July 4, 1910, 6.

106. "Stover Wants No Park Wading Pools," 3.

107. "The Central Park Plans," *New York Times*, July 4, 1910, 6.

108. On the social geography of New York City at the time, see DeForrest and Veiller, *Tenement House Problem.*

109. "Mayor Sees Swimmin'-Hole Site," *New York Evening Post*, July 7, 1910, 3.

110. "Protecting the Park," *New York Times*, July 9, 1910, 6; "Confusion about Central Park," *New York Times*, July 8, 1910, 6; *New York Times*, July 16, 1910, 6.

111. "Gaynor Going Slow on Park Changes," *New York Times*, July 8, 1910, 7.

112. Manheimer, "Studies on the Sanitation of Swimming Pools"; Manheimer, "Essentials of Swimming Pool Sanitation"; "Purifying Water for City Bathing Pools," *Survey* 32 (May 9, 1914): 183.

113. Manheimer, "Studies on the Sanitation of Swimming Pools," 170.

114. "Swimming Pool Cleaner," *New York Times*, May 16, 1911, 11; Manheimer, "Studies on the Sanitation of Swimming Pools," 160–61, 170, 171.

115. The city's third pool opened in 1911 on East 54th Street, in the heart of the East Side tenements. New York City opened another pool in 1914, on West 28th Street in Chelsea. See M. Williams, *Washing "The Great Unwashed,"* 57.

116. *Playground*, April 1908, 4.

117. Cavallo, *Muscles and Morals*, 36–38.

118. See Foster, "An Article for Small Parks."

119. "City Baths Ready Aug. 1," *New York Times*, July 23, 1911, 2.

120. Kasson, *Amusing the Million*, 50.

121. McGerr, *A Fierce Discontent*, esp. xiv.

122. Peiss, *Cheap Amusements*, 6.

123. See Zunz, *Making America Corporate*, 116–21; Barth, *City People*, 110–47; Powers, *Faces along the Bar*, 26–41.

INTERLUDE

1. I interpret St. Louis as a "northern" city for two main reasons. First, the social composition of St. Louis's population at the time was similar to that of more northern cities in that it had a large immigrant, industrial working class. Second, the history of the city's municipal pools closely resembles the development and use of municipal pools in more northern cities.
2. St. Louis Park Commissioner, *Annual Report* (1908–9), 39–41.
3. "All Races and Creeds Flock to Public Bath," *St. Louis Post-Dispatch*, August 11, 1907, 6.
4. St. Louis Park Commissioner, *Annual Report* (1912–13), 36. After 1911 the recreation commission stopped reporting separate attendance statistics for blacks and whites.
5. Ibid., 37.
6. "'Come on in,' Says Society, 'the water is fine,'" *St. Louis Post-Dispatch*, July 18, 1909, 13.
7. St. Louis Park Commissioner, *Annual Report* (1912–13), 29; "Splash! Jump into Our Big New Pond and Be Cool," *St. Louis Post-Dispatch*, July 20, 1913.
8. "To Change Hourly Playground Pool," *St. Louis Republican*, July 17, 1913, 2; "Thirteen of 25,000 in Bathing Rescued," *St. Louis Globe-Democrat*, July 21, 1913, 4; St. Louis Park Commissioner, *Annual Report* (1913–14), 6.
9. "Splash! Jump into Our Big New Pond and Be Cool," 4.
10. See Mrozek, "Sport in American Life," 18.
11. St. Louis Park Commissioner, *Annual Report* (1913–14), 4.
12. St. Louis Park Commissioner, *Annual Report* (1914–15), 23.
13. Mrozek, "Sport in American Life," 18.
14. "Thousands See Dedication of Fairground Park Swimming Pool," *St. Louis Globe Democrat*, July 16, 1913, 3.
15. "To Change Hourly Playground Pool," 2; "More Than 12,000 Persons a Day Take the Plunge," *St. Louis Post-Dispatch*, July 20, 1913, 6.
16. "Splash! Jump into Our Big New Pond and Be Cool," 4.
17. "Thirteen of 25,000 in Bathing Rescued," *St. Louis Globe-Democrat*, July 21, 1913, 4.
18. "Bathers Indiscreet Officials Are Told," *St. Louis Globe-Democrat*, July 20, 1913.
19. "More Than 12,000 Persons a Day Take the Plunge," *St. Louis Post-Dispatch*, July 20, 1913, 6.
20. "Thirteen of 25,000 in Bathing Rescued," 4.
21. "More Than 12,000 Persons a Day Take the Plunge," 6.
22. "Thin Bathing Suits Are Barred at New Fairground Pool," *St. Louis Post-Dispatch*, July 23, 1913, 1.
23. Ibid.
24. Ibid. The Fairgrounds Pool regulations were actually quite progressive. Unfor-

tunately, a comparison with another mixed-gender pool in the United States at the time is not possible, because no other U.S. city permitted males and females to swim together in pools. Gender integration did not become common practice in the United States until the mid-1920s. There was, however, a municipal pool in Battersea, England, that was gender integrated at the time, and a comparison between the policies governing it and Fairgrounds Pool reveals just how liberal they were in St. Louis. At Battersea, men and women seeking admission had to be a preapproved member of a "mixed-bathing club." To become a member, the prospective swimmer had to apply at town hall and have the backing of "a member of the [town] council, the town clerk, or any two ratepayers." Furthermore, each swimmer had to be accompanied by one and only one member of the opposite sex, except in the case of children who came with their parents. The pool rules also stipulated that "on leaving their dressing boxes bathers shall immediately enter the water and only approach the diving board directly from the water. When leaving the water bathers shall immediately go to their dressing boxes, and when dressed immediately leave the baths." In a quite heavy-handed way, these rules and regulations limited mixed-gender swimming to a select, known, and approved body of citizens and ensured that the pool was thoroughly unsocial and would not become a place for singles to meet. See "Our No. 1 Swimming Pool Is 40 Years Old," *Wilmington Journal Every Evening*, June 11, 1938, 6.

25. See Peiss, *Cheap Amusements*, 11–33.
26. For an astute assessment of the mixed-gender interaction that occurred at commercial venues at the time, see Kasson, *Amusing the Million*, 42–49, 59–61.
27. Horwood, "'Girls Who Arouse Dangerous Passions,'" 655.
28. "Extra Guards at Pool at Report of Negro Rush," *St. Louis Post-Dispatch*, July 27, 1913, 2.
29. Ibid.
30. Bederman, *Manliness and Civilization*, 8–9, 46; Douglas, *Terrible Honesty*, 256. On the southern origins of this stereotype, see Hodes, *White Women, Black Men*, 147–208; Fredrickson, *Black Image in the White Mind*, 256–82.

CHAPTER FOUR

1. "One of the Mermaids in Water Carnival to Close Avalon Pool," *Pittsburgh Press*, September 2, 1934, 8; "Races, Beauty Contest to Feature Carnival as Avalon Closes Pool for 1934," *Pittsburgh Press*, August 31, 1934, 34.
2. *New York Times*, June 5, 1940, 24.
3. The *Municipal Index* counted 117 outdoor municipal pools in the United States in 1916 and 61 indoor. Philadelphia operated 20 of them and Chicago 19. See "Swimming Pools and Other Public Bathing Places," *Municipal Index* (1931), 542. The editors gave the 1916 statistics in this 1931 issue as a comparison.

4. Atlanta and New Orleans were two significant exceptions to this general pattern. Atlanta operated four outdoor municipal pools before 1920 and opened a fifth in 1921 for black residents. New Orleans also operated four outdoor municipal pools before 1920 and opened a segregated pool for black residents at Thomy Lafon Playground in 1924. See *Municipal Index* (1931), 547–48, 550.

5. *Municipal Index* (1927), 484; (1931), 545–46, 548, 550, 555, 557. Municipal pools in the South clearly demand more attention than they receive here.

6. A few suburban communities with populations under 30,000, such as Belmont, Massachusetts, and South Manchester, Connecticut, operated municipal swimming pools before 1920, but these cities were really extensions of the larger metropolises, Boston and Hartford, respectively. Pendleton, Oregon, population 6,621, operated a pool beginning in 1913, but it was a unique case. Beginning in 1909, Pendleton hosted an annual rodeo sponsored by the Roundup Association. The association along with local businesses paid for the pool and then donated it to the town. The rodeo organizers even paid for the pool's upkeep out of their profits. See "A Municipal Natatorium," *American City*, April 1923, 171.

7. "An Unusual Small-Town Swimming Pool," *American City*, April 1923, 364.

8. "The Clairton Park Municipal Swimming Pool: An Outstanding Park Development," *American City*, October 1930, 109–10.

9. *Municipal Index* (1931), 545–50.

10. Leuchtenburg, *Perils of Prosperity*, 178–203.

11. Rodgers, *Work Ethic in Industrial America*, 106.

12. See Nasaw, *Going Out*, 221–40; Leach, *Land of Desire*, esp. 263–97.

13. "Swimming Pools and Other Public Bathing Places," *Municipal Index* (1931), 542. These numbers do not represent the exact number of municipal pools in 1916 and 1929. While close, they slightly understate the actual number. The *Municipal Index* admitted that despite its best research efforts, it could not identify all the municipal pools in the country.

14. "Clairton Park Municipal Pool," 110.

15. Wesley Bintz, "Public Swimming and Wading Pools at Pontiac, Ill.," *American City*, April 1926, 421; L. S. Johnson, "How Pana Is Financing and Building Its Community Swimming Pool," *American City*, March 1925, 306–7; "City's Pool Opens, Jammed at Once," *Elizabeth Daily Journal*, June 24, 1930, 22; Frank L. Bertschler, "Completely Equipped Municipal Plunge," *American City*, February 1927, 220–21.

16. Badger, *New Deal*, 190–215.

17. "2,419 Swimming and Wading Pools Built by WPA-PWA," *American City*, April 1938, 83.

18. "Nation-Wide Survey of WPA Pool and Beach Development," *Swimming Pool Data and Reference Annual* (1937), 52–56. The fourteen pools were built in Leav-

enworth (population 19,220), Pittsburgh (17,571), Ellsworth (2,227), Linn (395), Abilene (5,671), Concordia (6,255), Wellington (7,246), Hays (6,385), Englewood (377), Garden City (6,285), Ulysses (824), Sublette (582), Fowler (563), and Holton (2,885). The population statistics are for the year 1940. See U.S. Bureau of the Census, *Seventeenth Census*, vol. 1, part 16, 22–24.

19. Federal Writers Project, *WPA Guide to 1930s Kansas*, 120.

20. "East Side Cheers as City Opens Pool," *New York Times*, June 25, 1936, 23; "Pool Is Dedicated in McCarren Park," *New York Times*, August 1, 1936, 11; "25,000 at Opening of Harlem Pool," *New York Times*, August 9, 1936, 6; "40,000 at Opening of Red Hook Pool," *New York Times*, August 18, 1936, 21.

21. Caro, *Power Broker*, 454.

22. Ibid., 456; "40,000 at Opening of Red Hook Pool," 21; "25,000 at Opening of Harlem Pool," 6.

23. "10,000 See Swim Pool Dedicated," *Warren Tribune Chronicle*, July 12, 1934, 1.

24. In many conversations I have had with people who lived through the 1930s in small communities, my mention of swimming pools invariably evoked a sentimental story about the New Deal pool opened in their town or city.

25. "1937 Attendance Reports," *Swimming Pool Data and Reference Annual* (1938), 30.

26. "Bathers Flock to Park Pool," *Pittsburgh Sun-Telegraph*, July 15, 1932, 20; "Swimming Pool Receipts for Five Days $962, Far above All Expenses," *Warren Tribune Chronicle*, July 16, 1934, 1; "Mercury Here Hits 96, May Go Higher," *Warren Tribune Chronicle*, July 21, 1934, 1.

27. "Swimming . . . the New Great American Sport," *Fortune*, June 1934, 81, 85.

28. National Recreation Association, *Leisure Hours of 5,000 People*, 10–11.

29. Hiking ranked fifteenth overall, with 2,152 total participants and 768 frequent hikers. Only 1,282 people played baseball; 542 did so regularly. Bicycling was even less common with 547 total participants and 186 frequent bicyclists. See ibid.

30. All the respondents were adults, and most (59 percent) were women. Women and adults in general were the least likely to be natural-water swimmers. Second, the vast majority of respondents lived in noncoastal cities. They obviously could not easily or frequently visit the shore to "swim" in the waves. Finally, almost all the respondents were working class and middle class. Some may have swum at YMCA or YWCA pools, but few could have afforded to swim at private pools. See National Recreation Association, *Leisure Hours of 5,000 People*, 6–9.

31. See ibid., 7–8.

32. Ibid., 6, 60, 21.

33. "Swimmer's Invade City's 39 Pools," *Philadelphia Evening Bulletin*, June 26, 1934, "Swimming Pools" newspaper clip file, Urban Archives.

34. C. E. Miles, "The Evolution of a Swimming Pool," *American City*, September 1927, 322.

35. "The Trend of Swimming Pools," *Beach and Pool*, February 1934, 3.

36. Flamm, *Good Life in Hard Times*, 105; Charles Drew, "The Francis Swimming Pools of the Welfare and Recreational Association of Public Buildings and Grounds, Inc.: Season of 1932: Report of the Manager, Charles Drew," Charles Drew Papers, Moorland-Springarn Research Center.

37. Newspaper and magazine reports about pools during this period invariably emphasized the "modern" sanitation equipment and procedures in order to reassure concerned swimmers. See "Sanitation Used at Rahway Pool," *Elizabeth Daily Journal*, August 2, 1930, 2.

38. "Swimming . . . the New Great American Sport," 81.

39. Ibid., 83.

40. "East End District Has 8 City Pools," *Pittsburgh Press*, August 9, 1931, 4.

41. Charles Hall Page and Associates, "Documentation of Historic, Cultural, and Architectural Importance of the Fleishhacker Pool" (1977), 1, 6, 7, Vertical File Collection, Loeb Library; George W. Braden, "Some of California's Municipal Swimming Pools," *American City*, May 1927, 593–94; Flamm, *Good Life in Hard Times*, 104.

42. "An All-Year-'Round Swimmin' Hole," *American City*, June 1925, 660.

43. "Large Modern Swimming Pool a Gift to Wood River," *American City*, February 1927, 218; W. F. Corry, "Largest Municipal Pool in New England," *American City*, February 1941, 69.

44. "Sanitation Used at Rahway Pool," *Elizabeth Daily Journal*, August 2, 1930, 2.

45. "Investigation Wanted," *New York Times*, July 30, 1937, 18.

46. See Banner, *American Beauty*, 277; Peiss, *Hope in a Jar*, 150.

47. "Children Appeal to President to Save Swimming Pools Here," *Washington Star*, March 23, 1935, A-16.

48. Leeuwen, *Springboard in the Pond*, 78.

49. Ibid., 82–86.

50. Ibid., 98–107, 118–23.

51. Ibid., 195–96, 141–45, 176–87.

52. *Beach and Pool*, June 1934.

53. *Life*, May 24, 1937, 79.

54. Still photos of the *Palmy Days* and *Dancing Lady* scenes appear in Leeuwen, *Springboard in the Pond*, 157, 184. The analysis of them, however, is my own.

55. "Splashes," *Beach and Pool*, November 1939, 13.

56. "Swimming Pool to Open," *Wilmington Morning News*, June 2, 1898, 1; "New Bathhouse Opens," *Wilmington Morning News*, June 19, 1905, 1; "Little Ones Like Wading Pool," *Wilmington Morning News*, July 17, 1909, 1; "Bathing Pools Open, Small Boy 'Out of Misery,'" *Wilmington Evening Journal*, June 1, 1914, 6; Wilmington Board of Park Commissioners, *Report* (1920), 14.

57. "Wilmington's New Park to Have a Big Natatorium," *Wilmington Every Evening*, April 2, 1924, 3.

58. "Mayor to Receive Price's Run Pool," *Wilmington Morning News*, July 3, 1925.

59. "Resulting from Annual Drives City Now Has Splendid Pools," *Wilmington Sunday Star*, June 15, 1930, 9.

60. Mintz and Kellogg, *Domestic Revolutions*, 113.

61. "Another Pool for the City," *Wilmington Every Evening*, July 11, 1925, 6.

62. "First Free Bathhouse in City Opened to Public 35 Years Ago," *Wilmington Journal Every Evening*, June 11, 1938, 6.

63. "1900 Bathe in Price Run Pool," *Wilmington Evening Journal*, July 7, 1925, 13; "Price Run Pool Not to Be Open during Sundays," *Wilmington Every Evening*, July 15, 1925, 10.

64. "Labor Wants Sunday Swim," *Wilmington Evening Journal*, July 8, 1925, 11.

65. "More Than 1900 Persons Drawn to Price's Run Pool," *Wilmington Morning News*, July 7, 1925, 1.

66. "20,000 First Week Price's Run Pool," *Wilmington Every Evening*, July 11, 1925, 4.

67. "1900 Bathe in Price Run Pool," 13; "Nearly 3,000 Use Price's Run Park Pool in One Day," *Wilmington Every Evening*, July 7, 1925, 1.

68. In 1924, Leila Houghteling interviewed 467 "fully employed" unskilled and semiskilled workers in Chicago. Only 3 percent had cars. Referenced in Cohen, *Making A New Deal*, 103. In their study of "Middletown," Robert and Helen Lynd found much higher rates of automobile ownership among the "working class" in Muncie, Indiana, but it was clustered at the high end of the working-class income scale. See Lynd and Lynd, *Middletown*, 516–18.

69. "Another Pool for City!," *Wilmington Every Evening*, July 11, 1925, 6.

70. Bethlehem, *First Annual Message*, 21 (emphasis in original).

71. "Saucon Park 'Working Bee' a Great Success Yesterday," *Bethlehem Globe*, July 1, 1919, 1.

72. Bethlehem, *Third Annual Message*, 7.

73. "Saucon Park Pool Crowded," *Bethlehem Globe*, June 16, 1925, 9; "Saucon Park Swimming Pool Most Popular Place These Days," *Bethlehem Globe*, June 22, 1925, 8.

74. "Saucon Park Swimming Pool Most Popular Place These Days," 8. Bethlehem's population in 1930 was 57,892. See U.S. Bureau of the Census, *Fifteenth Census*, vol. 3, part 2, 685.

75. On levels of European immigration, see Daniels, *Coming to America*, 121–26, 288–90. On immigrants seeming less foreign to native-born Americans, see Roediger, *Working toward Whiteness*.

76. Cross, *An All-Consuming Century*, 59. Also see Zunz, *Why the American Century?*, 74–80. On working-class suburbs and working-class families moving out of urban slums, see Biggott, *From Cottage to Bungalow*; Crawford, *Building the Workingman's Paradise*; Nicolaides, *My Blue Heaven*.

77. On the public health campaigns of the period and declining rates of disease among the northern working class, see Tomes, *Gospel of Germs*, 204, 219, 242–43; Hoy, *Chasing Dirt*, 121, 123–49.

78. For example, an article on the opening of a municipal pool in Rahway, New Jersey, began: "Sanitation and health are the paramount considerations of the Union County Park Commission staff responsible for the Rahway swimming pool's administration. Not only is the water thoroughly chlorinated by the most modern chlorination plant, always in operation, but the pool is emptied, scrubbed and disinfected on the average of three times a week during the warm summer period." See "Sanitation Used at Rahway Pool," *Elizabeth Daily Journal*, August 2, 1930, 2.

79. Nasaw, *Going Out*, 60.

80. Guterl, *Color of Race in America*, esp. 6–13.

81. Elden R. Shaw, "Ellsworth—2,100 Population—Builds a Municipal Swimming Pool," *American City*, June 1924, 668–69.

82. "Swimming Pool Opens on Fourth," *Palmerton Press*, June 27, 1929, 1; Joseph Plechavy Jr., interview by Jeff Wiltse, April 16, 2001, notes with author, Palmerton Public Library, Palmerton, Pennsylvania; "Legion Community Picnic, July 27," *Palmerton Press*, July 17, 1930, 1; "Special Diving at Kunkle's Grove Sunday," *Palmerton Press*, June 26, 1930, 8.

83. "1900 Bathe in Price Run Pool," *Wilmington Evening Journal*, July 7, 1925, 13.

84. Nadine Brozan, "A Crumbling Pool Divides a Neighborhood," *New York Times*, July 30, 1990, B-1.

85. "Restoration of the WPA Era Pools in New York City," "Sports-swimming" vertical file, Irma and Paul Milstein Division, New York Public Research Library.

86. Dumenil, *Modern Temper*, 12.

87. Lynd and Lynd, *Middletown*, 480.

88. "1900 Bathe in Price Run Pool," 13.

89. "Bathing Suits: They Have Come a Long Way but Cannot Go Any Further," *Life*, July 9, 1945, 55–56; Chicago Special Park Commission Committee, *Annual Report*, 37–39.

90. Kidwell, "Women's Bathing and Swimming Costumes," 28.

91. "Sew Up Chicago Bathers," *New York Times*, June 19, 1921, 18.

92. "Bathing Suits: They Have Come a Long Way," 55; "As to Bathing Suits," *New York Times*, June 27, 1920, II-11; Kidwell, "Women's Bathing and Swimming Costumes," 25–26.

93. *Harper's Bazaar*, June 1920, 138. Quoted in Kidwell, "Women's Bathing and Swimming Costumes," 28.

94. "Rotarians to the Rescue," *New York Times*, June 10, 1921, 12.

95. For a thorough account of the changing role, attitude, and perception of American

woman in the 1920s, see Cott, *Grounding of Modern Feminism*; Dumenil, *Modern Temper*, 98–144.

96. "Suits with Skirts at Bathing Pools, New Edict Issued," *Washington Evening Star*, April 25, 1921, 1. District officials permitted mixed-gender swimming all summer long later in the decade.

97. "Nearly 3,000 Use Price's Run Park Pool in One Day," 1; "4500, Old and Young in Pool," *Wilmington Evening Journal*, July 8, 1925, 1.

98. "Bathing-Suits and Bathing-Beach Regulations," *American City*, June 1923, 569–70.

99. "Bathing Suits: They Have Come a Long Way," 56–57; "Yes, My Daring Daughter: The Saga of the American Bathing Girl from Voluminous Pantaloons to Diminutive Trunks," *Saturday Evening Post*, August 5, 1944, 24–25.

100. "Bathing Suits: They Have Come a Long Way," 55.

101. Paul Huedepohl, "Trunks without Uppers Need Not Be Objectionable Unless Extreme Streamlining Gives a 'Gorilla' Appearance," *Beach and Pool*, April 1939, 7, 16.

102. When Philadelphia imposed suit restrictions in 1921, for example, pool attendants simply told any female dressed immodestly to go home and put on a two-piece suit. "Ban 1-Piece Suits in Free City Pools," *Philadelphia Evening Bulletin*, June 27, 1921, "Swimming Pool" newspaper clip file, Urban Archives.

103. "Atlantic City Rival Entices Mermaids," *New York Times*, June 5, 1921, 7. The *Times* suggested that Crissey also made the decision for economic reasons, figuring he could entice summer consumers away from nearby Atlantic City.

104. "Bare Legged Bathers Start Row for Mayor," *New York Times*, June 6, 1921, 13; "Now the Rotarians Ask One-Piece Suit," *New York Times*, June 8, 1921, 20.

105. "Upholds One-Piece Suits," *New York Times*, June 28, 1926, 6.

106. Kidwell, "Women's Bathing and Swimming Costumes," 30.

107. For an astute examination at the way advertising shaped American tastes and culture early in the twentieth century, see Leach, *Land of Desire*.

108. Basinger, *A Woman's View*, 115.

109. *Life*, June 14, 1937, 78–79. For more substantial analyses on Americans' tendency to imitate movie stars during this period, see Sklar, *Movie-Made America*, 134–40; Basinger, *A Woman's View*.

110. As to the power of movies to shape American cultural attitudes, especially during the 1920s and 1930s, see Sklar, *Movie-Made America*.

111. Quoted in Kasson, *Rudeness and Civility*, 123.

112. Ibid., 129–30.

113. "Want to Bar 'Sea Vamp,'" *New York Times*, February 15, 1922, 3.

114. "Price Run Pool Not to Be Open during Sundays," *Wilmington Every Evening*, July 15, 1925, 10.

115. Huedepohl, "Trunks without Uppers," 16.

116. Peoria Board of Trustees, *Thirty-Fifth Annual Report*, 53.

117. "Races, Beauty Contest to Feature Carnival as Avalon Closes Pool for 1934," *Pittsburgh Press*, August 31, 1934, 34.

118. "Garbo Gaily Swims in Downtown Pool," *Philadelphia Evening Bulletin*, July 18, 1932, "Swimming Pools" newspaper clip file, Urban Archives.

119. "Saucon Park Swimming Pool Most Popular Place These Days," 8.

120. "More Than 1900 Persons Drawn to Price's Run Pool," 1; "Sunday Opening of Price Run Pool Not Yet Decided," *Wilmington Every Evening*, July 8, 1925, 2.

121. "Swimming . . . the New Great American Sport," 81.

122. "Dormont Residents Enjoy Splashes in Municipal Pools," *Pittsburgh Press*, July 10, 1932, 7; "Keystone Pool Affords Vacation Dips," *Pittsburgh Press*, July 9, 1932, 3.

123. "Heat Brings Crowds to South Park Pool," *Pittsburgh Post-Gazette*, July 11, 1932, 3.

124. Fass, *Damned and the Beautiful*, 5.

125. As to the redefinition of gender ideals, see Brumberg, *Body Project*, esp. xx–xxvi, 97–107; Kimmel, *Manhood in America*, 210–12; Rotundo, *American Manhood*, 222–24.

126. See Brumberg, *Body Project*, esp. xvii–xxxiii, 97–107.

127. Ibid., 107.

128. Fox and Lears, *Culture of Consumption*, x.

129. After New York City opened its eleven WPA pools in 1936, for example, local private pool owners tried to sell their facilities to the city because they were no longer profitable.

130. "Swimming . . . the New Great American Sport," 81.

131. Kasson, *Amusing the Million*; Peiss, *Cheap Amusements*; Erenberg, *Steppin' Out*.

CHAPTER FIVE

1. Kusmer, *A Ghetto Takes Shape*, 157–73; Spear, *Black Chicago*, 149–46; Osofsky, *Harlem*, 127–49.

2. See Tuttle, *Race Riot*, 74–207. A teenage Langston Hughes was wandering around Chicago one Sunday when he ventured "beyond Wentworth" into an Irish neighborhood. According to Hughes, he "was set upon and beaten by a group of white boys, who said they didn't allow niggers in that neighborhood." Quoted in Grossman, *Land of Hope*, 118. See also Chicago Commission on Race Relations, *Negro in Chicago*, 278–80, 288–95.

3. Essig, "Race Riots," 667. See also Tuttle, *Race Riot*.

4. Tomes, *Gospel of Germs*, 11, 111, 128, 131; Kraut, *Silent Travelers*, 78–135.

5. Grossman, *Land of Hope*, 153.

6. McBride, *From TB to AIDS*, 35–39; Hoy, *Chasing Dirt*, 117–21.

7. On the sexual stereotypes of black men, see Bederman, *Manliness and Civili-*

zation, 8–9, 46; Douglas, *Terrible Honesty*, 256; Drake and Cayton, *Black Metropolis*, 129–32. On the southern origins of this stereotype, see Hodes, *White Women, Black Men*, 147–208; Fredrickson, *Black Image in the White Mind*, 256–82.

8. See Bederman, *Manliness and Civilization*, esp. 1–31, 170–215. Quotation from p. 8.

9. Guterl, *Color of Race in America*, 6.

10. "East End District Has 8 City Pools," *Pittsburgh Press*, August 9, 1931, 4.

11. "East End Citizens Aroused," *Pittsburgh Courier*, August 8, 1931, 1.

12. "Police Unable to Prevent Highland Pool Race Clashes," *Pittsburgh Post-Gazette*, August 6, 1931; "Facts Submitted by the National Association for the Advancement of Colored People. IN RE: Disturbance at Highland Park Swimming Pool"; "Pittsburgh Swim Pool Disorders Taken to Court by N.A.A.C.P."; both in Pittsburgh Branch File, box G-190, Part I: 1909–39, NAACP Papers, Library of Congress.

13. "Facts Submitted by the National Association for the Advancement of Colored People."

14. In an August 11 incident, for example, the charges were upheld against David Beasley because officers found a small knife in his pocket, which the magistrate could construe as indicating malicious intent. See "Facts Submitted by the National Association for the Advancement of Colored People."

15. "Protection Promised by Mayor Kline after Conference," *Pittsburgh Courier*, August 29, 1931, 1; "4 Fined after Riot at Pool in Park," *Pittsburgh Sun-Telegraph*, August 21, 1931, 2; "Officer Stabbed, Bathers Hurt in Riot at City Pool," *Pittsburgh Post-Gazette*, August 21, 1931, 1.

16. "Officer Stabbed, Bathers Hurt in Riot at City Pool," 1; "4 Fined after Riot at Pool in Park," 2.

17. "2 Negro Swimmers Attacked by Mob," *Pittsburgh Press*, July 9, 1932, 16.

18. "East End Citizens Aroused," 1.

19. "Council Hears Pool Complaint," *Pittsburgh Courier*, July 16, 1932, 4; "Scores of Pools Open Today," *Pittsburgh Post-Gazette*, June 18, 1932, II-2.

20. "Council Hears Pool Complaint," 4.

21. Ibid.

22. "No Swimming, No Votes Edict," *Pittsburgh Courier*, August 15, 1931, 1; "Council Hears Pool Complaint," 1, 4.

23. "No Swimming, No Votes, Edict," 1, 4.

24. "Logan and Sams Are Winners," *Pittsburgh Courier*, November, 7, 1931, 1.

25. "2 Negro Swimmers Attacked by Mob," 16; "Council Hears Pool Complaint," 1, 4; Ernest Rice McKinney, "Views and Reviews," *Pittsburgh Courier*, July 23, 1932, 10.

26. "Negroes to Swim at Highland Park Pool; 'Protection' Given," *Pittsburgh Courier*,

June 24, 1933, 1; "DeRosa, Officials 'On Spot' after Pool Outrage," *Pittsburgh Courier*, July 22, 1933, 1.

27. "Voters' Protest Hit Politicians in Pool Outrage," *Pittsburgh Courier*, July 29, 1933, 1.

28. "Democratic Win Pleases Voters and Party Chiefs," *Pittsburgh Courier*, November 11, 1933, 1.

29. "A Jim Crow Pool—Whitewashed," *Pittsburgh Courier*, June 16, 1934, 1; "Tired of Stalling," *Pittsburgh Courier*, June 30, 1934, 2.

30. "Cops Turn Backs as Whites Attack Girl Scouts at Pool," *Pittsburgh Courier*, July 20, 1935, 1. At the time, Pennsylvania did not have a state civil rights law protecting black Americans' access to public facilities. The state finally passed such a law on June 24, 1939, after decades of effort on the part of civil rights advocates.

31. "Police Look on as Whites Beat Youth at Pool," *Pittsburgh Courier*, July 13, 1935, 1.

32. Johnson, *Along This Way*, 170.

33. As to the origins and southern history of the hypersexualized black man stereotype, see Hodes, *White Women, Black Men*, 147–208; Fredrickson, *Black Image in the White Mind*, 274–82.

34. Guterl, *Color of Race in America*, 13.

35. Sklar, *Movie-Made America*, 58–59.

36. McBride, *From TB to AIDS*, 10, 15–16, 17, 18–20, 48.

37. Douglas, *Terrible Honesty*, 256.

38. Wallenstein, *Tell the Court I Love My Wife*, 136–37, 146.

39. On the prevailing attitudes of northern whites and blacks toward interracial sex and marriage during this period, see K. Mumford, *Interzones*, 157–71; Kennedy, *Interracial Intimacies*, 79–92; Drake and Cayton, *Black Metropolis*, 133–45; Myrdal, *An American Dilemma*, 55.

40. Kevin J. Mumford examines several means northern whites used to prevent interracial relationships and marriages during the 1920s in *Interzones*. See esp. pp. 157–71.

41. Ibid., 93–117, 133–56.

42. See Kimmel, *Manhood in America*, 117–55, 210–12; Rotundo, *American Manhood*, 222–24, 239–44.

43. Bederman, *Manliness and Civilization*, 10–23.

44. On the consequences of the Johnson-Jeffries fight, see K. Mumford, *Interzones*, 6–18; Bederman, *Manliness and Civilization*, 1–10.

45. Elizabeth City Council, *Minutes* (1927), 169; Elizabeth Board of Recreation Commissioners, "Minute Book," August 27, 1975, Department of Recreation Office, Elizabeth City Hall; "Exclude Negroes from Dowd Pool," *Elizabeth Daily Journal*, August 4, 1930, 1. Given the paper's subsequent coverage of the racial conflict

at the pool, it was probably intentional that the headline of this article read as a command rather than a description. Elizabeth Board of Recreation Commissioners, "Minute Book," August 8, 1930, Department of Recreation Office.

46. "Race Riot Near at Dowd Pool," *Elizabeth Daily Journal*, August 11, 1930, 1.

47. Ibid.

48. Elizabeth City Council, *Minutes* (1938), 235.

49. "Municipal Pool to Stay Closed," *Elizabeth Daily Journal*, July 19, 1938, 9.

50. Elizabeth City Council, *Minutes* (1938), 235.

51. "Trouble Flares at Natatorium," *Elizabeth Daily Journal*, August 16, 1938, 13.

52. Elizabeth City Council, *Minutes* (1938), 235.

53. "Playfield, Pool Success Shown," *Elizabeth Daily Journal*, September 14, 1939, 21.

54. See Kusmer, *Ghetto Takes Shape*, 162; Spear, *Black Chicago*, 17.

55. Several factors intensified residential segregation in northern cities during this period. As black migrants arrived, they naturally and understandably chose to settle in areas already populated by African Americans. At the same time, working-class whites moved out of racially diverse neighborhoods, both to escape the inflow of southern migrants and because some could afford nicer homes and apartments. See Kusmer, *A Ghetto Takes Shape*, 163. Housing discrimination also played a crucial role in defining rigid racial boundaries in northern cities. White property owners refused to sell or rent homes and apartments in white neighborhoods to black families. Some white communities formed homeowners' associations whose principal, if not sole, function was to prevent blacks from living in their neighborhood. When black families slipped past the neighborhood covenants and agreements with real-estate companies, the white homeowners' associations often resorted to intimidation and even violence to force their new black neighbors out. See Spear, *Black Chicago*, 20–27; Kusmer, *A Ghetto Takes Shape*, 167–71.

56. Kusmer, *A Ghetto Takes Shape*, 161–65.

57. Spear, *Black Chicago*, 142–46; Osofsky, *Harlem*, 127–49; Sugrue, *Origins of the Urban Crisis*, 22, 35.

58. "The Race Problem at Swimming Pools," *American City* 47 (August 1932): 77; "East Side Cheers as City Opens Pool," *New York Times*, June 25, 1936, 23; "Pool Is Dedicated in McCarren Park," *New York Times*, August 1, 1936, 11; "40,000 at Opening of Red Hook Pool," *New York Times*, August 18, 1936, 21. As to the localized use of the pools, see Caro, *Power Broker*, 456–57, 512–14.

59. Caro, *Power Broker*, 513–14 (emphasis in the original). There is a short videoclip housed at the New York City Parks Library showing blacks and whites swimming together at Highbridge Pool, located in the Washington Heights section of Manhattan. The rest of the footage, however, taken at New York's other municipal pools, shows blacks and whites swimming at separate pools. Likewise, photographs of the city's pools from the late 1930s show racially segregated

use. As a whole, therefore, the evidence indicates that mixed-race swimming in New York Municipal pools at the time was, at most, unique to Highbridge Pool, and the lone video clip cannot substantiate whether it was common at High-bridge Pool. Furthermore, historians at the Parks Library cannot precisely date the video footage. It might have been taken as early as 1938, in which case the mixed-race swimming is noteworthy, or as late as 1949, by which time munici-pal pools throughout the North were being desegregated. The author viewed the video at an exhibit at the Arsenal Gallery, New York City, titled "Splash! A 70th Anniversary Celebration of New York's W.P.A. Pools." The video footage is part of the 16mm Silent Film Collection, 1938–49. See also, Kathryn Shattuck, "Big Chill of '36: Show Celebrates Giant Depression-Era Pools That Cool New York," *New York Times*, August 14, 2006, E-1.

60. "The Race Problem at Swimming Pools," 76.

61. "Big Bathing Pools Planned for City," *Washington Evening Star*, September 17, 1925, 1; *Congressional Record*, 3629, 7949–50, 8232, 8747; "Beach Bill Passed with Color Line," *Washington Tribune*, April 30, 1926, 1.

62. "The Bathing Pool Bill," *Washington Tribune*, April 30, 1926, 4.

63. "Bathing Pool a Much Discussed Matter," *Washington Tribune*, May 21, 1926, 1.

64. When the commercial pool actually opened, black swimmers were met by "a fla-grant sign before the door announcing that it is strictly for white patronage." See "A 'White' Pool," *Washington Tribune*, July 16, 1926, 1.

65. "Bathing Pool Bill," 4.

66. "As Usual," *Washington Tribune*, May 14, 1926, 4.

67. In 1930 the total black population of Washington was 132,068. The total popula-tion of Anacostia (census tracts 29 and 30) was 29,432 — 11,838 black and 17,594 white. The city's black population was concentrated in tracts 10, 11, and 14. The 47,578 black Americans living in this area were 66 percent of the total. See U.S. Bureau of the Census, *Fifteenth Census*, vol. 3, part 1, 385, 390–91.

68. "Anacostia Demands Ban on Bathing Site," *Washington Star*, May 7, 1926, 3.

69. "Four Bathing Pool Sites Are Selected," *Washington Evening Star*, May 28, 1926, 2; "New Bathing Pool Policy Endorsed," *Washington Evening Star*, June 19, 1926, 1.

70. "Colored Bathing Pool Opens July 15," *Washington Evening Star*, June 28, 1928, 2.

71. "Swimming Pool Is Opened Today," *Washington Evening Star*, July 14, 1928, 12.

72. James G. Tyson, "The Francis Swimming Pools of the Welfare and Recreational Association of Public Buildings and Grounds, Inc.: Season of 1939," James G. Tyson Papers, Moorland-Spingarn Research Center.

73. Charles Drew, "The Francis Swimming Pools of the Welfare and Recreational Association of Public Buildings and Ground, Inc., Summer of 1932: Report of the Manager, Charles Drew," Charles Drew Papers, Moorland-Spingarn Research

Center; "Mixed Swimming Will Be Allowed at All Times," *Washington Tribune*, July 6, 1928, 9; "Society Views Splash Events at Swim Meet: Many Prominent in Baltimore and Washington Social Circles at Francis Pool," *Washington Tribune*, September 14, 1928, 3.

74. Tyson, "Francis Swimming Pools," 3.
75. Ibid.
76. "Fatty, Skinny, and All the Gang Were There, and What Fun!," *Washington Tri-bune*, June 28, 1934, 1.
77. "20 More Pools for Wading and Swimming Held Urgent," *Washington Star*, March 20, 1935, B-1.
78. U.S. Bureau of the Census, *Fifteenth Census*, vol. 3, part 1, 385.
79. "Discrimination Closes D.C. Pool," *St. Louis Argus*, August 6, 1940, 20.
80. Sitkoff, *New Deal for Blacks*, 216–43.
81. On the exodusters, see Painter, *Exodusters*.
82. Federal Writers Project, *WPA Guide to 1930s Kansas*, 261–63; U.S. Bureau of the Census, *Fifteenth Census*, vol. 3, part 1, 856.
83. Samuel Ridley, "Colored Taxpayers Forced into Court," press release, undated; Sam Ridley to McCulley Ashlock, Mayor, August 17, 1935; both in "Discrimi-nation—Swimming Pools and Beaches" folder, box C-280, Part I: 1909–39, NAACP Papers.
84. Samuel Ridley to McCulley Ashlock, Mayor, August 17, 1935.
85. Ibid.; Ridley, "Colored Taxpayers Forced into Court."
86. Elisha Scott to Thurgood Marshall, July 27, 1937, "Discrimination—Swimming Pools and Beaches" folder, box C-280, Part I: 1909–39, NAACP Papers.
87. *Kern v. City Commissioners*, 100 P. 2d 710–11.
88. Ibid., 711.
89. Ibid.
90. Ibid.
91. *Kern v. City Commissioners*, 147 Kan. 472.
92. At the time, the future U.S. Supreme Court justice was just four years out of Howard Law School and one year into his tenure as assistant special counsel for the national NAACP office in New York City. See J. Williams, *Thurgood Marshall*, 59, 84–85.
93. E. E. Clark to Thurgood Marshall, July 16, 1937; "A Resolution Ordering the City Manager to Cause to Be Prepared Plans and Specifications for a Swimming Pool for Colored People as a Park Improvement in the City of Newton, Harvey County, Kansas," 29 June 1937; Thurgood Marshall to Samuel Ridley, July 20, 1937; all in "Discrimination—Swimming Pools and Beaches" folder, box C-280, Part I: 1909–39, NAACP Papers.
94. Ridley to Marshall, July 23, 1937, "Discrimination—Swimming Pools and Beaches" folder, box C-280, Part I: 1909–39, NAACP Papers.

95. As to national protest strategies at the time, see Sitkoff, *New Deal for Blacks*, 216–22, 237–40.
96. *Kern v. City Commissioners*, 147 Kan. 480–81.
97. *Kern v. City Commissioners*, 100 P. 2d 710.
98. Ibid., 714.
99. Samuel Ridley to Thurgood Marshall, April 13, 1940, "Discrimination—Swimming Pools and Beaches" folder, box C-280, Part I: 1909–39, NAACP Papers.
100. The city finally integrated Athletic Park Pool in 1951. Newton City Council, *Minutes*, August 15, 1951.
101. Quoted in Madison, *A Lynching in the Heartland*, 131–32.
102. "Resent Leasing of Jim-Crow Pool after Season for Whites Closes," *Pittsburgh Courier*, September 8, 1934, 1.
103. McBride, *From TB to AIDS*, 16–30, 34–40; Hoy, *Chasing Dirt*, 119.
104. Grossman, *Land of Hope*, 153.
105. Chicago Commission on Race Relations, *Negro in Chicago*, 303.

CHAPTER SIX

1. "6 Outdoor Pools for Whites Only," *Baltimore Afro-American*, July 25, 1953, 8.
2. Pangburn and Allen, *Long Range Recreation Plan*, 97.
3. "6 Outdoor Pools for Whites Only," 8.
4. "Boy, 13, Drowns for Lack of Pool," *Baltimore Afro-American*, August 8, 1953, 13; "Lack of Swimming Pool Causes 2 More Deaths," *Baltimore Afro-American*, August 29, 1953, 20.
5. "Park Board refuses to Change Policy on Outdoor Pool," *Baltimore Afro-American*, September 5, 1953, 8; *Dawson v. Mayor and City Council*, 123 F. Supp. 194–95.
6. "Decision Awaited in Md. Pool Cases," *Baltimore Afro-American*, July 3, 1954, 8; *Dawson v. Mayor and City Council*, 123 F. Supp. 202.
7. *Dawson v. Mayor and City Council*, 220 F. 2d 387; "Integration Delays Swim Pool Opening in City of Baltimore," *Washington Evening Star*, May 20, 1956, A-15.
8. *Baltimore Sun*, June 24, 1956, 38.
9. *Baltimore Afro-American*, July 7, 1956, 8.
10. "1 Druid Hill Park City Pool Closed," *Baltimore Sun*, July 24, 1956, 13; "Integrated Baltimore Pool Shut, Another Suffers Loss," *Washington Star*, July 23, 1956, B-2; "Baltimore Reports Attendance Drop at Integrated Pools," *Washington Star*, August 27, 1956, B-2.
11. "2 Negro Orphans Jeered Out of Baltimore Pool," *New York Times*, June 25, 1963, 13.
12. See Dudziak, *Cold War Civil Rights*, 7–10; Gleason, *Speaking of Diversity*, 153–87.
13. For an expansive assessment of the courts' role in desegregating public facilities, see Kluger, *Simple Justice*, 239–84.
14. In July 1946, for example, black and white members of the Paterson, New Jersey,

American Youth for Democracy began an organized effort to integrate Circle Swimming Pool. Under the leadership of Doris Berman and Rebecca Turgelsky, the group initiated a lawsuit, held a community meeting, and organized picketing parties at the pool. See Doris Berman to Franklin Williams, August 2, 1946, "Discrimination—Beaches and Swimming Pools" folder, box A-234, Part II: 1940–55, NAACP Papers, Library of Congress. At the same time, another pool protest was occurring in Lincoln, Nebraska. A group of black and white citizens called on Mayor Lloyd J. Marti in late July 1946 to protest racial exclusion at the city's municipal pool. When the mayor refused to desegregate the pool, the group wrote to the American Civil Liberties Union asking for advice on "the legal aspects of the situation." See George V. Oberlender to American Civil Liberties Union, August 7, 1946, "Discrimination—Beaches and Swimming Pools" folder, box A-234, Part II: 1940–55, NAACP Papers.

15. "Trial Brief for the Appellants [sic]," *James Culver, v. City of Warren*, In the Court of Appeals, Case No. 1183, 1–2; "Brief of Appellees," *Culver v. City of Warren*, In the Court of Appeals, Case No. 1183, 9–10; both in Trumbull County Archives.

16. "Trial Brief for the Appellants [sic]," *Culver v. Warren*, 1–2, Trumbull County Archives; "Memorandum," Marian Wynn Perry to Messrs. Marshall, Dudley, and Williams, January 12, 1948, "Discrimination—Swimming Pools—Warren, Ohio, Correspondence, 1947–49" folder, box B-66, Part II: 1940–55, NAACP Papers.

17. "Brief of Appellees," *Culver v. Warren*, 10–11, Trumbull County Archives.

18. "Trial Brief for Appellants [sic]," *Culver v. Warren*, 2–3, Trumbull County Archives; *Culver v. City of Warren*, 84 Ohio App. 377–79.

19. W. M. Howard to Thurgood Marshall, June 11, 1947; Thurgood Marshall to W. M. Howard, October 6, 1947; both in "Discrimination—Swimming Pools—Warren, Ohio, Correspondence, 1947–49" folder, box B-66, Part II: 1940–55, NAACP Papers.

20. "Trial Brief," *Culver v. City of Warren*, In the Court of Common Pleas, Case No. 54609, 2–4; "Opinion," *Culver v. City of Warren*, In the Court of Common Pleas, Case No. 54609, 14–16; both in Trumbull County Archives.

21. "Answer," *Culver v. City of Warren*, In the Court of Common Pleas, Case No. 54609, "Discrimination—Swimming Pools—Warren, Ohio, Correspondence, 1947–48" folder, box B-66, Part II: 1940–55, NAACP Papers; "Opinion," *Culver v. City of Warren*, 14–16, Trumbull County Archives.

22. "Opinion," *Culver v. City of Warren*, 2–5, 10–15, Trumbull County Archives.

23. "Memorandum," Perry to Marshall, Dudley, and Williams; Thurgood Marshall to W. M. Howard, February 6, 1948, "Discrimination—Swimming Pools—Warren, Ohio, Correspondence, 1947–48" folder, box B-66, Part II: 1940–55, NAACP Papers.

24. *Lawrence v. Hancock*, 76 F. Supp. 1005.

25. Ibid., 1005–6; T. G. Nutter to Thurgood Marshall, July 23, 1947, "Discrimina-

tion—Swimming Pools—West Virginia, 1940–48" folder, box B-66, Part II: 1940–55, NAACP Papers.

26. *Lawrence v. Hancock*, 76 F. Supp. 1006; *Anderson Brown v. Board of Education of Charleston*, 106 W. Va. 476.

27. T. G. Nutter to Thurgood Marshall, July 23, 1947.

28. T. G. Nutter to Thurgood Marshall, July 17, 1947, "Discrimination—Swimming Pools—West Virginia, 1940–48" folder, box B-66, Part II: 1940–55, NAACP Papers.

29. In a letter to Thurgood Marshall dated July 17, 1947, Nutter explicitly referenced the Newton case. See ibid.

30. "Complaint," *Lawrence v. Hancock*, In the District Court of the United States For the Southern District of West Virginia, "Discrimination—Swimming Pools—West Virginia, 1940–48" folder, box B-66, Part II: 1940–55, NAACP Papers.

31. "The Separate Answer of Montgomery Park Association to Plaintiff's Complaint," *Lawrence v. Hancock*, "Discrimination—Swimming Pools—West Virginia, 1940–48" folder, box B-66, Part II: 1940–55, NAACP Papers.

32. *Lawrence v. Hancock*, 76 F. Supp. 1004, 1007–8.

33. J. H. White to T. G. Nutter, February 17, 1948, "Discrimination—Swimming Pools—West Virginia, 1940–48" folder, box B-66, Part II: 1940–55, NAACP Papers.

34. Marian Wynn Perry to W. M. Howard, March 4, 1948, "Discrimination—Swimming Pools—Warren, Ohio, Correspondence, 1947–48" folder, box B-66, Part II: 1940–55, NAACP Papers.

35. *Culver v. City of Warren*, 84 Ohio App. 384, 386.

36. *Warren Tribune Chronicle*, June 16, 1948, 1.

37. "Court Rules on Pool Case," *Warren Tribune Chronicle*, July 3, 1948, 4.

38. St. Louis Division of Parks and Recreation, "Bathhouses and Swimming Pools," *Annual Report* (1944–45), no page number.

39. The black population of St. Louis was 108,649 in 1940 and 153,766 in 1950. See U.S. Bureau of the Census, *Sixteenth Census*, 1940, vol. 2, part 4, 455; U.S. Bureau of the Census, *Seventeenth Census*, 1950, vol. 2, part 25, 70.

40. George Schermer, "The Fairgrounds Park Incident: A study of the factors which resulted in the outbreak of violence at the Fairgrounds Park Swimming Pool on June 21, 1949, and account of what happened, and recommendations for corrective action," July 27, 1949, p. 8, "Discrimination—Swimming Pools—St. Louis" folder, box B-66, Part II: 1940–55, NAACP Papers.

41. Morris, *Lift Every Voice and Sing*, 37.

42. Schermer, "Fairgrounds Park Incident," 11.

43. "Joseph M. Darst, 64, St. Louis Ex-Mayor," *New York Times*, June 9, 1953, 27.

44. Schermer, "Fairgrounds Park Incident," 8, 12.

45. Ibid., 12.

46. "Pools and Playgrounds Opened to Both Races," *St. Louis Globe-Democrat*, June 21, 1949, 1.
47. "Negroes Will Not Be Denied a Swim in Any City Pool," *St. Louis Post-Dispatch*, June 21, 1949.
48. "Wrong O'Toole Gets Threats Aimed at Welfare Director," *St. Louis Globe-Democrat*, June 22, 1949, 2.
49. "Mayor Restores Old Swim Rules; Disturbances in Fairgrounds Park," *St. Louis Post-Dispatch*, June 22, 1949, 1; Schermer, "Fairgrounds Park Incident," 13.
50. "The Fairgrounds Incident," *St. Louis Argus*, June 24, 1949, 1 "Men Stabbed in Race Quarrels," *St. Louis Globe-Democrat*, June 22, 1949, 1; Schermer, "Fairgrounds Park Incident," 13–15.
51. "15 Injured in Clash over Pools; City Order Revoked," *St. Louis Star-Times*, June 22, 1949, 1, 4; "Fairgrounds Incident," 1; "Mayor Restores Old Swim Rules," 3; Schermer, "Fairgrounds Park Incident," 17.
52. Schermer, "Fairgrounds Park Incident," 16–17.
53. "15 Injured in Clash over Pools; City Order Revoked," 4.
54. Ibid., 4, 6.
55. Ibid., 6; Schermer, "Fairgrounds Park Incident," 19.
56. "Text of Darst's Statement Rescinding O'Toole's Order," *St. Louis Star-Times*, June 22, 1949, 4.
57. "Mayor Restores Old Swim Rules," 1.
58. "New Council Set Up to Ease Tension Following Pool Clash," *St. Louis Star-Times*, June 23, 1949, 1.
59. "Major Restores Old Swim Rules," 1.
60. Schermer, "Fairgrounds Park Incident," 22.
61. "O'Toole Was Right!," *St. Louis Argus*, July 1, 1949, 14.
62. "Weeding Out Prejudice," *St. Louis Post-Dispatch*, June 24, 1949, 2C.
63. "Dangerous Sparks," *St. Louis Globe-Democrat*, June 23, 1949, 2C.
64. Schermer, "Fairgrounds Park Incident," 20, 25, 26.
65. Henry F. Chadeayne to Joseph M. Darst, August 1, 1949, "Discrimination—Swimming Pools—St. Louis" folder, box B-66, Part II: 1940–55, NAACP Papers.
66. "Darst Abolishes Segregation at Two City Pools," *St. Louis Post-Dispatch*, April 15, 1950.
67. "Urban League Sends Letter of Protest to Mayor Darst," *St. Louis American*, April 13, 1950, 10; "League of Women Voters Ask Mayor Darst to Open Pools to Everyone," *St. Louis American*, May 18, 1950, 1.
68. "Refusal of Admittance to Fairgrounds Pool Witnessed by City's Top Officials," *St. Louis American*, June 22, 1950, 1.
69. "NAACP Backs Negroes Who Got 'Brush' on Monday," *St. Louis Argus*, June 23, 1950, 1.

70. "Shot Kills Judge in Tax Plot Case," *New York Times*, July 8, 1956, 36.

71. "Finding of Fact," *Draper v. City of St. Louis*, "Discrimination—Swimming Pools—St. Louis" folder, box B-66, Part II: 1940–55, NAACP Papers.

72. "Police Chief Says Dept. Could Take Care of Situation If City Opens Swim Pools," *St. Louis American*, July 13, 1950, 1, 16; "Race Relations Council Member Supports City's Bias Stand on Pools," *St. Louis Argus*, July 14, 1950, 1, 10.

73. *Draper v. City of St. Louis*, 92 F. Supp. 549.

74. Ibid., 548. Decided on June 5, 1950, the McLaurin case severely limited the separate-but-equal doctrine. The court ruled that a black graduate student at the University of Oklahoma had been denied his constitutional rights because he was forced to sit at a designated desk in class, eat at a particular table in the cafeteria, and study at a particular table in the library; whereas white students could choose freely where to sit, eat, and study. It was not enough, the court ruled, that McLaurin was permitted to attend the same classes, eat in the same cafeteria, and use the same library. He must, the court ruled, be treated the same as all the other students. See *McLaurin v. Oklahoma State Regents*, 339 U.S. 637.

75. *Draper v. City of St. Louis*, 92 F. Supp. 550.

76. "Transcript of Proceedings," *Draper v. City of St. Louis*, pp. 3, 12, "Discrimination—Swimming Pools—St. Louis" folder, box B-66, Part II: 1940–55, NAACP Papers.

77. The original note was still attached to the "Transcript of Proceedings" in NAACP Papers.

78. "City Thrice Denied Stay Order in One Day," *St. Louis American*, July 30, 1950, 20; "Judge Refuses to Delay Opening Pools to Negroes," *St. Louis Post-Dispatch*, July 18, 1950, 3.

79. "All Races Swim at Fairgrounds Citizens Alert," *St. Louis Argus*, July 21, 1950, 1, 16; "Police Reserves Called Out at Fairground Pool," *St. Louis Post-Dispatch*, July 19, 1950, 1; "Eight Arrested in Disturbance at Fairground Pool," *St. Louis Post-Dispatch*, July 20, 1950, 3.

80. "90 More Police to Be Stationed at Pools Today," *St. Louis Post-Dispatch*, July 23, 1950, 3.

81. St. Louis Division of Parks and Recreation, *Annual Report* (1934–40), (1946–56).

82. St. Louis Division of Parks and Recreation, *Annual Report* (1954), 18.

83. St. Louis Division of Parks and Recreation, *Annual Report* (1958), 1–2.

84. "Pools for Everybody," *St. Louis Post-Dispatch*, July 25, 1950, B-2.

CHAPTER SEVEN

1. "City to Build Swimming Pool in North End of Central Park," *New York Times*, August 21, 1961, 1.

2. "Park Swimming Pool Backed," *New York Times*, August 29, 1961, 30.

3. As to the municipal fiscal crisis of the 1970s, see Teaford, *Rough Road to Renaissance*, 200–252.

4. By one count, there were 1,200 private club pools in the United States in 1950. See "Data on Swimming Pools," *Recreation* 45 (March 1952): 575.

5. "Everybody's Taking the Plunge," *Washington Post*, July 10, 1999, G-5; "Data on Swimming Pools," 575.

6. Putnam, *Bowling Alone*, 288.

7. New York City opened fifteen pools during the 1930s. See "Parks for Seven Million: A Vision Realized," *New York Times*, August 16, 1936, VII-11; "Pools Will Open Today," *New York Times*, May 29, 1940, 10. Lasker Pool, which opened in 1963, was the first outdoor municipal pool opened in New York City during the postwar period. Four pools opened in Washington, D.C., between 1930 and 1935. See "D.C. Recreation Pools Seek More Swimmers," *Washington Evening Star*, July 13, 1943, A-12. No new pools opened in Washington between 1935 and 1963. See "D.C. Supports Plan to Provide 15 Public Pools," *Washington Evening Star*, September 25, 1963, B-1.

8. When Kansas City opened Swope Pool in 1942, it operated three pools: Swope, Grove, and Paseo. It operated those same three pools in 1957, although Paseo Pool was renamed Parade Pool. See "Into a Glittering Pool," *Kansas City Times*, July 30, 1942, 3; "Grove Pool Is Closed," *Kansas City Times*, October 21, 1957, 3.

9. "New Pool Dedicated in Fairground Park," *St. Louis Post-Dispatch*, September 4, 1959, C-3.

10. In St. Louis, white attendance before desegregation typically approached 500,000 a year. St. Louis did not keep track of separate numbers for black and white swimmers after desegregation, but an optimistic estimate is that 50,000 to 75,000 whites swam in the city's pools after desegregation. See St. Louis Division of Recreation, *Annual Report* (1949); (1954), 19. In Washington, D.C., overall white attendance dropped from 346,000 in 1948 to 146,000 in 1950. See "Board Asks Interior's Estimate of Success of Interracial Pools," *Washington Star*, September 16, 1950, A-20. In Kansas City, white attendance at the city's primary pool, Swope Pool, dropped from an average of 150,000 a year to about 30,000. See "Pool Total of 48,301," *Kansas City Times*, September 9, 1954.

11. In Peoria, Illinois, for example, the amount of public recreation space per person in black neighborhoods in 1968 was one-tenth of the average for the city as a whole. As the city's Urban League complained, the city's largest black neighborhood was "the most recreationally deprived area in the park system." See "Park Board Gives OK to South Side Pool," *Peoria Journal-Star*, May 9, 1968.

12. "Integrated in 1954: A Ho-Hum Anniversary," *Kansas City Star*, June 16, 1974; "The Pools Inadequate? The West Side Picture," *Chicago News*, July 16, 1966, "Swimming Pools—Chicago" newspaper clip file, Municipal Reference Collec-

tion, Harold Washington Library; "Neglected Neighborhoods Tell the Story," *Detroit News*, July 25, 1987, A-10.

13. "McKinley Pool, in Bad Condition, to Be Shut Down," *Washington Star*, March 30, 1962, A-3; "Pickets Ask Reopening of Closed Pool," *Washington Star*, July 6, 1963, A-16.

14. "Grove Pool Is Closed," *Kansas City Times*, October 21, 1957; "Adieu to Grove Pool," *Kansas City Times*, October 29, 1957.

15. "3 Councilmen Want More Swim Pools," *Philadelphia Evening Bulletin*, July 19, 1966, "Swimming Pool" newspaper clip file, Urban Archives.

16. Button, *Black Violence*, 10.

17. "Police Get 12-Hour Duty in Westside Uproar," *Chicago Defender*, July 16–22, 1966, 1, 2; "Loot Stores in W. Side Unrest," *Chicago Tribune*, July 13, 1966, 1.

18. "Police Get 12-Hour Duty in Westside Uproar," 2.

19. Ibid., 1, 2; "Loot Stores in W. Side Unrest," 1, 6; "7 Cops Hurt by Teens on West Side," *Chicago Tribune*, July 14, 1966, 1, 4; "118 Seized in Outbreak of Violence," *Chicago Tribune*, July 15, 1966, 1, 4; "1500 Troops Go to Area Ready to Shoot," *Chicago Tribune*, July 16, 1966, 1, 2.

20. "Police Get 12-Hour Duty in Westside Uproar," 2.

21. "Here's How a Westsider Explains the Outbreak," *Chicago Defender*, July 16–22, 1966, 1; "The Pools Inadequate? The West Side Picture," *Chicago News*, July 16, 1960, "Swimming Pools—Chicago" newspaper clip file, Municipal Reference Collection, Harold Washington Library.

22. "Guard Patrol Is Cut in Chicago Ghetto; City Buys 10 Pools," *New York Times*, July 18, 1966, 17; "Race Riot in Chicago," *New York Times*, July 31, 1960, 15.

23. Chicago Commission on Race Relations, *Negro in Chicago*, 275, 280, 288–92; Drake and Cayton, *Black Metropolis*, 102–5.

24. As to residential segregation in northern cities during this period, see Sugrue, *Origins of the Urban Crisis*, 179–258; Hirsh, *Making the Second Ghetto*.

25. "Guard Patrol Is Cut in Chicago Ghetto; City Buys 10 Pools," 17; "Goal: A Pool for Every Neighborhood," *Chicago News*, July 19, 1967, "Swimming Pools—Chicago" newspaper clip file, Municipal Reference Collection, Harold Washington Library.

26. "32 New Pools to Help Chicago Keep Its Cool," *Chicago News*, March 13, 1968, "Swimming Pools—Chicago" newspaper clip file, Municipal Reference Collection, Harold Washington Library.

27. "Program Rushed for Slum Youth," *New York Times*, August 7, 1966, 48.

28. "City Opens First of 10 Pools Planned for Slum Areas," *New York Times*, August 3, 1967, 23; "20 New Minipools Planned in Slums," *New York Times*, March 24, 1968, 61; "Lindsay Smiles His Way through City," *New York Times*, August 14, 1971, 29.

29. "20 New Minipools Planned in Slums," 61.

30. "Summer Job Plan May Be Extended," *New York Times*, August 16, 1966, 43.

31. "Swimming Pools to Cool Hot Tempers," *Chicago News*, June 10, 1967, "Swimming Pools—Chicago" newspaper clip file, Municipal Reference Collection, Harold Washington Library; "8 Areas Turn Down Daley's Swim Pools," *Chicago News*, July 13, 1968, "Swimming Pools—Chicago" newspaper clip file, Municipal Reference Collection, Harold Washington Library.

32. As to the conditions in northern inner cities, see Sugrue, *Origins of the Urban Crisis*.

33. "Lindsay Smiles His Way through City," 29; "32 New Pools to Help Chicago Keep Its Cool"; "8 Areas Turn Down Daley's Swim Pools"; "Cool Minipools for the Hot Summer," *American City*, April 1968, 81–83.

34. "Pool Opens in Bedford-Stuyvesant," *New York Times*, July 11, 1971, 33; "Florida Architect Is Designing a Pool for Brooklyn Ghetto," *New York Times*, November 23, 1966, 30; "How a Pool Grew in Brooklyn," *New York Times*, August 13, 1972, II-18; "Bedford Stuyvesant Community Pool," *Architectural Record* 155 (June 1974): 98–99.

35. Teaford, *Rough Road to Renaissance*, 200–252.

36. "Troubled Waters: Swimming Pool Vandals Spoil Kids' Splashing Good Time," *Detroit News*, August 3, 1989, B-1.

37. Pool attendance in 1948, 1956, 1965, and 1969 was 203,491; 191,693; 228,412; and 221,304, respectively. See "City Pools Set Record," *Youngstown Vindicator*, September 5, 1948; Youngstown Park and Recreation Commission, *Annual Report* (1956), (1965), (1969).

38. "City Reverses Decision, Plans to Open All Pools," *Youngstown Vindicator*, June 27, 1981, 1; "Pools to Close Aug. 9," *Youngstown Vindicator*, July 25, 1981, 1.

39. "City Pools Receipts Drop 33%; '85 Closings Eyed," *Youngstown Vindicator*, August 17, 1984, 20; "City to Operate Only 7 Pools Because of Lifeguard Shortage," *Youngstown Vindicator*, June 16, 1985, 1.

40. "Youngstown Pool Attendance Takes a Dip; One May Close in '89," *Youngstown Vindicator*, August 19, 1988, 1; "Closing of Pool Approved," *Youngstown Vindicator*, October 28, 1988, 19.

41. "Ask More Police at Parks, Pools," *Youngstown Vindicator*, June 26, 1983, 25.

42. "Strict Security Measures Follow Skirmish at Pool," *Youngstown Vindicator*, July 8, 1988, 1.

43. "Youngstown May Close 2nd City Pool," *Youngstown Vindicator*, April 21, 1989, 1.

44. See pictures in Youngstown Parks and Recreation Commission, *Annual Report* (1957), (1965), (1969), (1972), (1973); "Youngstown May Close 2nd City Pool," 1.

45. "Youngstown May Close 2nd City Pool," 1.

46. Ibid.

47. "Overall Pool Attendance Takes a Dive in Youngstown," *Youngstown Vindicator*, August 11, 1989, 1; "Official Wants Pools to Merge," *Youngstown Vindicator*, July 12, 1991, A-1.
48. Youngstown Parks and Recreation Commission, *Annual Report* (2004), 4.
49. "In the Swim of Things," *New York Times*, November 30, 1981, III-2.
50. "Goldin Cites Hazards at Swimming Pools," *New York Times*, April 1, 1985, B-4.
51. "A Crumbling Pool Divides a Neighborhood," *New York Times*, July 30, 1990, B-1; "City Pools? '99.9 Percent Peaceful,'" *New York Times*, August 7, 1994, XIII-14.
52. "Make City Pools Private, Councilman Proposes," *Pittsburgh Post-Gazette*, November 16, 1995; Pittsburgh Parks and Recreation Department, "Swimming Pool List," <http://www.city.pittsburgh.pa.us/parks/html/swimming_pools.html#list.>
53. "The Talk of the Town," *New Yorker*, August 5, 1991, 23–24.
54. "Use of District Pools Cut in Half since '48," *Washington Star*, July 19, 1959, C-7.
55. On postwar mass suburbanization, see Jackson, *Crabgrass Frontier*; Baxandall and Ewen, *Picture Windows*; Duany, Plater-Zyberk, and Speck, *Suburban Nation*; Nicolaides, *My Blue Heaven*.
56. "County Rejects Plea in Donaldson Run for Swimming Pool," *Washington Star*, April 3, 1955, A-8; "County Widens Segregation Bar," *Washington Star*, June 11, 1955, A-1.
57. On the Levittown pools, see "Up from the Potato Fields," *Time*, July 3, 1950, 69.
58. "Montgomery Heated on Community Swimming Pools," *Washington Star*, July 11, 1954, A-13; "Pool Co-ops Take Work, But Pay Off Generously," *Washington Star*, May 22, 1955, A-31; "Use of District Pools Cut in Half since '48," C-7.
59. "Communities Are Pooling Their Interests for Everyone's Benefit," *Philadelphia Evening Bulletin*, April 6, 1958, "Swimming Pools" newspaper clip file, Urban Archives.
60. "The Cooperative Family Swim Club," *Swimming Pool Data and Reference Annual* (1959), 17; "Communities Are Pooling Their Interests for Everyone's Benefit."
61. "Montgomery Readies First County Pool," *Washington Star*, July 14, 1968, B-5.
62. "It's Hard for Most to Get in the Swim," *Washington Post*, May 26, 1974, B-1.
63. "Booming Public Pools Lag behind Rise in Swimmer Population," *Philadelphia Inquirer*, July 30, 1964, "Swimming Pools" newspaper clip file, Urban Archives. The title of the article is inexplicably misleading. The text of the article emphasizes the absence of public pools in suburban Philadelphia and the boom in private pools.
64. "County Rejects Plea in Donaldson Run for Swimming Pool," A-8.
65. "Glenwood Play Club Calls Meeting for Tomorrow," *Washington Star*, March 20, 1955, A-19; "Swimming Pool Finally OK'd," *Washington Star*, November 18, 1955,

A-21; "Pool Dedicated by 3 Communities in Prince Georges," *Washington Star*, September 9, 1956, A-16.

66. "Communities Are Pooling Their Interests for Everyone's Benefit."

67. "Chevy Chase Club Explains Stand On Membership," *Washington Star*, January 17, 1962, A-17; "Integration Vote Fails at Bethesda Swim Club," *Washington Star*, August 2, 1966, B-3; "Fairfax Club Affirms Barring of Negro Family," *Washington Star*, July 30, 1965, C-2.

68. *Tillman v. Wheaton-Haven Recreation Association*, 410 U.S. 432–33. Many other club pools located in the outer reaches of suburban Washington similarly passed explicit bylaws during the mid- to late 1960s. See "Integration Effort Fails at Virginia Hills Pool," *Washington Star*, August 11, 1966, B-3; "Club in New Carrollton Excludes Negro Family," *Washington Star*, July 14, 1968, B-4.

69. "Club in New Carrollton Excludes Negro Family," B-4.

70. "Civic Federation Asks Two $150,000 Montgomery Pools," *Washington Star*, March 15, 1955, A-10.

71. "Pool Program to Share Budget Hearing Interest," *Washington Star*, June 14, 1955, A-16.

72. "Montgomery Heated on Community Swimming Pools," A-13.

73. "Fairfax Club Affirms Barring of Negro Family," *Washington Star*, July 30, 1965, C-2; *Sullivan v. Little Hunting Park*, 396 U.S. 229–30.

74. *Tillman V. Wheaton-Haven Recreation Association*, 451 F. 2d 1213.

75. "Attorneys Plan Appeal Today of Wheaton-Haven Ruling," *Washington Star*, July 10, 1970, B-1; *Tillman v. Wheaton-Haven Recreation Association*, 451 F. 2d 1213; "After 5 Years, Humiliation Still Recalled," *Washington Post*, February 28, 1973, A-12.

76. "Attorneys Plan Appeal Today of Wheaton-Haven Ruling," B-1; *Tillman v. Wheaton-Haven Recreation Association*, 451 F. 2d 1212, 1220–21.

77. *Tillman v. Wheaton-Haven Recreation Association*, 410 U.S. 431–34.

78. "After Five Years, Humiliation Still Recalled," A-12. Some community pools in the Washington area voluntarily admitted black members, although not without opposition. In January 1966 the membership of the Kemp Hill Swim Club in Montgomery County overruled its board of directors and voted overwhelmingly (193 to 36) to admit a black family. The family had recently purchased a $30,000 house in a nearby subdivision. The *Washington Star* noted that "several months of dispute and muted opposition" preceded the meeting. The black family no doubt benefited from a preliminary vote as to whether the membership vote should be open or secret ballot. The proponents of an open vote barely triumphed, 122 to 111. The fact that the membership vote was not nearly so close suggests some members did not feel comfortable publicly expressing their opposition to admitting the black family. See "Kemp Mill Swim Club Admits Negro Family," *Washington Star*, January 7, 1966, B-4.

79. On the importance of social status at the time, see Packard, *Status Seekers*.
80. "Data on Swimming Pools," 575.
81. "Swimming Pool Trade Buoyant on Outlook for Backyard Boom," *New York Times*, December 25, 1955, III-7.
82. "Why More and More Americans Are Saying: 'I'm buying a home with a swimming pool,'" *Beach and Pool* 28 (December 1954): 17.
83. "Boom in Backyard Pools," *St. Louis Post-Dispatch*, August 12, 1956.
84. "Backyard Pool Salesmen Expect 600-Million Year Despite Slump," *New York Times*, May 11, 1958, VIII-1; "Sales Splash," *New York Times*, February 12, 1959, 40; "Buyers Plunge to Get into Swim as Installation of Pools Widens," *New York Times*, January 11, 1960, 95; "Backyard Pools Gaining Favor," *Philadelphia Evening Bulletin*, June 8, 1957, "Swimming Pools" newspaper clip file, Urban Archives.
85. Coontz, *The Way We Never Were*, 24–26.
86. Ibid., 24–25.
87. Leeuwen, *Springboard in the Pond*, 183–85; "Swimming Pool Boom Bigger Than Ever," *Philadelphia Evening Bulletin*, October 10, 1953, "Swimming Pools" newspaper clip file, Urban Archives.
88. "Backyard Pool Salesmen Expect 600-Million Year Despite Slump," 1.
89. Coontz, *The Way We Never Were*, 24. See also, May, *Homeward Bound*, esp. 58–91, 35–182.
90. "More Taking the Plunge," *Philadelphia Evening Bulletin*, July 31, 1955, "Swimming Pools" newspaper clip file, Urban Archives; "Every Yard Can Have a Pool," *Philadelphia Evening Bulletin*, May 22, 1957, "Swimming Pools" newspaper clip file, Urban Archives.
91. Sylvia Porter, "Boom in Swimming Pools," *Washington Star*, May 22, 1957, B-22.
92. "They're All Swimming in the Backyard," *New York Times*, August 12, 1956, 23.
93. Ibid.
94. Ibid.
95. "We Took the Plunge and Love It!," *Philadelphia Evening Bulletin*, May 21, 1965, "Swimming Pools" newspaper clip file, Urban Archives; "Swimming-Pool Sales Making a Bigger Splash," *Philadelphia Evening Bulletin*, October 23, 1971, "Swimming Pools" newspaper clip file, Urban Archives.
96. "We Took the Plunge and Love It!"; "Swimming-Pool Sales Making a Bigger Splash."
97. "Status Is a Thousand-Dollar Splash in the Backyard," *New York Times*, April 23, 1967, III-20.
98. Margaret Dana, "If a Backyard Pool Is Your Wish, Get Facts before Taking the Plunge," *Philadelphia Evening Bulletin*, July 20, 1967, "Swimming Pools" newspaper clip file, Urban Archives.

99. *Wall Street Journal*, February 14, 1974, 1; "The Pool Business Is Back in the Swim," *New York Times*, May 30, 1976, III-13. On the economic conditions of the mid-1970s, see Levy, *Dollars and Dreams*, esp. 60–65.

100. "Swimming Pool: Buying for the Back Yard," *Washington Post*, July 10, 1975, D-10.

101. "In the Swim," *Wall Street Journal*, August 19, 1985, 17; "Pool Sales Will Sparkle," *New York Times*, July 26, 1987, III-1; "All About Swimming Pools," *New York Times*, September 13, 1992, III-10; "Pool Sales Booming in State," *New York Times*, August 14, 1988, XII-8.

102. "Everybody's Taking the Plunge," *Washington Post*, July 10, 1999, G-5.

103. "Pools Worthy of Boom Times," *New York Times*, April 1, 2000, B-1.

104. "Paradise Found: Catching the New Wave of Dramatic Home Pools," *Chicago Tribune*, May 19, 2000, B-1.

105. "Pool Problems? Not If There Are Pool Rules," *New York Times*, July 24, 1976, 14.

106. "In the Swim: Backyard Pools or Private Clubs," *Philadelphia Evening Bulletin*, May 30, 1976, "Swimming Pools" newspaper clip file, Urban Archives.

107. "The Pool: No Longer So Cool," *Boston Globe*, April 10, 2001, 1, 15.

108. Putnam, *Bowling Alone*, 247–76, 280, 283–84.

109. Quoted in Sennett, *Fall of Public Man*, vii.

110. "L.I. Dispute: Are 2 Pools 1 Too Many?," *New York Times*, June 4, 1988, 29.

111. "A Crumbling Pool Divides a Neighborhood," *New York Times*, July 30, 1990, B-1.

CONCLUSION

1. "1900 Bathe in Price Run Pool," *Wilmington Evening Journal*, July 7, 1925, 13.

2. Joseph Plechavy Jr., interview by Jeff Wiltse, April 16, 2001, notes with author, Palmerton Public Library, Palmerton, Pennsylvania.

3. "Splashes," *Beach and Pool*, November 1939, 13.

4. L. Mumford, *City in History*, 512–13.

5. Sugrue, *Origins of the Urban Crisis*, 231–58.

6. "Police Report Sex Assault of Girl, 14, in Bronx Pool," *New York Times*, July 6, 1993, B-3; "A Menacing Ritual Is Called Common in New York Pools," *New York Times*, July 7, 1993, A-1; "New York Police Report Sex Assault at Another Pool," *New York Times*, July 12, 1993 B-3; "Police Investigate Reported Incidents of Sexual Abuse at Two City Swimming Pools," *New York Times*, July 5, 1994, B-3; "Girl Is Sexually Assaulted in Public Pool in Bronx," *New York Times*, July 6, 1994, B-3; "Girl, 12, Is Groped at a Pool in Queens," *New York Times*, July 24, 1995, B-3.

7. Mary B. W. Tabor, "New York Police Report Sex Assault at Another Pool," *New York Times*, July 12, 1993, B3.

8. "Swimming . . . the New Great American Sport," *Fortune*, June 1934, 81.

9. Michael Marriot, "A Menacing Ritual Is Called Common in New York Pools," *New York Times*, July 7, 1993, A-1.

10. This general trend is clearly evident in suburban St. Louis. St. Charles, a suburban city about twenty miles northwest of St. Louis, opened an elaborate aquatic center in 1992 that contained twisting slides, stepping-stone "lily pads," water cannons, and mushroom-shaped "raindrop" waterfalls. To build it, the city demolished the traditional pool that had occupied the space previously. Over the next several years, St. Peters, Lake Saint Louis, St. Vincents, Granite City, and Webster Grove all funded similar water theme parks rather than swimming pools. "Everyone into the Pool, Er . . . Complex," *St. Louis Post-Dispatch*, May 18, 1993, A-1; "Cool Pools," *St. Louis Post-Dispatch*, August 15, 1995, D-1.

BIBLIOGRAPHY

ARCHIVAL MATERIAL

Boston Public Library, Boston
    Government Documents Reading Room
Chicago Historical Society, Chicago
    Special Collections
Elizabeth City Hall, Elizabeth, New Jersey
    Department of Recreation Office
Harold Washington Library, Chicago
    Municipal Reference Collection
Library of Congress, Washington, D.C.
    Manuscript Division
        National Association for the Advancement of Colored People Papers
Loeb Library, Harvard University, Cambridge, Massachusetts
    Vertical File Collection
Moorland-Spingarn Research Center, Howard University, Washington, D.C.
    Charles Drew Papers
    James G. Tyson Papers
National Archives and Records Administration, Waltham, Massachusetts
    Manuscript Census
New York City Parks Library, New York
    16mm Silent Film Collection, 1939–49
New York Public Research Library, New York
    Irma and Paul Milstein Division of United States History, Local History, and
    Genealogy
Philadelphia City Archives, Philadelphia
Trumbull County Courthouse, Warren, Ohio
    County Archives
Urban Archives, Temple University, Philadelphia
    Newspaper Clippings Collections

COURT CASES

Anderson Brown v. Board of Education of Charleston, 106 W. Va. 476 (1928).
Culver v. City of Warren, 84 Ohio App. 373 (1948).
Dawson v. Mayor and City Council of Baltimore, 123 F. Supp. 193 (1954).
Dawson v. Mayor and City Council of Baltimore, 220 F. 2d 387 (1955).
Draper v. City of St. Louis, 92 F. Supp. 546 (1950).
Kern v. City Commissioners of City of Newton, 147 Kan. 471 (1938).

Kern v. City Commissioners of City of Newton, 100 P. 2d 709 (1940).

Lawrence v. Hancock, 76 F. Supp. 1004 (1948).

McLaurin v. Oklahoma State Regents, 339 U.S. 637 (1950).

Sullivan v. Little Hunting Park, 396 U.S. 229 (1969).

Tillman v. Wheaton-Haven Recreation Association, 451 F. 2d 1211 (1971).

Tillman v. Wheaton-Haven Recreation Association, 410 U.S. 431 (1973).

GOVERNMENT RECORDS AND PUBLICATIONS

Bethlehem, Pennsylvania. *First Annual Message of Mayor Archibald Johnston to the Members of Council and Citizens of Bethlehem, Pa., and Reports of Superintendents of the Various City Departments.* Bethlehem, 1918.

———. *Third Annual Message of Mayor Archibald Johnston to the Members of Council and Citizens of Bethlehem, Pa., and Reports of the Superintendents of the Various City Departments.* Bethlehem, 1920.

Boston City Council. *Notes on the Proceedings.* 1898.

———. *Report of the Proceedings.* 1896, 1898, 1902.

Boston Committee on Bathing. *Report.* 1868, 1869, 1870, 1876.

Boston Department of Baths. "Free Municipal Baths in Boston: History and Description of the System." In *Annual Report*, Boston. 1898.

Boston Joint Special Committee on Free Bathing Facilities. *Report.* 1866.

Boston Joint Special Committee on Public Bathing Houses. *Report.* 1860.

Boston Joint Standing Committee on Bathing. *Report.* 1867.

Boston Park and Recreation Department. *Annual Report.* 1917–18.

Boston. *The By-Laws and Town-Orders of the Town of Boston, Made and Passed at Several Meetings in 1785 and 1786.* 1786.

Breen, Daniel, ed. *Historical Register of the Twenty-Two Superseded Park Districts, Chicago Park District.* Vol. 1. Washington, D.C.: Works Progress Administration, 1941.

Brookline Building Committee and Committee on Care and Management. "Brookline Public Bath." In *Report*, Brookline, Massachusetts. 1897.

Brookline Committee on Bath-Houses. "Report." *Brookline Town Report.* 1884, 1885, 1887.

Brookline Committee on Care and Management of the Public Bath. "Report." In *Report*, Brookline, Massachusetts, 1901.

Brookline, Massachusetts. *Report.* 1884, 1885, 1887, 1890, 1894, 1897, 1898, 1900, 1904.

Chicago Special Park Commission Committee on Parks, Playgrounds, and Beaches for the City of Chicago. *Annual Report.* 1916.

Elizabeth City Council. *Minutes.* 1927, 1938.

Federal Writers Project. *WPA Guide to 1930s Kansas.* Lawrence: University of Kansas Press, 1984. Originally published in 1939.

Massachusetts Bureau of Statistics of Labor. *Twenty-Eighth Annual Report*. 1898.

New York City Board of Estimate and Apportionment. *Minutes, Financial, and Franchise Matters*. 1910.

New York, New York. *Laws and Ordinances, Ordained and Established by the Mayor, Aldermen, and Commonality of the City of New-York*. 1808.

Newton City Council. *Minutes*. 1951.

Peoria Board of Trustees of the Pleasure Driveway and Park District. *Thirty-Fifth Annual Report*. 1931.

Philadelphia. *Annual Report*. 1897, 1883, 1884, 1888, 1889, 1891, 1897.

Pittsburgh Parks and Recreation Department. "Swimming Pool List." <http://www.city.pittsburgh.pa.us/parks/html/swimming_pools.html#list>. May 10, 2006.

South Park Commissioners. *Annual Report*. 1909.

St. Louis Division of Parks and Recreation. *Annual Report*. 1934–40, 1945–58.

St. Louis Park Commissioner. *Annual Report*. 1908–9, 1912–13, 1913–14, 1914–15.

U.S. Bureau of the Census. *Fifteenth Census of the United States: 1930*. Vol. 3, *Population*. Washington, D.C.: U.S. Government Printing Office, 1932.

———. *Seventeenth Census of the United States: 1950*. Vol. 1, *Population*. Washington, D.C.: U.S. Government Printing Office, 1952.

———. *Seventeenth Census of the United States: 1950*. Vol. 2, *Population*. Washington, D.C.: U.S. Government Printing Office, 1952.

———. *Sixteenth Census of the United States: 1940*. Vol. 2, *Population*. Washington, D.C.: U.S. Government Printing Office, 1943.

U.S. Congress. *Congressional Record*. 69th Cong., 1st sess. Washington, D.C., 1926.

U.S. Department of Commerce and Labor. "Public Baths in the United States." *Bulletin of the Bureau of Labor* 54 (September 1904): 1245–1367.

West Chicago Park Commissioners. *Annual Report*. 1900.

———. *Proceedings of the Board, January 8, 1895 to December 30, 1895*.

Wilmington Board of Park Commissioners. *Report*. 1920, 1924.

Youngstown Parks and Recreation Commission. *Annual Report*. 1956, 1957, 1965, 1969, 1972, 1973, 2004.

PERIODICALS

American City
Architectural Record
Art Exhibit of Fashion
Baltimore Afro-American
Baltimore Sun
Beach and Pool
Bethlehem Globe
Boston Columbian Sentinel

Boston Daily Globe
Boston Evening Transcript
Boston Globe
Brickbuilder
Brookline Chronicle
Chicago Defender
Chicago Journal
Chicago News

Chicago Record
Chicago Times-Herald
Chicago Tribune
Detroit News
Elizabeth Daily Journal
Fortune
Godey's Lady's Book
Harper's Bazaar
Kansas City Star
Kansas City Times
Life
Milwaukee Sentinel
Municipal Index
New England Magazine
New York Evening Post
New York Herald
New York Times
New Yorker
Palmerton Press
Peoria Journal-Star
Philadelphia Evening Bulletin
Philadelphia Inquirer
Pittsburgh Courier
Pittsburgh Post-Gazette
Pittsburgh Press
Pittsburgh Sun-Telegraph
Playground

Recreation
Roxbury Gazette and South End
  Advertiser
Saturday Evening Post
St. Louis American
St. Louis Argus
St. Louis Globe-Democrat
St. Louis Post-Dispatch
St. Louis Republican
St. Louis Star-Times
Swimming Pool Data and Reference
  Annual
Time
Wall Street Journal
Warren Tribune Chronicle
Washington Evening Star
Washington Post
Washington Star
Washington Tribune
Water-Cure Journal
Wilmington Evening Journal
Wilmington Every Evening
Wilmington Journal Every Evening
Wilmington Morning News
Wilmington Sunday Star
Youngstown Vindicator

PUBLISHED SOURCES

Addams, Jane. "Public Recreation and Social Morality." *Charities and the Commons* 18 (August 3, 1907): 492–94.

———. "Recreation as a Public Function in Urban Communities." *American Journal of Sociology* 17 (March 1912): 615–19.

Altherr, Thomas, ed. *Sports in North America: A Documentary History*. Vol. 1, Part 2, *Sports in the New Republic, 1784–1820*. Gulf Breeze, Fla.: Academic International Press, 1997.

Anbinder, Tyler. *Five Points: The 19th-Century New York City Neighborhood That Invented Tap Dance, Stole Elections, and Became the World's Most Notorious Slum*. New York: Free Press, 2001.

Aron, Cindy. *Working at Play: A History of Vacations in the United States*. New York: Oxford University Press, 1999.

Badger, Anthony J. *The New Deal: The Depression Years, 1933–1940*. New York: Hill and Wang, 1989.

Banner, Lois W. *American Beauty*. Chicago: University of Chicago Press, 1983.

Barth, Gunther. *City People: The Rise of Modern City Culture in Nineteenth-Century America*. New York: Oxford University Press, 1980.

Basinger, Jeanine. *A Woman's View: How Hollywood Spoke to Women, 1930–1960*. New York: Alfred A. Knopf, 1993.

Baxandall, Rosalyn, and Elizabeth Ewen. *Picture Windows: How the Suburbs Happened*. New York: Basic Books, 2000.

Bederman, Gail. *Manliness and Civilization: A Cultural History of Gender and Race in the United States, 1880–1917*. Chicago: University of Chicago Press, 1995.

Biggott, Joseph. *From Cottage to Bungalow: Houses and the Working Class in Metropolitan Chicago, 1869–1929*. Chicago: University of Chicago Press, 2001.

Blodgett, Geoffrey. *The Gentle Reformers: Massachusetts Democrats in the Cleveland Era*. Cambridge, Mass.: Harvard University Press, 1966.

———. "Josiah Quincy, Brahmin Democrat." *New England Quarterly* 38 (December 1965): 435–53.

Boyer, Paul. *Urban Masses and Moral Order in America, 1820–1920*. Cambridge, Mass.: Harvard University Press, 1979.

Bridenbaugh, Carl. "Baths and Watering Places of Colonial America." *William and Mary Quarterly* 3 (April 1946): 151–81.

Brumberg, Joan Jacobs. *The Body Project: An Intimate History of American Girls*. New York: Random House, 1997.

Button, James W. *Black Violence: Political Impact of the 1960s Riots*. Princeton, N.J.: Princeton University Press, 1977.

Carbaugh, Harvey. *Human Welfare Work in Chicago*. Chicago: A. C. McClung, 1917.

Caro, Robert. *The Power Broker: Robert Moses and the Fall of New York*. New York: Vintage, 1974.

Cavallo, Dominic. *Muscles and Morals: Organized Playgrounds and Urban Reform, 1880–1920*. Philadelphia: University of Pennsylvania Press, 1981.

Cheape, Charles W. *Moving the Masses: Urban Public Transportation in New York, Boston, and Philadelphia, 1880–1912*. Cambridge, Mass.: Harvard University Press, 1980.

Chicago Commission on Race Relations. *The Negro in Chicago: A Study of Race Relations and a Race Riot*. New York: Arno Press, 1968. Originally published in 1922.

Chudacoff, Howard P., and Judith E. Smith. *The Evolution of American Urban Society*. 6th ed. Upper Saddle River, N.J.: Pearson Prentice Hall, 2005.

Cohen, Lizabeth. *Making A New Deal: Industrial Workers in Chicago, 1919–1939*. New York: Cambridge University Press, 1990.

Considine, Bob, and Fred Jarvis. *The First Hundred Years*. New York: Macmillan, 1969.

Coontz, Stephanie. *The Way We Never Were: American Families and the Nostalgia Trap*. New York: Basic Books, 1992.

Cott, Nancy. *The Grounding of Modern Feminism*. New Haven: Yale University Press, 1987.

Crawford, Margaret. *Building the Workingman's Paradise: The Design of American Company Towns*. New York: Verso, 1995.

Cross, Gary. *An All-Consuming Century: Why Commercialism Won in Modern America*. New York: Columbia University Press, 2000.

Daniels, Bruce C. *Puritans at Play: Leisure and Recreation in Colonial New England*. New York: St. Martin's Press, 1995.

Daniels, Roger. *Coming to America: A History of Immigration and Ethnicity in American Life*. 2d ed. New York: Perennial, 2002.

DeForrest, Robert W., and Lawrence Veiller, eds. *The Tenement House Problem*. New York: Macmillan, 1903.

Denehy, John William. *A History of the Town of Brookline, from First Settlement of Muddy River until the Present Time, 1630–1906*. Brookline, Mass.: Brookline Press, 1906.

Douglas, Ann. *Terrible Honesty: Mongrel Manhattan in the 1920s*. New York: Farrar, Straus, and Giroux, 1995.

Drake, St. Clair, and Horace R. Cayton. *Black Metropolis: A Study of Negro Life in a Northern City*. Chicago: University of Chicago Press, 1993. Originally published in 1945.

Duany, Andres, Elizabeth Plater-Zyberk, and Jeff Speck. *Suburban Nation: The Rise of Sprawl and the Decline of the American Dream*. New York: North Point Press, 2000.

Dudziak, Mary L. *Cold War Civil Rights: Race and the Image of American Democracy*. Princeton, N.J.: Princeton University Press, 2000.

Duis, Perry. *Challenging Chicago: Coping with Everyday Life, 1837–1920*. Urbana: University of Illinois Press, 1998.

Dumenil, Lynn. *Modern Temper: American Culture and Society in the 1920s*. New York: Hill and Wang, 1995.

Elias, Norbert. *The Civilizing Process: A History of Manners*. Translated by Edmund Jephcott. New York: Urizen Books, 1978.

Erenberg, Lewis. *Steppin' Out: New York Nightlife and the Transformation of American Culture*. Chicago: University of Chicago Press, 1981.

Essig, Steven. "Race Riots." In *The Encyclopedia of Chicago*, edited by James Grossman, Ann Durkin Keating, and Janice L. Reiff, 667. Chicago: University of Chicago Press, 2004.

Fass, Paula. *The Damned and the Beautiful: American Youth in the 1920s*. New York: Oxford University Press, 1977.

Flamm, Jerry. *Good Life in Hard Times*. San Francisco: Chronicle Books, 1977.

Fox, Richard Wightman, and T. J. Jackson Lears, eds. *The Culture of Consumption: Critical Essays in American History, 1880–1980*. New York: Pantheon Books, 1983.

Fredrickson, George M. *The Black Image in the White Mind: The Debate on Afro-American Character and Destiny, 1817–1914*. Middletown, Conn.: Wesleyan University Press, 1971.

Gleason, Philip. *Speaking of Diversity*. Baltimore: Johns Hopkins University Press, 1992.

Goodman, Cary. *Choosing Sides: Playgrounds and Street Life on the Lower East Side*. New York: Shocken Books, 1979.

Green, Harvey. *Fit for America: Health, Fitness, Sport, and American Society*. New York: Pantheon, 1986.

Griscom, John H. *The Sanitary Condition of the Laboring Population of New York. With Suggestions for Its Improvement*. New York: Harper and Brothers, 1845.

Grossman, James R. *Land of Hope: Chicago, Black Southerners, and the Great Migration*. Chicago: University of Chicago Press, 1989.

Guterl, Matthew Pratt. *The Color of Race in America, 1900–1940*. Cambridge, Mass.: Harvard University Press, 2001.

Handlin, Oscar. *Boston's Immigrants: A Study in Acculturation*. New York: Athenaeum, 1974. Originally published in 1941.

Hardy, Stephen. *How Boston Played: Sport, Recreation, and Community, 1865–1915*. Boston: Northeastern University Press, 1982.

Higginson, Thomas Wentworth. "Gymnastics." *Atlantic Monthly* 7 (March 1861): 283–302.

———. "Saints and Their Bodies." *Atlantic Monthly* 1 (March 1858): 582–95.

Higham, John. "The Reorientation of American Culture in the 1890s." *Writing American History: Essays on Modern Scholarship*, 73–102. Bloomington: Indiana University Press, 1970.

Hirsh, Arnold R. *Making the Second Ghetto: Race and Housing in Chicago, 1940–1960*. Chicago: University of Chicago Press, 1983.

Hodes, Martha. *White Women, Black Men: Illicit Sex in the Nineteenth-Century South*. New Haven, Conn.: Yale University Press, 1997.

Holloran, Peter C. *Boston's Wayward Children: Social Service for Homeless Children, 1830–1930*. Boston: Northeastern University Press, 1994. Originally published in 1989.

Hopkins, C. Howard. *History of the Y.M.C.A. in North America*. New York: Association Press, 1951.

Horwood, Catherine. "'Girls Who Arouse Dangerous Passions': Women and Bathing, 1900–39." *Women's History Review* 9 (2000): 653–73.

Howe, Daniel Walker. "American Victorianism as a Culture." *American Quarterly* 27 (December 1975): 507–32.

————. "Victorian Culture in America." In *Victorian America*, edited by Daniel Walker Howe, 3–29. Philadelphia: University of Pennsylvania Press, 1976.

————, ed. *Victorian America*. Philadelphia: University of Pennsylvania Press, 1976.

Hoy, Suellen. *Chasing Dirt: The American Pursuit of Cleanliness*. New York: Oxford University Press, 1995.

Jackson, Kenneth T. *Crabgrass Frontier: The Suburbanization of the United States*. New York: Oxford University Press, 1985.

Johnson, James Weldon. *Along This Way: The Autobiography of James Weldon Johnson*. New York: Viking Press, 1933.

Kasson, John. *Amusing the Million: Coney Island at the Turn of the Century*. New York: Hill and Wang, 1978.

————. *Rudeness and Civility: Manners in Nineteenth-Century Urban America*. New York: Hill and Wang, 1990.

Kennedy, Randall. *Interracial Intimacies: Sex, Marriage, Identity, and Adoption*. New York: Pantheon, 2003.

Kidwell, Claudia. "Women's Bathing and Swimming Costume in the United States." *United States National Museum Bulletin* 250 (1968): 2–32.

Kimmel, Michael. *Manhood in America: A Cultural History*. New York: Free Press, 1996.

Kirkbride, Franklin B. "Private Initiative in Furnishing Public Bath Facilities." *Annals of the American Academy of Political and Social Sciences* 13 (March 1899): 280–84.

Kisseloff, Jeff. *You Must Remember This: An Oral History of Manhattan from the 1890s to World War II*. Baltimore: Johns Hopkins University Press, 1989.

Kluger, Richard. *Simple Justice: The History of Brown v. Board of Education and Black America's Struggle for Equality*. New York: Random House, 1975.

Kraut, Alan M. *Silent Travelers: Germs, Genes, and the "Immigrant Menace."* New York: Basic Books, 1994.

Kusmer, Kenneth. *A Ghetto Takes Shape: Black Cleveland, 1870–1930*. Urbana: University of Illinois Press, 1976.

Leach, William. *Land of Desire: Merchants, Power, and the Rise of a New American Culture*. New York: Pantheon Books, 1993.

Leeuwen, Thomas A. P. van. *The Springboard in the Pond: An Intimate History of the Swimming Pool*. Cambridge, Mass.: MIT Press, 1998.

Leuchtenburg, William. *The Perils of Prosperity, 1914–1932*. Chicago: University of Chicago Press, 1958.

Levy, Frank. *Dollars and Dreams: The Changing American Income Distribution*. New York: Russell Sage Foundation, 1987.

Lewinson, Edwin R. *John Purroy Mitchel: Boy Mayor of New York*. New York: Astra Books, 1965.

Lubove, Roy. "The New York Association for Improving the Condition of the Poor:

The Formative Years." *New York Historical Association Quarterly* 43 (July, 1959): 307–27.

Lynd, Robert S., and Helen Merrell. *Middletown: A Study in Modern American Culture*. New York: Harcourt Brace, 1929.

Madison, James H. *A Lynching in the Heartland: Race and Memory in America*. New York: St. Martin's, 2001.

Manheimer, Wallace. "Essentials of Swimming Pool Sanitation." *United States Public Health Service Reports*, September, 17, 1915, 1–16.

———. "Studies on the Sanitation of Swimming Pools." *Journal of Infectious Diseases* 15 (July 1914): 159–82.

May, Elaine Tyler. *Homeward Bound: American Families in the Cold War Era*. New York: Basic Books, 1988.

McBride, David. *From TB to AIDS: Epidemics among Urban Blacks since 1900*. Albany: State University of New York Press, 1991.

McGerr, Michael. *A Fierce Discontent: The Rise and Fall of the Progressive Movement, 1870–1920*. New York: Free Press, 2003.

McGreevy, John T. *Parish Boundaries: The Catholic Encounter with Race in the Twentieth-Century Urban North*. Chicago: University of Chicago Press, 1996.

Mintz, Steven, and Susan Kellogg. *Domestic Revolutions: A Social History of American Family Life*. New York: Free Press, 1988.

Moore, Lawrence R. "Directions of Thought in Progressive America." In *The Progressive Era*, edited by Lewis L. Gould, 35–53. Syracuse, N.Y: Syracuse University Press, 1974.

Morris, Ann, ed. *Lift Every Voice and Sing: St. Louis African Americans in the Twentieth Century*. Columbia: University of Missouri Press, 1999.

Mrozek, Donald J. "Sport in American Life: From National Health to Personal Fulfillment, 1890–1940." In *Fitness in American Culture: Images of Health, Sport, and the Body, 1830–1940*, edited by Kathryn Grover, 18–48. Amherst: University of Massachusetts Press, 1989.

Mumford, Kevin J. *Interzones: Black/White Sex Districts in Chicago and New York in the Early Twentieth Century*. New York: Columbia University Press, 1997.

Mumford, Lewis. *The City in History: Its Origins, Its Transformations, and Its Prospects*. New York: Harcourt, Brace, and World, 1961.

Muths, Guts. *Gymnastics for Youth; or, A Practical Guide to Healthful and Amusing Exercises. For the Use of Schools*. Philadelphia: P. Byrne, 1803.

Myrdal, Gunnar. *An American Dilemma: The Negro Problem and Modern Democracy*. New York: Harper and Brothers, 1944.

Nasaw, David. *Children of the City: At Work and at Play*. New York: Oxford University Press, 1985.

———. *Going Out: The Rise and Fall of Public Amusements*. New York: Basic Books, 1993.

National Cyclopaedia of American Biography. New York: J. T. White, various years.

National Recreation Association. *The Leisure Hours of 5,000 People: A Report of a Study of Leisure Time Activities and Desires.* New York: National Recreation Association, 1934.

New York Association for Improving the Condition of the Poor. *Eighteenth Annual Report.* New York, 1861.

———. *Ninth Annual Report.* New York, 1852.

———. *Tenth Annual Report.* New York, 1853.

Nicolaides, Becky M. *My Blue Heaven: Life and Politics in the Working-Class Suburbs of Los Angeles, 1920–1965.* Chicago: University of Chicago, 2002.

Novak, William J. *The People's Welfare: Law and Regulation in Nineteenth-Century America.* Chapel Hill: University of North Carolina Press, 1996.

Osofsky, Gilbert. *Harlem: The Making of a Ghetto, Negro New York, 1890–1930.* New York: Harper and Row, 1968. Originally published in 1963.

Packard, Vance. *The Status Seekers.* New York: David McKay, 1959.

Pacyga, Dominic, and Ellen Skerrett. *Chicago: City of Neighborhoods.* Chicago: Loyola University Press, 1986.

Painter, Nell Irvin. *Exodusters: Black Migration to Kansas after Reconstruction.* New York: Alfred A. Knopf, 1976.

Pangburn, Weaver, and F. Ellwood Allen. *Long Range Recreation Plan, City of Baltimore, Maryland.* Baltimore, 1943.

Peiss, Kathy. *Cheap Amusements: Working Women and Leisure in Turn-of-the-Century New York.* Philadelphia: Temple University Press, 1986.

———. *Hope in a Jar: The Making of America's Beauty Culture.* New York: Metropolitan Books, 1998.

Philpott, Thomas Lee. *The Slum and the Ghetto: Neighborhood Deterioration and Middle-Class Reform, Chicago, 1880–1930.* New York: Oxford University Press, 1978.

Playground Association of Philadelphia. "The Advance of the National Playground Movement." *Annual Report.* Philadelphia, 1909.

———. "Play as Citizen Maker." *Annual Report.* Philadelphia, 1909.

Powers, Madelon. *Faces along the Bar: Lore and Order in the Workingman's Saloon, 1870–1920.* Chicago: University of Chicago Press, 1998.

Putnam, Robert. *Bowling Alone: The Collapse and Revival of American Community.* New York: Simon and Schuster, 2000.

Quincy, Josiah. "The Development of American Cities." *Arena* 17 (March 1897): 529–37.

Rodgers, Daniel T. *The Work Ethic in Industrial America, 1850–1920.* Chicago: University of Chicago Press, 1974.

Roediger, David. *Working toward Whiteness: The Strange Journey from Ellis Island to the Suburbs.* New York: Basic Books, 2005.

Rosenzweig, Roy. *Eight Hours for What We Will: Workers and Leisure in an Industrial City, 1870–1920.* New York: Cambridge University Press, 1983.

Rosenzweig, Roy, and Elizabeth Blackmar. *The Park and the People: A History of Central Park.* Ithaca, N.Y.: Cornell University Press, 1992.

Rotundo, E. Anthony. *American Manhood: Transformations in Masculinity from the Revolution to the Modern Era.* New York: Basic Books, 1993.

Ryan, Mary. *Women in Public: Between Banners and Ballots, 1825–1880.* Baltimore: Johns Hopkins University Press, 1990.

Sennett, Richard. *The Fall of Public Man.* New York: Norton, 1974.

Sitkoff, Harvard. *A New Deal for Blacks: The Emergence of Civil Rights as a National Issue.* New York: Oxford University Press, 1978.

Sklar, Robert. *Movie-Made America: A Cultural History of American Movies.* Revised and updated edition. New York: Vintage Books, 1994.

Smith, Robert A. *A Social History of the Bicycle: Its Early Life and Times in America.* New York: American Heritage Press, 1972.

Spear, Allan. *Black Chicago: The Making of a Negro Ghetto, 1890–1920.* Chicago: University of Chicago Press, 1967.

Stevenson, Louise L. *The Victorian Homefront: American Thought and Culture, 1860–1880.* New York: Twayne Publisher, 1991.

Stewart, Jane A. "Boston's Experience with Municipal Baths." *American Journal of Sociology* 7 (November 1901): 416–22.

Sugrue, Thomas J. *The Origins of the Urban Crisis: Race and Inequality in Postwar Detroit.* Princeton, N.J.: Princeton University Press, 1996.

Taylor, Graham Romeyn. "Recreation Developments in Chicago Parks." *Annals of the American Academy of Political and Social Science* 35 (March 1910): 304–21.

Teaford, Jon. *The Rough Road to Renaissance: Urban Revitalization in America, 1940–1985.* Baltimore: Johns Hopkins University, 1990.

Todd, Robert. "Four New City Baths and Gymnasiums." *Survey* 23 (February 5, 1910): 680–83.

———. "The Municipal Baths of Manhattan." *Charities and the Commons* 19 (October 19, 1907): 896–903.

Tomes, Nancy. *The Gospel of Germs: Men, Women, and the Microbe in American Life.* Cambridge, Mass.: Harvard University Press, 1998.

Tuttle, William M., Jr. *Race Riot: Chicago in the Red Summer of 1919.* New York: Athenaeum, 1970.

Veblen, Thorstein. *The Theory of the Leisure Class.* New York: Penguin Books, 1987. Originally published in 1899.

Veiller, Lawrence. "A Statistical Study of New York's Tenement Houses." In *The Tenement House Problem,* edited by Robert W. DeForrest and Lawrence Veiller, 191–240. New York: Macmillan, 1903.

Wallenstein, Paul. *Tell the Court I Love My Wife: Race, Marriage, and Law—An American History*. New York: Palgrave, 2002.

Watkins, Mel. *Dancing with Strangers: A Memoir*. New York: Simon and Schuster, 1998.

Williams, Juan. *Thurgood Marshall: American Revolutionary*. New York: Times Books, 1998.

Williams, Marilyn. *Washing "The Great Unwashed": Public Baths in Urban America, 1840–1920*. Columbus: Ohio State University Press, 1991.

Worman, Clark. *History of the Brooklyn and Queens Young Men's Christian Association, 1853–1949*. New York: Association Press, 1952.

Young Men's Era. *Book of Young Men's Christian Association Buildings*. Chicago: Young Men's Era, 1895.

Zunz, Olivier. *Making America Corporate, 1870–1920*. Chicago: University of Chicago Press, 1990.

———. *Why the American Century?*. Chicago: University of Chicago Press, 1998.

UNPUBLISHED SOURCES

Charles Hall Page and Associates. "Documentation of Historic, Cultural, and Architectural Importance of the Fleishhacker Pool." San Francisco, 1977.

Hantzmon, R. Clark. "Forestalling: The Enforcement of Market Regulations in Massachusetts, 1820–1860." Unpublished paper, Brandeis University, 1996.

Osborn, Marian Lorena. "The Development of Recreation in the South Park System of Chicago." M.A. thesis, University of Chicago, 1928.

Schermer, George. "The Fairgrounds Park Incident: A study of the factors which resulted in the outbreak of violence at the Fairgrounds Park Swimming Pool on June 21, 1949, and account of what happened, and recommendations for corrective action." St. Louis, 1949.

INDEX

Chicago Athletic Association, 29
Chicago Commission on Race Relations, 64, 152
Cincinnati, Ohio, 140
Cities: nineteenth-century development of, 17; class-divided social geography of, 17, 22, 24–25, 32, 48–49, 57–58, 62–63, 71–73, 79, 186–87; middle-class perceptions of, 17–18; race-divided social geography of, 25, 63–64, 123, 139–40, 144, 145, 155, 167, 175, 186–87; early twentieth-century conditions in, 48, 57–58; cultural geography of, 75; fiscal crisis in during 1970s, 189–90
Civil rights laws, 135, 146, 147, 159, 162, 197, 198. *See also* Fourteenth Amendment
Clairton, Pa., 91
Class: health and cleanliness prejudices based on, 18, 20, 25, 34, 40–41, 73, 76, 106, 124, 151–52; municipal pools as social levelers, 27, 32, 104, 208; exclusion of working-class swimmers from municipal pools, 32–34, 43–44, 44–45; weakening of prejudices related to during interwar years, 89, 104, 106–7. *See also* Class conflict; Class divisions; Class integration of municipal pools; Social values: assumptions about public recreation based on
Class conflict: over access to municipal pools, 8; over proper use of municipal pools, 9, 23, 26, 34, 37, 41, 42–43, 75–76; over the location of municipal pools, 51, 70–73. *See also* Class: exclusion of working-class swimmers from municipal pools
Class divisions: in use of municipal pools, 1, 3, 24–25, 37, 40–41, 44, 48–

49, 57–58, 62–63, 65, 76, 79, 209; in natural-water swimming, 14–15, 16; in use of river baths, 21–22
Class integration of municipal pools, 3, 4, 32, 78, 81–82, 88–89, 103–4, 105–7, 145
Cleveland, Ohio, 139
Columbus, Ohio, 96–97
Commercial recreation, 3, 48, 76–77, 84, 92, 107, 120
Community life: municipal pools as centers of, 6, 61, 89, 94–95, 106, 107–9, 206, 207–8; privatization of swimming pools degrades quality of, 6, 183, 183–84, 201, 204–5; municipal pools as venues for events important to, 87, 89, 108; public discourse at municipal pools, 108–9; closure of municipal pools degrades quality of, 193, 206; Putnam's argument about "civic disengagement," 204–5
Coney Island (New York City), 75
Coolidge, Calvin, 143
Cultural agency of ordinary Americans, 6, 208–9, 215 (n. 7); working-class children establish a pleasure-centered culture at municipal pools, 5, 9, 26, 29, 46, 52, 61–62; Americans redefine standards of public decency, 5, 82–83, 83–84, 111–12, 113–14
Cultural values, 4–5; cleanliness, 1, 9, 18–19, 22, 24, 55, 62; public sexuality, 5, 83–84, 109, 114–17, 212; pools as symbols of the "good life," 5, 103, 119, 206; consumerism, 6, 118–19; standards of public decency, 10, 11–13, 14, 50, 82–84, 89–90, 109–12, 113–14, 118, 216 (n. 14); masculinity, 12, 16, 27, 36, 117, 124–25, 134–35, 144; prejudices against swimming and exercise, 14–15; pleasure-cen-

tered justification of recreation, 53–54, 80–81; public objectification of women's bodies, 89–90, 114–17, 118, 212–13; importance of physical appearance, 117–18; democratic production of public culture, 208–9. *See also* Exhibitionism and voyeurism; Nudity; Swimsuits

Daley, Richard, 187
Dallas, Tex., 90–91
Darst, Joseph, 168, 169, 174, 179
Detroit, Mich., 140, 141, 187
Diseases: germ theory of, 1, 34, 34–35; as threat to public health, 18, 20; zymotic theory of, 20; concerns about transmission of in pools, 73, 97; among working-class whites, 107; among black Americans, 124, 133, 152
Drowning deaths, 67, 156
Du Bois, W. E. B., 25

Economic conditions: during 1920s, 91–92; during 1970s, 182, 189–90, 202; during post–World War II era, 199–200
Ederle, Gertrude, 97
Elizabeth, N.J.: race relations and Dowd Pool, 135, 137–40
Ellsworth, Kans., 107
Ethnicity: perceptions of differences in regard to, 3, 83, 106–7; pools intended to alleviate conflict based on, 61; pools intended as instruments of assimilation, 61; mixed-ethnic use of pools, 62–63, 79; conflict between ethnic whites and black Americans, 123, 128
Exercise and physical fitness, 15–16, 29–30, 31, 34, 36, 134

Exhibitionism and voyeurism, 37–38, 83, 89, 97, 110, 111–12, 114–17, 118, 212. *See also* Beauty contests

Fairgrounds Park Pool (St. Louis, Mo.), 78, 132; designed as leisure resort, 79–81; class-integrated use of, 81–82; gender integration of, 82; cultural crisis resulting from gender integration of, 82–84; swimsuit regulations at, 83–84; regulation of male-female interaction at, 84; black Americans excluded from, 85, 167–68, 176; racial desegregation of, 166, 167–79; race riot precipitated by racially integrated use of, 169–73, 174–76; racial desegregation of leads to gender segregation of, 179; declining white use of after desegregation, 179–80; closure of, 180. *See also* St. Louis, Mo.
Federal government, 93–95, 142–43, 158–59, 185, 187, 198
Fleishhacker Pool (San Francisco, Calif.), 97, 98, 99
Flint, Mich., 98
Fort Worth, Tex., 90
Foster, J. Frank, 59–60, 62, 74
Fourteenth Amendment (U.S. Constitution), 146, 148, 165, 178
Fox, Richard, 5, 6, 119

Gaynor, William, 71, 73, 74
Gender: swimming in natural water as a male activity, 12, 13–14; masculinity, 12, 15, 16, 27, 36, 117, 124–25, 134–35, 144; early pools as male spaces, 26, 27–30; mixed-gender socializing, 76–77, 84, 125; regulation of male-female interaction at gender-integrated pools, 84; women

as visual objects, 89–90, 114–17, 118, 212–13; increased use of pools by women, 96, 97; racial segregation as means of limiting women's sexual and social choices, 124, 133–34; Gender violence at municipal pools, 211–12. *See also* Cultural values: importance of physical appearance; Cultural values: public objectification of women's bodies; Cultural values: public sexuality; Gender integration; Gender segregation

Gender integration: of municipal pools, 3, 4, 78, 82, 88–89, 103–5, 106, 145, 212, 227–28 (n. 24); cultural crisis resulting from, 82–84; as cause of racial segregation and exclusion at municipal pools, 85–86, 121, 124, 128–30

Gender segregation: at municipal pools, 1, 3, 4, 14, 22, 32, 48, 52, 65, 76, 209, 212; at private-club pools, 16; at river baths, 21; as solution to racial conflict at municipal pools, 129; racially integrated use of pools as a cause of, 179

Generation: children and youths as primary users of municipal pools, 23, 26, 27, 52, 59–60, 62, 97, 188, 219 (n. 79); increased adult use of pools, 32, 34, 44, 88–89, 96, 97; intergenerational use of pools, 32, 82, 104; age-based segregation at municipal pools, 97. *See also* Youths: pool swimming culture

Glen Echo Amusement Park (Montgomery County, Md.), 99

Government, proper role of, 23, 49–50, 53, 55, 80–81, 217 (n. 43), 218–19 (n. 66). *See also* Federal government

Great Black Migration, 3, 107, 123, 124, 139, 152

Great Depression, 88, 93, 146, 205

Great Gatsby, The, 102

Great Migration. *See* Great Black Migration

Griscom, John H., 18

Gulick, Luther, 74

Higginson, Thomas Wentworth, 14–15, 15–16

Howard, William M., 160, 161, 162, 165

Hulen, Rubey M., 176–79

Immigrants, 58; bathing habits of, 12–13; as users of public baths, 22, 218 (n. 57); as users of municipal pools, 24–25; pools intended as instruments of assimilation, 48; assimilation and acculturation of, 106

Immigration, 3, 10, 17, 106, 124

Johnson, Jack, and Jim Jeffries boxing match, 135

Johnson, James Weldon, 132

Johnson, Lyndon B., 187

Kansas City, Mo., 184, 185

Kansas Supreme Court, 164, 165

Kasson, John, 3, 75, 120, 218 (n. 66)

Kearns, Daniel, 1, 25

Kellerman, Annette, 97, 110

Kerner, Otto, 186

King, Martin Luther, Jr., 187

Kline, Charles, 127, 129

Ku Klux Klan, 175

Leach, William, 5, 6

Lears, T. J. Jackson, 5, 6, 119

Livingston, Mamie, 154, 155, 158

Los Angeles, Calif., 90

MacFadden, Bernarr, 36, 134

Marion, Ind., 151

Marshall, Thurgood, 149, 151, 160, 162, 163, 165, 178

McLaurin v. Oklahoma State Regents for Higher Education, 178

Milwaukee, Wisc.: natural-water swimming in, 10; controversy over natural-water swimming and bathing in, 11–13; population of, 17; municipal pools in, 26–27; social use of municipal pools in, 27–29

Mini-pools, 187–88, 189, 211

Mitchel, John Purroy, 67–69

Montgomery, W.Va., 162–65

Moore, Ben, 164–65

Moses, Robert, 94, 140

Movies, 103, 112–13

Mumford, Lewis, 209

Muscular Christianity, 15–16

Nasaw, David, 3

Nashville, Tenn., 90

National Association for the Advancement of Colored People (NAACP), 158; Pittsburgh, Pa., branch, 128–29, 129, 131; Elizabeth, N.J., branch, 135; national office, 146, 151, 162, 163, 165, 178; Newton, Kans., branch, 147, 149, 151; Baltimore, Md., branch, 156; Warren, Ohio, branch, 160; Montgomery, W.Va., branch, 162; St. Louis, Mo., branch, 176

National Recreation Association, 5, 96

New Deal swimming pools, 88, 93–95, 108, 206

Newton, Kans.: characteristics of population in, 146–47; racial exclusion at Athletic Park Pool, 147; legal challenge to racial exclusion at Athletic Park Pool, 147–51; Athletic Park Pool in 2000, 207, 208

New York, N.Y.: law against natural-water swimming in, 10; natural-water swimming in, 10–11, 66–67; lack of baths in slums, 35; Progressive Era municipal pools in, 65–66; mixed-race use of municipal pools in, 65–66, 238–39 (n. 59); 1910 swimming pool in Central Park controversy, 68–74; social geography of, 70–73, 139–40; play reformers in, 71–72, 74; lack of outdoor municipal pools in during Progressive Era, 74, 75; cultural geography of, 75; New Deal pools in, 94, 108, 206; de facto racial segregation at municipal pools in, 121, 140, 238–39 (n. 59); Lasker Pool, 181–82; building of municipal mini-pools in, 187–88; Bedford-Stuyvesant People's Pool, 188–89; dilapidated condition and closure of municipal pools in, 192; controversy over McCarren Pool, 206; "whirl-pooling" incidents at municipal pools in, 212–13

New York Association for Improving the Condition of the Poor (AICP), 19, 60

New York Athletic Club, 29

New York Society for Parks and Playgrounds, 71

New York Times, 72, 73, 75

Nudity, 10–11, 12, 13, 14, 27, 66, 220 (n. 87)

Nutter, T. Gillis, 163–65

Olmsted, Frederick Law, 69–70, 218 (n. 66)

Olympic View Swimming Pool (Seattle, Wash.), 213

O'Toole, John, 168–69

Palmerton, Pa., 107–8, 208
Peiss, Kathy, 3, 77, 120
Pendleton, Ind., 91
Philadelphia, Pa.: municipal bathing
pools in, 1, 24–26; racially integrated use of municipal pools in, 1,
25–26; Twelfth and Wharton Bath,
8–9, 24–25; private-club pools in,
16; nineteenth-century population
of, 17; river baths in, 24; social geography of, 24–25; class segregated use
of municipal pools in, 25; use of municipal pools in for amusement, 26;
dilapidated condition of municipal
pools in, 48; number of Progressive
Era municipal pools in, 74, 90; use
of municipal pools in by women,
96; closure of municipal pools in,
185
Pittsburgh, Pa.: Highland Park Pool,
95, 98, 125–26, 132; racial discrimination at Highland Park Pool, 126;
racial violence at Highland Park
Pool, 126–28, 130–31; gender integration as cause of racial conflict at
Highland Park Pool, 128; racially
integrated use of pools in, 128;
political protest over racial conflict at
Highland Park Pool, 129–30, 130–31;
official racial segregation at municipal pools in, 131; racial violence at
gender-segregated municipal pools
in, 131; Shady Grove Park, 151; closure of municipal pools in, 192–93,
213
Playground Association of America
(PAA), 59, 74
Playgrounds, 54, 60, 71–72, 145–46,
167
Plessy v. Ferguson, 165
Pool building industry, 92–93

Pool sanitation, 1, 40–41, 62, 73–74, 97,
107, 144, 202, 233 (n. 78)
Pools, municipal: as leisure resorts, 1, 4,
78, 79–81, 88–89, 97–100, 145, 180,
210; as public baths, 1, 8, 9, 17, 19–
20, 22–29, 34, 52, 53, 66, 79, 210;
as Victorian reforms, 9, 17, 19, 24,
36–37, 42; as public amusements,
9, 26, 27, 53, 55, 56; as exercise
and sport facilities, 31–34, 36, 38–
40, 44, 53; opposition to, 35, 38, 49,
50–51, 54–56, 69–72, 75–76; as
Progressive reforms, 46, 48, 56–
57, 58–64, 74–75; as recreation
asylums for urban youths, 59–61,
181, 184, 187–88, 210; popularity/
proliferation of during interwar
years, 88, 90–91, 92, 93–99, 109,
119–20
—decline of, 193; pool closures, 180,
184–85, 190–91, 192; dilapidated
condition of, 182, 184–85, 190, 192,
206; crime at, 182, 191, 206; slow-
down in new construction of, 183,
184; declining attendance at, 184,
190–91, 192; lack of municipal pools
in suburbs, 194–95, 196, 213
Pools, private-club, 2, 6; in nineteenth
century, 16, 29–30; class-exclusive
use of, 29–30, 195; municipal pools
converted to in order to exclude
black Americans, 147, 160, 162–63;
racial exclusion at, 161, 195–97;
building of spurred by racial desegregation of public pools, 180, 183,
193, 198; post–World War II proliferation of, 182, 193–94; social function of, 194; racial desegregation of,
196–98, 250 (n. 78); as signs of civic
disengagement, 205; social divisions
reflected at, 209–10

Pools, public school, 56, 144

Pools, residential, 2, 6; in nineteenth century, 100–101; in early twentieth century, 101–3; cultural identity of, 103, 206; post–World War II proliferation of, 182, 198–203, 205; economic factors that enabled post–World War II proliferation of, 199–200; social appeal of, 200, 201, 203; as emblems of success and upward mobility, 200–201, 202; above-ground models, 202; social isolation at, 203–4; as signs of civic disengagement, 205

Pools as intimate spaces, 3, 4, 6, 26, 76, 85, 108, 109, 129, 132, 150, 156

Pools as sexualized spaces, 4, 5, 84–85, 87, 89, 109–17, 212–13

Progressive reform, 60–62, 68, 74–76, 224 (n. 60)

Public health, pools as threats to, 35, 73, 222 (n. 6)

Putnam, Robert, 204–5

Quincy, Josiah, 1, 25, 49–54, 59

Race: hardening of black-white social divide in the North, 4, 107, 125, 215 (n. 6); sex prejudices based on, 85–86, 124, 132–33; social construction of whiteness, 107; conflict between black Americans and ethnic whites, 123, 128; health and cleanliness prejudices based on, 124, 126, 148, 151–52; gender segregation as solution to conflicts related to at pools, 129; spread of prejudice based on, 131–32; impact of World War II on white northerners' attitudes about, 158, 159. *See also* Race riots; Racial desegregation; Racial discrimination;

Racially integrated use of municipal pools; Racial violence; Social values: assumptions about public recreation based on

Race riots, 123, 169–73, 182, 185–86. *See also* Racial violence

Racial desegregation, 2, 4, 157–59; as spur to building of private-club pools, 2, 180, 183, 193, 198; social efforts toward, 137–38, 154, 167–69; public officials close pools in response to, 138, 165, 174, 159; social resistance to, 138–39, 157, 158, 169–73; legal efforts toward, 147–51, 156–57, 160–62, 163–66, 176–79; as a cause of declining use of municipal pools by white Americans, 157, 159, 160, 166, 179–80, 184, 193, 205; contributions to by white Americans, 158, 159, 160, 176, 177, 241–42 (n. 14); political efforts toward, 159–60; as a cause of gender segregation at pools, 179; of private-club pools, 196–98, 250 (n. 78). *See also* Racially integrated use of municipal pools; Racial violence

—court cases related to: *Kern v. Newton*, 147–51, 164, 165; *Dawson v. Mayor and City Council of Baltimore*, 156; *Culver v. City of Warren*, 161–62, 165–66; *Lawrence v. Hancock*, 163–65; *Draper v. City of St. Louis*, 176–79; *Tillman v. Wheaton-Haven Recreation Association*, 197–98

Racial discrimination, 3–4, 121–23, 141–42, 209; reasons for success of, 4, 152–53; inconsistency of de facto segregation at municipal pools, 140–41; acceptance of segregated municipal pools by black Americans,

143–44, 145, 147; justifications of, 148, 156, 177
—causes of: gender integration and race-based sex prejudices, 78, 85–86, 121, 124–25, 128–29, 132–35, 156; race-based health and cleanliness prejudices, 124, 151–52; concerns about black masculinity, 124–25, 134–35; restricting black men's social access to white women, 133–34
—forms of: segregated municipal pools in the North, 2, 129, 131, 142–43, 144, 145, 154–56, 167–68, 176; unequal provision of municipal pools for black Americans, 25, 63–64, 145–46, 154–56, 166–67, 177, 186–87; exclusion of black Americans from municipal pools, 78, 85, 126, 135, 147, 160, 162–63; segregated municipal pools in the South, 90–91, 229 (n. 4); de facto segregation at municipal pools in the North, 130, 131, 135–41, 157, 187; cities lease municipal pools to private citizens to circumvent civil rights laws, 147, 160, 162
—resistance to: segregation and exclusion, 4, 85, 126–31, 137–38, 143, 147, 152; unequal provision of segregated municipal pools, 145–46, 154–56, 166–67
Racially integrated use of municipal pools: during late nineteenth and early twentieth centuries, 1, 3, 25–26, 48, 64, 65, 65–66, 79; during interwar years, 128, 137–38, 140–41, 238–39 (n. 59); during second half of twentieth century, 157, 160, 166, 169, 179, 207. See also Racial desegregation
Racial violence: at municipal pools, 4,

64, 121, 126–28, 130–31, 137–38, 169–73; condoned by public officials, 126, 127, 128, 138–39, 153, 170; black victims of arrested by police, 126, 127, 174. See also Race riots
Ridley, Samuel, 147, 165, 207
Roosevelt, Franklin D., 93, 100, 176
Roosevelt, Theodore, 101

St. Louis, Mo.: population of, 17; gender segregation at municipal pools in, 78–79; racially integrated use of municipal baths and pools in, 78–79; Marquette Park Pool, 166, 177, 179; unequal provision of segregated pools for black Americans, 166–67; social geography of, 167, 175; Council on Human Relations, 174, 175, 176, 178; declining white attendance at municipal pools in after racial desegregation, 184; increased use of pools in by black Americans after desegregation, 187. See also Fairgrounds Park Pool
Sandow, Eugen, 36
Sanitation at pools. See Pool sanitation
Schermer, George, 175–76
Scott, Elisha, 147
Smith, Gerald L. K., 174–75
Social values: assumptions about public recreation based on, 23, 51, 53–54, 59–61, 188, 210–11, 218 (n. 66); emphasis on family, 104, 200, 205; privacy, 194, 199, 201, 203–4, 205, 206. See also Class; Gender; Race
Somers Point, N.J., 111–12
Spokane, Wash., 90
Stover, Charles, 71–72, 74, 210
Suburbs, 17–18, 193–94, 200, 209

jections to swimsuits worn at Price Run Pool, 113

World War II, 158, 162, 205